ASTRØLØGICAL
INTELLIGENCE

ASTRØLØGICAL INTELLIGENCE

A PRACTICAL SYSTEM

FOR ILLUMINATING

LIFE'S EVERYDAY

CHOICES

Andrea Valeria
with Sherri Rifkin

Three Rivers Press   New York

Published by Three Rivers Press, a division of Crown
Publishers, Inc., 201 East 50th Street, New York, New York
10022. Member of the Crown Publishing Group.

Random House, Inc. New York, Toronto, London,
Sydney, Auckland
www.randomhouse.com

THREE RIVERS PRESS is a registered trademark of
Random House, Inc.

Printed in the United States of America

Design by Donna Sinisgalli

Library of Congress Cataloging-in-Publication Data
Valeria, Andrea.
Astrological intelligence: a practical system for illuminating
life's everyday choices / Andrea Valeria.—1st pbk. ed.
p. cm.
Includes index.
1. Astrology. 2. Decision-making—Miscellanea. I. Title.
BF1701.V294 1999
133.5—dc21 98-25143
CIP

ISBN: 0-609-80161-9

10 9 8 7 6 5 4 3 2 1

First Edition

C⊕NTENTS

ACKNOWLEDGMENTS:
ANDREA

Putting this book together has been a delightful assembly of people falling into place and words overwhelming my brain. Everything seemed and seems to have a cause and an effect. I would have to thank all those kinsmen whom I have passed on the street, at movie houses, in libraries, or in bookstores, who have, for some reason, given me that special insight that makes a person's day! I must include the light that sometimes dances on the tree in a Tenth Street garden, a cardinal that keeps returning to chirp a warning, a blue jay and his family, and many others.

Instead of taking a long, winding road to explain why I am thankful to all the above and below, names that most people do not read anyway, I would like to give a gift of some well-written words in this small space, for those who have seen me, heard me, and suffered with me through the thick and thin of this grand production. These quotations should last at least until the next wave of recognition comes along!

For those who are Aries: "Nothing exists except atoms and empty space; everything else is opinion"—Democritus.

(To Christiane Grautoff, my mother, and Cesar Vallejo, whose words I cherish.)

For those who are Taurus: "Give me a firm spot on which to stand, and I will move the earth"—Archimedes.
(To Christianne Gout, one of my daughters who is a beloved star, if there ever was one!)

For those who are Gemini: "Angels can fly because they take themselves lightly"—G. K. Chesterton.
(To Miles Davis, Lord Byron, and a toast to the EZLN, not exactly with me but helping me to stay in there.)

For those who are Cancer: "Gratitude is a burden upon our imperfect nature"—G. K. Chesterson.
(Even so, it is a pleasure to thank Anne Edelstein, my agent, who has always, with grace and intelligence, not only answered all my phone calls, but also pushed and shoved me the right way; Gwendollyn Gout, one of my daughters and my favorite Cancer person; Sherri Rifkin, her insight, intelligence, and poise, who knows what I really want to say; New York, *the* city; and last but not least, Julie Palau de Terrazas, no longer here but ever so present.)

For those who are Leo: "That little spark of celestial fire— conscience"—George Washington.
(To Corinna Sneider, proud carrier of her sign; Fritz (Peter)

Landshoff, whose light seems to be around; Will and Gerda Schaber, who used the best part of this sign for a full life; and Ted Byfield, who, although is not a Leo, does have that spark in his cosmic persona.)

For those who are Virgo: "The spirits of the wise sit in the clouds and mock us"—William Shakespeare.
(To Everardo Gout, my son, who is the best of all possible Virgos in the best of all possible worlds.)

For those who are Libra: "Veni, vidi, vici"—Julius Caesar.
(To Abigail Agranat, who found the eureka to my illuminations; the city of Cuernavaca, a longtime favorite. I also feel that I must mention the great unbeliever [in astrology], Joyce Buñuel, who is always somewhere, charming other unbelievers.)

For those who are Scorpio: "Time present and time past/Are both perhaps present in time future"—T. S. Eliot.
(To Leopoldo Gout, my son, who knows that Scorpios are my beloved favorites; Norbert Guterman, father figure and figure favorite; Robert Dreesen, whose timely intelligence is always an asset.)

For those who are Sagittarius: "A little folly outlives wisdom and honor"—Bible
(To Susana Slagt, a great friend through thick and thin.)

For those who are Capricorn: "I like trees because they seem more resigned to the way they have to live than other things do"—Willa Cather.
(To Lauren Klein, an uncommon soul as well as a fine artist.)

For those who are Aquarius: "Moments are sparks of eternity"—David Hofstein.
(To my sikhote-alin individual, my piece of meteor, and for anyone else who has one, for being an Aquarius can carry you through anything, even space.)

For those who are Pisces: "A writer is someone who can make a riddle out of an answer"—Karl Kraus
(My father was a Pisces, my love is a Pisces, my best friend is a Pisces: Valeriu Marcu, Leon Garcia Soler, and Marely—lots of love, but I still will not listen to reason.)

ACKN⊕WLEDGⅢENTS: SHERRI

I'd like to thank my former colleagues and friends at Harmony Books—Leslie Meredith, Joanna Burgess, and Peter Guzzardi—for making this book possible and treating it with such care, as well as the people at Crown who miraculously transformed a manuscript into a book. I am also grateful to Anne Edelstein, who introduced Andrea and this book into my life, an act which unwittingly allowed and influenced me to make major changes in that life. Thanks to my parents, who brought me into this world as a true Cancer the Crab. A special "Shout Out" to my brother, Alan, whose gave his support, love, and patience through this and other life projects without hesitation, something for which I will always be grateful. You're the best, man! I love ya like a brother!

And, of course, a heartfelt, cosmic, and illuminated thank-you to Andrea Valeria, whose guidance, wit, intelligence, sensitivity, wisdom, and love made this one of the most pleasurable, educational, and satisfying experiences of my life. I am honored to be a part of something that gives others even just a slice of all the wonderful things that are Andrea.

ASTRØLØGICAL
INTELLIGENCE

BEGINNINGS:
AN INTRODUCTION

"Whether it favors him or not, the calendar is man's master."
—Fernand Braudel

I have always viewed astrology as a practical tool. Don't get me wrong, I love the mystical and mysterious energy that the cosmos holds for us, but what good does that do us if we can't *use* it every day of our lives if we want or need to? In my thirty years as an astrologer plus another fifteen years of association with the field before then, I have always searched for the most practical way to apply the ideas of astrology to making everyday choices and decisions. People, hundreds and perhaps thousands of them, come to me because I help them see how they can use astrology to make essential everyday selections: whether or not they should take that job offer, how they should approach that real estate agent, if they should ask somebody out for a date, when to start their fitness program, and so on—issues that feel important to them and that could influence the course of their lives. Helping my clients, friends, and family find their own answers is one of my greatest joys because I see not only how well it works but also how much happier they are when they make carefully plotted decisions.

Most people come to me with questions. I always tell people that the right answers are already within them. To find those answers they just have to learn a little bit about their astrological sign and make the connection to it. By doing so, they can apply the energy of this powerful combination to any situation.

Think of an equation like this one: astrology + your choices = a better chance.

One of the things that astrology is about is interpretation. Astrology is a language, and just as no two translators translate the same poem from one language to another in exactly the same way, no two people interpret the message of the stars in exactly the same way. Astrology is about breaking down boundaries, not creating them. Because of that, I decided that words and their cosmic interpretations were the best and easiest way to introduce and connect people to the joys of astrology.

Your choices are the building blocks of life, which I have broken down into six components that can be used in sequence or juggled around. Albert Einstein, a Pisces, said that "life is what man is thinking about all day," so I have chosen the following six words specifically to be the touchstone of the system of *Astrological Intelligence* that I call illuminating your choices. After making my own illuminated choice, I decided that these six words best represent the six stages of decision-making, either for what you are "thinking about all day" or for a larger continuum, such as the arc of our lives that takes us from or through one point to another.

Here are the six stages:

1. *Approaching:* whenever you begin something
2. *Questioning:* when you find yourself asking
3. *Strategies:* when you start devising a plan
4. *Negotiating:* when you actually begin relating
5. *Bonding:* when you make the connection
6. *Building:* when you start thinking about tomorrows

You were born with a very special password that allows you to jump right into this unique system: your sun sign, or astrological sign, which is determined by the day you were born. We all have one, so no one is excluded from being able to give this a try. Every one of us is either an Aries, a Taurus, a Gemini, a Cancer, a Leo, a Virgo, a Libra, a Scorpio, a Sagittarius, a Capricorn, an Aquarius, or a Pisces. (You may already know your sign, but if you don't, not to worry: I will show you how to determine your sign and anyone else's a little later.) The wonderful, complex, rich mythology and history of each sign has been woven into the texture of this book. By using *Astrological Intelligence,* you will get comfortable with your sign, so you can make it part of your identity, almost like an alternative name, as you go out into the world and relate to everything and everyone around you. Whether you make snap judgments (as Aries tends to do) or plot out hundreds of choices on a spreadsheet and ponder the various possibilities for months (a common Taurus trait), you still move through at least part of the process at one time or another. Each astrological sign has a unique way of relating to these six stages through words of his or her own, as I will show you.

I know that everyone can benefit from this relationship. If you use this system, your decisions will always be given a boost in the right direction. The best way to find out that the system works is to try it for yourself and give it a chance. Just the other day, the lovely daughter of a friend looked up the combination of Pisces and Leo in the "Bonding" section. The advice for Pisces was to get Leo to believe in something that she had not created. "That's exactly what I have been trying to do and it hasn't been working!" she said, in an almost accusing tone. I made her keep on reading, and she realized that the advice that she should let the Leo, who happened to be her mother, shove her around a bit could fit into her lovely Piscean scheme if she gave it a chance.

I am fully aware of the ongoing debate between those who believe and those who do not believe in some kind of message from the stars. Your decision to pick up this book would seem to indicate that your heart and mind are at least somewhat open to the possibility of accepting the fact that there is something to astrology. You are far from alone, by the way, because forty million other Americans believe the same thing. Whether you are already a devotee, a Curious George, or a complete nonbeliever, take a chance, pick a word, and open the door to amazing possibilities.

I understand and sometimes even enjoy the fact that this idea is not entirely clear to everyone else. For instance, a couple of years ago, I was at a very lovely luncheon in honor of my good friend's eighty-fifth birthday. The party was held in a swanky downtown duplex filled with an impressive art collection and an equally impressive guest list. I struck up an interesting and lively conversation with a gentleman who turned out to be a well-known psychoanalyst. When he asked, "Soooo . . . what do you do?" and I answered, "I am an astrologer," his reply was immediate: "But you seem so intelligent!" I had to laugh because this person, like many others, believed that astrology and intelligence were mutually exclusive entities.

I wonder what Ptolemy, Kepler, Copernicus, Democritus, Carl Jung, Alexander the Great, or even François Mitterrand, among many other great thinkers and famous figures, would have responded. The list of intelligent people who have shown an interest in astrology is almost as long as a list of those who are dead set against it. Even a very serious contemporary book, *The Oxford Companion to the Mind*, edited by Richard L. Gregory, notes about astrology that, "contrary to all common sense, it *seems* to work. That is to say, the personal characteristics that are supposed to be governed by the 'sun signs' often appear curiously accurate."

For some or for many reasons—be it the coming of the new millennium, the Pathfinder landing on Mars in July 1997, or the new feeling of the world being a global village thanks in part to the wonders of the Internet—lately there seems to be a shift in attitude about our connection to the universe, evidenced by our insatiable desire to understand our place within it. As an article that appeared last year in the *New York Times* about the fascinating or startling new cosmic realities that seem to be discovered every day admitted, "We earthlings may be connected to the space around us in ways we only dimly appreciate." I will grant that perhaps the venerable *New York Times* was not referring specifically to astrology, but *I* am.

I started using astrology at the age of fourteen. My mother introduced me to it, and since I idolized my mother, I jumped right into it without giving it a second thought. My mother was born into a family of well-known literati— in fact, one of Thomas Mann's stories was based on her father, who was a friend of Mann's. My mother was married at age sixteen to one of the best-known German-Jewish dramatists of the 1920s. She lived an abundant, wonderful, and unconventional life, filled with famous friends, interesting astrological charts, and some tragic moments. In fact, her autobiography, titled *The Goddess and Her Socialist*, was recently published in Germany. She became an astrologer in the 1950s while going through one of her difficult divorces. She was taught by a painter whom she later married and, of course, divorced. His paintings now hang in the Los Angeles Museum of Art. It wasn't until later that I came to understand how the art of astrology actually helped her get back on her feet.

Although my mother died too early, at the age of fifty-seven, I still keep many of her handwritten charts as treasures in my library not only because some of them belong to well-known people but also because her insight was uncanny. Mine is not so. I rely on the knowledge that my 4,000-book library contains. The books range from classic texts dating from 1640 to recent mass-market paperbacks. All of them are underlined and full of bookmarks. The experience of reading them all, writing articles and books in Mexico, and mapping out astrological charts has made me want to show others how practical, insightful, and rewarding the lore of the heavens can be for anyone who catches so much as a brief glimpse of what astrology has to offer.

I have a studio in Cuernavaca, Mexico, that looks out onto a pyramid, and I sometimes sit there and think about the first book on astrology I ever purchased myself. I bought at Mason's bookstore on Lexington Avenue in New York City in the 1960s. The building is still there, but sadly the bookstore is not. Mr. Mason, who was also an astrologer, drew up my chart and made me promise that I would never dare to give astrological advice to anyone until I had hung my chart above my bed and studied it for at least sixteen years. While I thought his advice was unreasonable, I ended up listening to him, and it wasn't until sixteen years later that I actually held my first consultation with somebody who worked at the city hall in my town (which happens to be the largest city in the world). This person later became the mayor of one of the largest cities in the world—something I predicted would happen. The word got around that I was a good graphic designer, which I was at the time, but that I was better at dealing with the stars.

So I began spending more of my time working with astrology, and people started to come to see me. I now have hundreds of clients with whom I consult in person, over the phone, by fax, and by E-mail in four languages—in addition to the language of astrology, which makes five. Doing readings in different tongues is a joyous challenge because each language has its own nuances, whether I am searching for simple words or describing complex relationships in which difficulties crop up when people least expect them, sometimes several of them at the same time! I sit at my desk, watching the sun play games with Teopanzolco, one of the oldest pyramids around, known to have been a central power source for the Tlahuicas in ancient Mexico. It is from living there and from many other wonderful and not so wonderful experiences in my life that I am so certain that people—and if push comes to shove, even things, like my laptop or the little piece of meteor I have sitting on my desk—have their own cosmic energy. The spirit of Tomoanchan, where the ancient Mexican calendar with its nine heavens was supposed to reside, has perhaps shown me the way to pick and choose the right word in Spanish, English, French, or German. Through language and astrology, I have come to understand why *"oui"* is not as easygoing as "yes" and why "Sí" has much more meaning than a simple translation can contain. In fact, my own lineage comprises a glorious mixture of cultures and religions: Romanian, Jewish, and German Aryan, with enough chili inside me to make me a hot-blooded Mexican.

Along with many others, I believe that astrology is not only a language but also an art. I like to call it the poetic side of astronomy. In fact, the art of astrology has been around ever since humans first looked up into the sky and wondered why they were able to even ask about the cosmos. The twelve signs of the Zodiac constitute only a tiny portion of the vast story and history of astrology. The word "astrology" comes from the Greek words *"astro"* and *"logos."* The combination of these two words is often translated as "speaking to the stars," which is further evidence that astrology is a language. And since history is a continuous—or, depending on your stars, discontinuous—narration of a never-ending story, a discussion of the history of astrology might begin with the question, "Do you look up at the sky, or does the sky look down on you?"

Astrology has made its historical journey through the ages hand in hand with art and poetry and, along the way, has become etched with wonder and awe in the memory of humankind. The correspondences between cosmic patterns and human experiences have been considered serious business for at least three thousand years. The innovative Babylonians, the ancient Egyptians, the wise Chinese, the wondrous Mayans, and the colorful Aztecs held astrology in high esteem and regarded it as an integral element of their cultures. Even Vedic literature and Icelandic lore have astrological themes, which the people of those cultures studied fervently. Many still do so.

I tend to agree with those who claim that there is a grand design to the universe. Within this scheme, there definitely is a place for astrology, which has been carried in humankind's soul for thousands of years and is retrieved in what scientists call eidetic memory (photographic memory) the moment we turn our heads and look up to the stars.

Astrology rides on history's caudal appendage (rear end) in the same way that a comet's tail streams behind it because of the sun's influence. Call it preordained harmony, call it circumstantial evidence, or call it significant eidos, astrology is in the human psyche just as the passing hours wake us up or put us to sleep every day. This, our created world, is, as Sir Thomas Browne says, "but a small parenthesis in eternity," and has no respite from the legends that our imaginations bring into being. So why should we not relate each of the zodiac's twelve signs to an idea or decision that helps us all lift our spirits?

Astrology has no expiration date: even though its history goes back to ancient times, and possibly before, astrology is a thoroughly modern practice as well. The system I have devised, and which I explain in this book, puts a modern spin on this ancient art by making it practical and useful. It also gives anyone and everyone an advantage by simplifying the history, harnessing the strength of each sign, and showing how to apply it to this decision-making process. In fact, this book could have been called *Your Personal Dictionary of Clues to Making a Better Choice at Any Time under Any Circumstances*. A good idea but a bad title—and way too long. Instead, why don't I now show you how to illuminate your choices through astrology by working with your very own cosmic adviser—yourself! This could be the beginning of a new relationship between your personal needs and the better side of happiness or bliss.

Working with Your Personal Cosmic Adviser

In keeping with the idea of no boundaries, *Astrological Intelligence* covers a wide spectrum—the spectrum that is life: business, family, friendships, romance, education, recreation, whatever you like: Should I look for a new job? Should I ask her to marry me? Should I wear the blue sweater or the green one? How can I negotiate better business deals? How can I console my daughter's broken heart? How can I tell my husband that I want us to move to a different city? There are hundreds of thousands of possible decisions and a multitude of answers.

You have an array of questions, so now you are ready to take the first step, which is finding your password, or sun sign. You might already know your sign or that of the person or people to whom you are relating, but in case you don't, here is an easy guide:

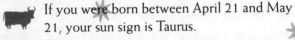

If you were born between March 21 and April 20, your sun sign is Aries.

If you were born between April 21 and May 21, your sun sign is Taurus.

If you were born between May 22 and June 21, your sun sign is Gemini.

If you were born between June 22 and July 22, your sun sign is Cancer.

If you were born between July 23 and August 23, your sun sign is Leo.

If you were born between August 24 and September 22, your sun sign is Virgo.

If you were born between September 23 and October 24, your sun sign is Libra.

If you were born between October 25 and November 22, your sun sign is Scorpio.

If you were born between November 23 and December 21, your sun sign is Sagittarius.

If you were born between December 22 and January 20, your sun sign is Capricorn.

If you were born between January 21 and February 18, your sun sign is Aquarius.

If you were born between February 19 and March 20, your sun sign is Pisces.

Please note, however, that the exact passing of the sun through one of the twelve signs of the zodiac sometimes varies year by year, so be sure to get in touch with a good astrologer or look up your year of birth in a reputable ephemerides book, which is an astronomical calculation of the degrees of the planets in the sky in relation to the earth at any given time, used by astronomers and astrologers alike. Think of your sun sign as a large, happy, loving, boisterous family that you are born into; you have brothers and sisters and cousins, but each of you has your own unique personality, even though you share the same ancestors.

Often people ask me, "What is the best sign?" My answer is always the same: the best astrological sign is, without a doubt, your *own*. If you are a Cancer, then Cancer is the best sign to be. If you are a Gemini, then Gemini is the best sign. Now, I know there are millions and millions of people who inhabit this beautiful planet of ours while there are only twelve astrological signs. But in addition to the day of birth, the precise time and place of birth also contribute to our astrological makeup and give each of us our moon sign and our ascending sign, which is one reason why no two Tauruses are exactly alike. Since complicated calculations are necessary to determine the moon and ascending signs, for the purpose of this book, all you need to know is your sun sign. You'll find a lot more about your sun sign in "Astrological Profiles" at the end of this section and throughout the book.

Now that you know your sign, the second step is relating it to any possible situation in your life—which also depends on what stage of that situation you are in—that is most closely represented by one of the six stages of decision-making represented by the words below:

- Approaching
- Questioning
- Strategies
- Negotiating
- Bonding
- Building

At the beginning of the six chapters, I present a general description of each stage to give you direction and help you narrow down your choices. You can look at these six words as the stages of a chronological, integrated process, going from the first to the last or, alternatively, as separate actions that you do at any time—but whichever way you choose to use the system, you must remember that each of the twelve astrological signs feels, smells, sees, tastes, and hears in its own unique way. To illustrate the difference between how the twelve signs relate to each of the six stages, I have chosen a particular word as a variation on, or a first cousin to, the umbrella word. Therefore each chapter is constructed so that as you turn to your sign, you will find a discussion of your sign's singular connection to that new word. By looking at the chart at the end of this chapter, you can instantly see what word your sign best relates to in each stage.

Lest you think that these words were chosen at random, I assure you that there is a method to this delightful madness. I chose these seventy-two possibilities because they help bring the practical side of this process into the picture. They have been carefully picked to be your sign's entrée into my version of what astrology has to offer. For example, Scorpio relates to the word "questioning" through "mystery" because Scorpio, the zodiac's magician, can pull a glowing response out of any old hat, while Capricorn relates to "questioning" through the word "waiting" because the more time goes by, the safer Capricorn feels. You can make your choices at random, but my system is not haphazard in any way.

Although knowing yourself better is imperative, it is not always enough, because we live in a world filled with other people who have their own agendas, dreams, desires, and needs and with whom we want and need to interact on a daily basis. As you get used to the language of your own sign, you will discover the best way to approach, question, strategize, negotiate, bond, and build for and by yourself, and you will also find tips for relating optimally with people of all the other signs. For instance, if you are a Virgo who needs to negotiate with an Aquarius, you can turn to the chapter entitled "Negotiating." There you will first find out that Virgo relates to negotiating through the word "bargain." Then you can look up the corresponding interaction between Virgo and Aquarius. To give yourself an added advantage, you can look up Aquarius in that same chapter to find out that it relates to "negotiating" through "exploring" and then read the flip side of your interaction between Aquarius and Virgo from Aquarius's point of view.

A good example of how well this can work is illustrated by the story of two of my Leo clients. Not too long ago, both of these Leos were cast aside by their significant others. Goodness, did they suffer! At that time they saw themselves as past their prime, had grown-up children, and found that they were on the threshold of a void that seemed to get darker and larger by the minute. They had questions to ask, and by looking at their astrological profiles, I showed them how to find their sense of direction by learning how to illuminate their own way. I explained to them that within the context of their signs, the two of them were suited to channel their pain into creative pursuits. I pointed out how they could *negotiate* with each other by tapping into their own powerful energy. As a result, they were able to *bond* by celebrating their newfound identities as they *built* on self-expression by writing a best-selling cookbook, which also built up their bank account.

The more you use the guidance in this book, the more clearly you will see the advantage of being intimate not only with your own sign and the cosmic energy associated with it but also with the people with whom you come into contact on any basis—intimate, platonic, professional, or familial. Knowing someone else's sign and working with him or her according to both of your astrological temperaments will allow the two of you to get into sync. You can make all of your interactions flow to your advantage—that is what

Astrological Intelligence is all about. I have found that through this handbook of cross-referential advice, we can find a way to look a little deeper into each other's eyes as we go about our daily endeavors, and we can relate to one another with that much more harmony and peace.

You can find out how to put your best foot forward with the flip of a page. Just remember that rather than telling you what you *should* do, modern astrology tells you what you *can* do, while you supply the quantity and the frame of reference. The system is now yours, for you to navigate around in. This book is intended to be a first step that helps you plan, implement, and improve on your initiatives—an added energy boost, if you will—and a practical way to leverage your freedom of choice.

ASTR⊕L⊕GICAL PR⊕FILES ⊕F THE TWELVE SIGNS

"When once you have taken the Impossible into your calculations, its possibilities become practically limitless."

—*H. H. Munro (Saki)*

ARIES
March 21 to April 20

Bursting with energy, you either light up other people's days or put them in their place. The best thing that can happen to the other eleven signs is to have the chance to work at your side, Aries, although they should be a little fearful when you are near. The zodiac begins with your sign, which is probably why you enjoy being first in anything you desire, dare, or need to prove. You usually turn out to be somebody's hero. But woe to the person who offends you, for you can intimidate with a sharp glance. You bring others the morning light to illuminate the world, so all other signs can see. You will do yourself a favor if you use your intellect to enlarge and expand things. Could it be that Mars, your astrological ruler, actually obtained Earth's close attention through sheer will? If Aries had anything to do with it, I wouldn't doubt this for a minute, because your sign has such strength that it can activate energy just by being there. For you, Aries, anything is possible!

TAURUS
April 21 to May 21

Taurus, you carry the universal medal of irresistible charm with caution and care. Neither time nor form can withstand your strength. When anyone mentions the word "determination," it means that you must be around, even if you are not within view. You can endure whatever is necessary, for you have a deep belief in yourself. If you haven't yet discovered your inner strength, it is simply because you have not yet discovered all that your sign has to give to you. You give other people the strength to count on the chance of a second time around. You know how to tame any kind of desire and store it within yourself for later use. If a non-Taurus is lucky enough to have you as a friend or a lover, it usually takes more than a century to get you out from under his or her skin, but often, after one century, most people want to renew their connections with you! You, Taurus, can bring all the other signs closer to their own natural abundance in joy, for your ability to donate bliss to others is quite remarkable.

GEMINI
May 22 to June 21

Those who listen to you, Gemini, will probably learn more than they were counting on, and they will surely see what matters in a new light or from a different perspective. Gemini can be called the eye-opener of the zodiac. You can be the world's clearest conveyer of anything you need to explain, communicate, or talk about. "Innovation" is your key word. When you are at the side of others, they can risk anything and everything, because you will help them understand the best way to satisfy their curiosity through change. You know how to present the best case for any side you choose to take because you can bestow whatever meaning on a word that you deem necessary at the moment. And moments for you, Gemini, have more than one place in time. You master perfect duality while showing others how to enjoy the two sides of every story. You have the grandest allure, and most people feel lucky when you're around!

CANCER
June 22 to July 22

Coming into one's own is a process that is done with the finishing touch of Cancer's spirit. Earth's mother, the moon, has carried your sign through thick and thin ever since astrology was first mentioned in human history. The vision of the everlasting glow of a moonbeam that leaves everything to the imagination is what others should thank you, Cancer, for leaving in the collective psyche. You are at your best when you take the time to show others what is for real, because you live surrounded by emotions and feelings to such a degree that your navigational skills of this terrain are

first class. If they weren't, you wouldn't last; you would run amok. You are the master of life's ceremonies. You show others what it is like to be in the right place at the right time. You also know how others experience their destiny because you have always been by their side. If things go wrong, your keen insight gives you the ability to trouble-shoot, get to the heart of the problem, and tell others what they need to weed out. Cancer, you thrive when you are nurturing others. The only reality check you need is a promise—any promise—that starts you on another quest.

LEO
July 23 to August 23

Leo, you are the king or queen of celebrating your own fate, so much so that all the other signs become vulnerable when they are in your arms or circle. You can make any other sign yield to you, because any man, woman, or child who comes within your sphere is in for a wonderful surprise, besides most probably being charmed right off his or her feet! The two words "wonder" and "surprise" were probably invented aeons ago when the sign of Leo came into being. People often learn something important about themselves by spending time with a Leo. You carry a magic and majestic field within you that enhances everything you come in con-tact with. Your sign is represented by an open heart that beats away and makes time valuable as it links ancient gods to human souls. However, you can have a real Atlas com-

plex, in that you sometimes try to prove that you hold the world on your shoulders. I'll admit that in some cases you actually do. When this happens, you know how to take the delicate balance that values life for all it's worth to the limit—and get away with it, as you, Leo, deserve to get away with anything!

VIRGO
August 24 to September 22

Everyone of us is unique. If you can relate to your uniqueness, Virgo, you will find your personal quest to be wrapped up in the history of what was once called the "virgin daughter of Babylon"—meaning someone close to perfection. Virgo, when you beg or pray, the gods will surely listen, because you always choose the appropriate words, and your timing is perfect. Even though it is rather difficult for you to deal with your inner demons and with the world's chaos, you know how to bargain with words and feelings in such a way that you come out a winner in the long run. Virgo, you do best when you answer only to yourself. Most people born under this incredibly understanding sign use worry as their identification tag, and those around them just have to deal with this. Virgo, you might be intrinsically divine, because your sign has the makings of a god or goddess, but since you don't really believe in mystery, you need consolation instead of devotion. You should already know this, Virgo, because you do have the ability to do the impossible.

LIBRA
September 23 to October 24

Welcome, delight, and take pleasure in being yourself, Libra, for no one can do this better than you. Your introspection goes so deep that you could almost be your own psychoanalyst and actually conquer yourself, if not others! If perfection is in the eyes of the beholder, then you are the one sign who can pretend perfectly that those you love are exactly what you need, whether you believe it or not, just to make them happy. You usually compromise your own needs and desires so that your loved ones not only find what they need but also solve their own difficulties. You take the time to understand others and point the way so that they can find their freedom with grace. As a result, you are at ease whether you are in the company of strangers, of those you love, or of both together, because your sign revels in giving of yourself.

SCORPIO
October 25 to November 22

The Bible says, "Seek and ye shall find." With you, Scorpio, any quest usually involves some soul-searching. Your passion can be summed up in the saying "Live and let live." You, Scorpio, help others discover the mystery inside themselves, because you are never afraid of even the hardest fall. And if you do fall, you know instinctively how to find the path that leads back up to the highest summit. Others should know that having a Scorpio dear or near to them is the best antidote to any difficulty, labor, or trouble. You can make anything possible—for yourself and for others. Scorpios have been dazzling people ever since Ptolemy called the star Antares, Scorpio's mentor, "so splendid," more than a thousand years ago! In ancient mythology, Scorpio was once related to the idea of time, because ancient sages said that Scorpio woke the human unconscious to the concept of evolution. There is no problem that you, Scorpio, cannot resolve, and that is your own mysterious satisfaction.

SAGITTARIUS
November 23 to December 21

Sagittarius, you are the great giver of joy, which you wrap in pleasure and use to help others through difficult moments and to bring them to safe ground. Centuries ago the sign of Sagittarius was divided into six groups (a bit like our umbrella words), each of which was supposed to define your journey in life and simplify your pursuits so you could show all other signs how to grow. These six groups—the philosophers, the prophets, the teachers, the athletes, the advisers, and the people who had a good time—turned you into the mentor of the zodiac. Those categories still stand strong today and show us the way to begin to understand the concept of "forever." Sagittarius, you were born to give to others and share, not material goods but ideals, ambitions, beliefs, and quests. The mind is your playground. And when others lean on you, they will do themselves a favor. Luck is usually on your side because Jupiter is your sign's planetary ruler, and Jupiter clears the way for the best possibilities. As long as you use your utopian sensibility, everyone will be safe.

CAPRICORN
December 22 to January 20

If you, Capricorn, let others stay around you long enough, they will learn the power of the word—perhaps not always the spoken word, but surely the durable one, the one that has longevity and relates to a realistic and incisive construction of life in general. Capricorn is the best sign to demonstrate the many ways that astrology may be the poetic side of astronomy or how it is neither fact nor folly. You, Capricorn, just need to give yourself a chance to relate to the wisdom of the sacred crocodiles that symbolized your sign on ancient Egyptian scrolls and pointed the way for humankind to deal with life. This means that even though you may not know it now, if you give yourself the chance you can make your wildest dreams come true. Capricorn, you can play the waiting game longer than anyone else. You will always turn up the winner in the long run because the time you invest in any quest or activity works to your advantage. Only you, Capricorn, know why. You also know how to build on a question and how to keep going and going while getting better and better. If I could have chosen, I would perhaps have elected to be a Capricorn myself.

AQUARIUS
January 21 to February 18

Aquarius, you need to declare your independence from your dreams so you don't keep all others guessing what you really want. At the same time you should never stop exploring your own individuality. The first thing might seem to contradict the other, but if you are an Aquarius, it does not. Oppositions create energy in your psyche. As an Aquarius, you can deal with anything. If you find that there is too much heat in the kitchen, don't get out! You were born with the ability to harness any or all cosmic forces that have ever been available in the universe. You can always deal with whatever surprises come your way. The motto "E pluribus unum," which is Latin for "from many, one," should help all the other signs understand how they can give in to your whims, leaving you the time to get in touch with the part of yourself that is part angel. That angelic part is supposedly 80 percent of you, which is why it is "the many." The other 20 percent—the "one"—should wake up. You, Aquarius, keep dreaming and help others find their guiding light.

PISCES
February 19 to March 20

You are master of it all, Pisces. You are at your best when you show others how to cope. You can blaze a trail for all the other signs, and you are always needed. You will go to the ends of the earth for someone else if you feel you should. You might do this so often that you sometimes seem to be escaping from yourself. However, you usually are not escaping; you are helping those around you assert themselves, and in doing so, you give the breath of life to those who need it. The consciousness of humankind might seem to rest on your shoulders—and at times it does—so you'd better start building your own self-esteem because the other astrological signs need you to lean on and to look up to. You have a great talent for showing others how to assert themselves, even if you do not agree with their ideals. You may be the last sign of the zodiac, Pisces, but without you, there would be no first sign. Perhaps that is why the word "quest" seems to fit you so well and why others manifest their destiny when they lean on you.

A HANDY CHART TO HELP YOU NAVIGATE YOUR DECISIONS

	APPROACHING	QUESTIONING	STRATEGIES	NEGOTIATING	BONDING	BUILDING
ARIES	to dare	to command	fear	to begin	to work	to obtain
TAURUS	caution	strength	to possess	endurance	to believe	to have
GEMINI	curiosity	listening	change	risk	duality	translate
CANCER	trouble-shooting	talking	leaving	reality check	giving	finishing
LEO	values	spending	yielding	vulnerability	having fun	self-expression
VIRGO	judging	to win	worrying	bargain	to answer	understanding
LIBRA	introspection	loving	to pretend	conquer	compromise	solve
SCORPIO	passion	mystery	to fall	imagination	searching	to know
SAGITTARIUS	to grow	pleasure	continue	to simplify	relating	ambition
CAPRICORN	power	waiting	counting	to invest	adding	staying
AQUARIUS	independence	guessing	giving in	exploring	anticipation	vitality
PISCES	self-esteem	assertion	escape	ideals	to create	pathways

CHAPTER 1

Approaching

Approaching is nearness. It is the first part of your plan, the beginning of a path, as well as a wake-up call. As Lewis Carroll wrote in *Alice in Wonderland,* "The time has come . . . to talk of many things." Approaching is the first cousin to the wee hours in the morning when you first wake up, just before you put your feet on the floor and seize the day.

We could drive ourselves crazy thinking too much (or not at all) about the mysteries of the universe, our place in it, relations, quantities, and feelings. I have an easier way. Consider a sentence that appeared in a *New York Times* editorial on Friday, May 30, 1997, "We earthlings may be connected to the space around us in ways we only dimly appreciate." I am not suggesting that the *New York Times* is in any way vouching for astrology, but this sentence is so perfect for this moment in time, that I cannot resist using it to illustrate "an approach."

I cannot go on without telling each one of you how very remarkable you are!

Aries, Taurus, Gemini, Cancer, Leo, Virgo, Libra, Scorpio, Sagittarius, Capricorn, Aquarius, and Pisces, more than 70 million years of natural chaos have made you into human beings who should carry with pride and joy that spark of cosmic DNA that can so easily help you along your way. All you have to do is decode it. Using this book is a good start. After decoding this personal information, you can start your approach at the right nanosecond of time and work on constructing the space you need to create your own personal silver lining.

Albert Einstein, a great Pisces individual, once said that "one has been endowed with just enough intelligence to be able to see clearly how inadequate that intelligence is when confronted with what exists." As a Pisces, his "approaching" mode incorporates self-esteem, as you will find out in the Pisces section of this chapter. Each astrological sign enables every one of us to bloom by getting us in touch with our own individual strengths. Accessing these strengths fortifies your psyche to approach situations and people with skill. This skill helps you convert abstract relations, concrete quantities, and feelings into tools to get a better hold on your possibilities. The approach you choose with this knowledge should also ease your necessary doubts.

And it gets better and better for you as you open yourself up to the energy of the stars. Everything we do has a story with a unique approach: a telltale beginning and a middle that carries you through to the end and the final outcome—all of it your own. It takes courage to carry anything through. Right now is the perfect time to start working on your own personal story and to approach anything you want with words, descriptions, reflections, narratives, and literary devices that use the wonderful language of the astrological sign that you were born with.

In this chapter I offer you a quick survey of the building blocks of the zodiac that can help you get on your way and prepare you for something that might be reasonable, useful, or instrumental to your life. I hope this information will make opportunities more accessible to you and give you the time you need. However, while figuring out your best approach, you may discover either a reason to litigate or incriminating evidence against someone or something. No matter what the eventual outcome or by-products of your approach, the self-conscious you will have an illuminated choice on which you can rely. Instead of being an ordeal, your approach will be part of a modern, more intelligent process that whispers in your ear, "You can trust yourself because you belong." Every one of us belongs to a larger cosmic whole that is just as strong as the sum of its parts. The "parts" are what you contribute, what you choose.

This first chapter, "Approaching," gets the ball rolling. This is the time when you ask yourself, "What's next?" Well, think of it this way: the answer is already encoded in your sign. I admit that there is not always a perfect solution to any problem, even a mathematical one. But if you can lean on the artistry of your sign for a split second or a little bit longer, then you can easily become the author of your own autobiography. All you need to do is rely on your inner glow and you will find yourself making the final approach to a well-written strategic moment—the one you are choosing right now! Doing all of this may not change your life drastically, but it will help you approach your decisions with pen and paper in hand.

ARIES

to dare

"If all men were just, there would be no need of valor."

—*Agesilaus*

The idea of daring is part of the boldness of your life's venture, Aries. For you, daring comes naturally. You rejoice while you defy. You start by challenging yourself, which is probably why so many astrological books describe Aries as the sign that goes straight through the wall without thinking about it first. This attitude is such an integral part of the Aries personality that Houdini (an Aries) never doubted that he could get himself out of any predicament, until of course, he couldn't! This intrepid daredevil approach goes with your sign because it is the first in the zodiac. You should engrave the phrase "first of all" in your favorite place and then dare anyone to try to wipe it off.

You should not forget that you inspire all the other signs to move ahead, because it is precisely that part of you that exists in all others that risks taking the first step. It is likely you will approach something or someone with a push, with a shove, with excitement, in a hurry, bravely, with courage, sometimes recklessly, with a whoop, with a snap of your fingers, audaciously, at times disobediently, and usually right under every one else's nose. Good for you! However, try to remember that the other eleven signs have different ways of approaching that first step. It's almost too easy for you to overwhelm others, and before they can take a second breath, you've already beat them to it. You need to give your mind a chance to catch up. Aries, your vivacious boldness dares all of us to follow you and learn something from your novel approach!

ARIES
to dare

ARIES & ARIES: Your approach should be as clean-cut as possible. However, don't jump to conclusions, because you might not be able to see as far into the future as you would like. It might be better to slow down and take stock of your situation. Try to remember that there is always a wall that you can bump into, so don't be brash, please.

ARIES & TAURUS: Like a teenager on a first date, be careful not to misplace a kiss, a word, or an action. In other words, watch your step and take it a bit easier than you normally would. You'll be doing Taurus a favor, and he or she will be grateful. Specifically, don't try a surprise approach, even if it *seems* worth the risk!

ARIES & GEMINI: Otto von Bismarck, an Aries, gave the best advice to this striking combination: "Better pointed bullets than pointed speeches." This means watch your words and don't be too sure that Gemini is offering a good thing. Follow your gut feeling—you probably are right this time!

ARIES & CANCER: When you approach Cancer, he or she may think you are pouncing or charging instead of honestly spending or investing your time. Aries, you always have to be careful around Cancer because you are capable of hurting his or her feelings. This is another sign with which you should not jump to conclusions.

ARIES & LEO: When it feels right, it probably is. If you feel safe, you probably are. The worst thing that could happen is that you'll have a lot of fun with Leo and be able to forget everything the next day if you want to. If things don't work out, adopt a new attitude—it just might work wonders or become a great solution.

ARIES & VIRGO: Do not overdo or oversimplify your approach. It is possible that you are invading Virgo's territory because you have not taken the time to explain what your approach is about. So, you need to make amends. Try to understand what Virgo would actually enjoy or be interested in without being your usual demonstrative self. Cool it!

ARIES & LIBRA: Remind yourself that you really are strong beneath your defiant exterior. You'll need this extra bit of insight when approaching your astrological opposite, Libra, who at times can see right through you. If you can get Libra to explain his or her point of view, you can use this to your advantage. Your innovative spirit could cure Libra's doubtfulness.

ARIES & SCORPIO: You two could fall into each other's arms like long-lost friends, go overboard together, and then have a serious falling-out. In the long run, however, Aries, may convince Scorpio that the falling-out was actually pleasant. Scorpio might take a long time to understand that riding this roller coaster along with you is actually a cleansing process for you both.

ARIES & SAGITTARIUS: The best way for you two to approach each other is to start an argument. I dare you to. You then will immediately see the best and worst side of each other, and your relationship may evolve into something that could work out on almost any terms. You both have a unique urgency to live life to the hilt. Try to meet each other halfway.

ARIES & CAPRICORN: Each of you must find the role that fits you best, as if you were acting on a stage, but don't go overboard with it. You need to use the word "coherence" when you are around a Capricorn, who will size you up more than you think. Whether or not you measure up to Capricorn's expectations is another story.

ARIES & AQUARIUS: You are both tuned in to whatever is really cool. "Does one have to look into the past to see the future?" might be the best question to get you going toward an approach that could stun others and turn out to be the find of the year or even the century (but perhaps not the millennium).

ARIES & PISCES: I have a deep respect for this combination. Have you heard of the Ourobouros, an emblematic crowned mythological dragon that is continually reborn from itself? Try to understand how much you can give to each other if you approach the task with enough respect. You can dare each other to go as far as trying to unify material and spiritual things.

TAURUS

caution

"Till all that it foresees, it finds."

—Henry Wadsworth Longfellow

It might be that caution is one of the best tactics for anybody born under the perpetually fascinating sign of Taurus to adhere to because it allows more calm to settle in. You, Taurus, have a worldly-wise sensitivity syndrome, meaning that you are aware of what is going on around you, but you tend to feel overwhelmed by this knowledge. At other times, the memories in your consciousness can sometimes appear to be the original thing instead of the related scenes that they should evoke. Memories processed by the five senses can seem like reality to you, Taurus. I would not go so far as to say that you have cryptomnesia, but you take things so much to heart that you dwell on what interferes with your own best interest instead of moving ahead with care. You do this only because you are so responsive to the needs of others.

So, Taurus, a cautionary approach is the best tactic you can take. However, just because your approach is caution-ary does not mean that it can't also be broad or far-reaching. Try to see things with the widest possible scope as you take your time. If you use caution to help you answer the ques-tion "why?" before you make your approach you will be opening up a world of possibilities. For instance, instead of approaching things with a reverberating and bullish "It is . . . !" why not take the lead from the TV game show *Jeopardy* and answer with a tempting "What is . . . ?" Then you will be in a win-win situation from the beginning.

Once you have settled down into your own time with caution, you can make use of your opinionated self. At the risk of seeming too sure of yourself before you even start on what you hope to continue, you will find that your worries diminish as you get more comfortable. As in a big jigsaw puzzle, the pieces, questions, and feelings will fall into place

because they fit. You need that extra caution to give yourself the time to work on your persona and to give yourself
the specific tools that will help you approach anything with
ease. Comfort for you, Taurus, is a necessity, even if it is
only while you sit in your chair. (I hope you were allowed
to be comfortable in your high chair!) It is imperative for
you, Taurus, to feel good standing, sitting, and musing
about the best way to approach something with all due caution. You will be the poet of the solar system if you let yourself go, because your emotional responses stir the
imagination. If you wear a tag that says "Handle with Care,"
the other eleven signs will use the proper caution when they
come into contact with you.

TAURUS
caution

TAURUS & ARIES: Be sure to show Aries that you have
already thought things over. Both of you should pay attention to the "Handle with Care" warning. Somewhere, somehow, heeding this warning will pay off. Once Aries
understands that you are actually approaching this situation
of your own free will, you will be able to benefit from the
Aries know-how.

TAURUS & TAURUS: Each of you should be a stepping-
stone for the other. However, you should take turns doing

so and do so as delightfully as a Haydn musical piece, meaning with style and pizzazz. You are both at your best when you are in a controlled environment, which means you can help each other through goodwill and careful planning.

TAURUS & GEMINI: You can be sure that Gemini will investigate the best method for getting whatever he or she wants. You do not need any fancy-schmancy wording to approach Gemini and grab his or her interest. Either you will click immediately or Gemini will snub you. Be careful not to make a mountain out of a molehill, something that you are prone to do with any sign.

TAURUS & CANCER: Approaching Cancer could be a calming experience as long as you stick to what you know and don't try anything too new or daring. Instead, make sure that there is something soothing in your approach that can make the surroundings, as well as the others involved, feel better because of what you have to offer. It may take a couple of tries to tie things down, but it is worth the effort.

TAURUS & LEO: You need to be cautious in your approach so you will not need any quick fixes, which could ruin long-term plans. Things might get superficially unmanageable, but never forget how good the two of you can be at fueling each other's flame. People around you should enjoy what's coming from the both of you.

TAURUS & VIRGO: A blessing in disguise might come out from under the woodwork without you two having to do much to make it happen. Chance is your best ally, because any new beginning between a Taurus and a Virgo can be worked out. Even if the result of your approach doesn't leave you with much, it is for a reason. Anyway Virgos are so cautious that you don't have to be.

TAURUS & LIBRA: Both of you are influenced by Venus, which is responsible for beauty, so your signs should find a classic way into or out of any situation, even if what you are thinking about is a bee farm—or anything else that could sting you if you are not careful. You will have to pay attention to each other's physical well-being, however, because without caution you might literally slip in the wrong place.

TAURUS & SCORPIO: Take your time. Then take some more time. You two are opposite signs, so you could get a bit fanatical about each other, especially while you are beginning your approach. One of you has to agree to be the anchorperson while the other should sit back and look great. I refuse to choose who does what—it's up to you.

TAURUS & SAGITTARIUS: The wisest thing you, Taurus, can do is to enlist in some environmental cause. The size of the cause doesn't matter at all; it could be earth-embracing or minuscule. The way the current flows between you two does matter, though; others who might be involved need to be able to see, hear, or feel it.

TAURUS & CAPRICORN: You can do a great deal for a Capricorn if you update your intellect and your knowledge. You can think low-budget here because a Capricorn always enjoys a penny saved. While you are at it, try to help Capricorn relax. In fact, have you ever been told that you could be someone's shaman?

TAURUS & AQUARIUS: If you two can work things out without either of you getting a little vexed at the start, you will win an award. So if you stumble, get right back into the ring and give Aquarius a chance to invite you over his or her house. You could end up launching something that doesn't even approach what you first had in mind, which could be quite a treat!

TAURUS & PISCES: This combination could be a chaotic surprise and has the cosmic ability to find any Web site without a search engine. Things just fall into place. You might give yourselves a boost by using a fantastic, if not a fantasy, approach, but be sure to use just a speck of caution so you don't send yourselves to the moon without having mapped out a way to come back.

GEMINI

curiosity

"Most people only want to know in order to talk."

—Blaise Pascal

"I just want to find out how" is a great mantra to follow if you always go for that one answer without wasting other people's time. Because, Gemini, if you really want to know something, you have to learn to ask the right questions. You can't beat around the bush, and if you leave your superficiality cloak in the closet, you can be one of the best teachers of how to approach the nearest star. Inquisitiveness starts in infancy: those who ask get to learn about everything. And curiosity is the best companion to the mind. Figuring out how a question can or should be answered is a great step forward, and you, Gemini, bathed in versatility and quick-wittedness, are the best one to approach this task.

You have a knack for scattering ideas, getting others interested, and helping to clarify oddities. Gemini, you should, as Robert Burns once wrote, "Gently scan your brother man," or conversely, rummage through a sale and get the best bargain. You can be the best of companions when you are at someone's side but then you are sorely missed when you are no longer around. Marilyn Monroe was my favorite Gemini, even though her life did not provide us with as much knowledge as did that of Adam Smith, a Gemini whose biting and inquisitive approach to wealth and capitalism influences our lives to this day. His statement in *Wealth of Nations*, "The real price of every thing, what every thing really costs to the man who wants to acquire it, is the toil and trouble of acquiring it," is perhaps a reason to tone down our search and ask our curious selves how far forward we should go on our quest, be it life-changing, mind-boggling, or a simple everyday pursuit.

So, Gemini, set the pace, let others follow, and ask yourself the probing question that will set others free from their taboos and meddlesome qualities. You can show others how to use their desire to investigate and learn. You can also help them laugh at themselves or, at least, not take themselves so seriously.

GEMINI
curiosity

GEMINI & ARIES: If you don't get frightened at the thought of jumping into something without forming an opinion at the beginning, then you will get all the more out of your approach to Aries. Pretend it's a quiz, not a quest. Catch the question and click on "view," as you would on your computer, to see what's there. What appears might not be what you expected, but you can't go wrong either way.

GEMINI & TAURUS: Don't get upset if Taurus appears to be cross-examining you. Taurus may seem uninterested in getting to the point. The trouble is that Taurus's point is as far away from yours as the nearest star is from earth. You shouldn't worry, because this doesn't mean you can't work things out. In fact, you ground each other.

GEMINI & GEMINI: You would be wise to have a lawyer nearby when you approach another Gemini, not because any litigation is imminent but because a dispute is bound to stem from the heart of a deeper meaning. In this combination, a good lawyer will be more advantageous than a psychotherapist.

GEMINI & CANCER: Your curiosity just might kill the cat if you are not straightforward with Cancer. If you want a simple answer, ask a simple question. Also, perhaps you would do best to play the kitten by pretending you do not know as much as you think you do. It could be that Cancer sees through to the end before you realize what is going on.

GEMINI & LEO: Being open in your communication is your best bet with Leo. Talk things over to find out why and how come. The cause and the reason are within your reach. All you have to do is grab Leo's attention. Do so with tact, however, or Leo will prove you wrong. Be aware that Leo, in order to connect, needs to enjoy whatever you are doing together.

GEMINI & VIRGO: According to the proverb, "The proof of the pudding is in the eating." Take this to heart and be as down-to-earth as you can. Virgos are well worth listening to, especially in the atmosphere of their own home. Take the comparative approach: What does this mean to you? What does it mean to me?

GEMINI & LIBRA: Libras are always weighing one matter against another. They usually put things in a place that seems more advantageous for them. For you, Gemini, this means that you just have to let go a bit in this combination. You two could get the best of good times rolling if you take turns at the wheel.

GEMINI & SCORPIO: Don't try too hard with a Scorpio. Scorpios do not enjoy being prodded, and they won't always admit that they are interested in your approach, which will seem curious to them. If it doesn't work out right now, try again during another season.

GEMINI & SAGITTARIUS: If you're not careful, you might exact the wrong kind of excitability from Sagittarius, since you are dealing with your opposite sign. If you are careful, if you are caring, and if you can hide your curiosity, you just may be able to hitch your wagon to Sagittarius's horse. Are you in for a ride!

GEMINI & CAPRICORN: Seriousness is always a good thing when you decide to take a Capricorn up on something. If you don't seem levelheaded, Capricorn might wipe you off his or her slate. If you seem too self-assured, however, Capricorn will be curious about why it's you, not him or her, basking in the light of power. So there you are—it's as clear as mud!

GEMINI & AQUARIUS: You might have to run a crooked mile to approach Aquarius, but curiously, this could be one of your most original, if not eccentric, approaches. You just might get more good out of it than you thought you could. At any rate, the approach depends a lot on you being the one who marches to the beat of a different drummer.

GEMINI & PISCES: This could be a real love-hate relation-ship, even if it is a superficial one. You would be wise, how-ever, to exchange that possibility for a bit of mischief and flip a coin when in doubt. Get out there together and com-pete at at sports, or take a gamble together by purchasing a lottery ticket. Don't keep your curiosity penned up or let yourself become overwhelmed by your approach. One of you will be luckier than the other. Who the lucky one will be depends on the moon.

CANCER
trouble-shooting
"What is now proved, was once only imagined."
—William Blake

At times, Cancer, approaching can be like an inside-out stream of consciousness. Why? Because it is so easy for you to get lost in yourself. First of all, you must understand that you, Cancer, are always on the rebound from yourself. If you are a Cancer, as I am, you will surely understand the familiar feeling of finding yourself looking in the "trouble-shooting" chapter in the user's manual before you even open the box. You think that you have a recognizable problem and you need to look at the indicators on your personal control panel, which stem from that microchip that gives a readout from the "rebounding mode" that we were all born with. When you are dealing with yourself, errors will not be displayed as they so comfortably are when something goes wrong on your computer. But then again, it is different when anyone is dealing with feelings instead of technology.

When you begin your approach, remember that your emotions should get you reasonably involved, not unreasonably aggravated. Ask yourself, "Am I facing reality up front?" It doesn't matter if you aren't, but if that is the case, don't pretend that you are. Recognizing reality as such should be your personal trouble-shooting mode. Take advantage of your moonlike, crabby spirit and dare to tell others how sure you are that your dreams will become a reality.

You, of all the known signs in the zodiac, have the ability to make good choices by feeling and putting your emotions up front. With the help of those feelings, you can acknowledge that what you wish you could pledge, promise, or show will be right there, at your disposal. All you have to do is to be a tiny bit more reckless than you thought you could be. Then your charm will fall into place and you will be where you should be: past the trouble-shooting mode at last and in the productive one, which is better for you. Things are usually much better than you think (that's your illuminated force)—you just need to get over the first emotional impact. You are not on your own. You have so much strength bestowed on you by moon-beams, starlight, and all those things that are not supposed to exist but do. So cuddle up to your dream and use what you can to begin on your path toward it. What do you care if people think elephants don't walk on the moon? Antoine de Saint-Exupéry, the author of *The Little Prince*, showed us that it is possible. He was a Cancer.

CANCER
trouble-shooting

CANCER & ARIES: You will meet your match in trouble-shooting reality here because neither of you will let the other off easily. Take it easy and accept the fact that perhaps the whole process will take more time. If Aries gives you any time, make the most of it. If not, find the right words to jolt Aries into seeing another side of you. You just might bring a bit of magic into his or her life.

CANCER & TAURUS: This could be a traditional, down-to-earth long-term relationship that uses give-and-take to work things out. It actually should, not just could, work. If it doesn't, it very well might be your fault, Cancer. You will have to give in and acknowledge the fact that Taurus can fix things that aren't working properly.

CANCER & GEMINI: Let yourself be cornered by Gemini, but don't show any gratitude as Gemini clears things up. Remember that there will always be someone else to take Gemini's place, no matter what he or she has already done for you. Do not crawl into your shell. Instead of letting Gemini get away with something, tell him or her to shove off if any trouble starts. Keep a record of your ideas—it could be useful later.

CANCER & CANCER: All you have to do to get another Cancer on your team is to find the right approach. This means that one of you needs to see the optimistic side and not let go of it, because when things do work out, you can be so supportive of each other. Your sensitivities are attuned to each other, so don't let another sign come between you. Of all the double cosmological whammies, this one can be the best!

CANCER & LEO: You both have such vivid imaginations that it might be difficult to pinpoint the right approach without a mediator. Give it a try, but if you estimate that things are taking too long, get a mediator or an agent . . . and make sure that he or she is neither a Cancer nor a Leo.

CANCER & VIRGO: Virgo is just the one you need if you want to get the money in the bag, even if you think your main interest is in something else. You should trust Virgo, and you can even be careless with your approach, because Virgo will always put you back on the right track. But whatever you do, don't get gloomy. If you do, you'll chase Virgo away!

CANCER & LIBRA: One of you will have to give in, and hopefully it will be you, Cancer. You will be giving your-self a break if you dare to do so, because Libra usually sees further ahead than you do (since that sign is not so affected by every little moonbeam). It just might be that for starters, Libra sees things in a clearer light than you do. . . .

CANCER & SCORPIO: Scorpios usually have a secret store of strength that comes with their being born within that sign. This is a good thing for you, Cancer, because it means that Scorpio can help you overcome any of your little vul-nerabilities that might make you over-anxious. So ask instead of wasting time assessing, and you will see how this gracious combination can fall into place.

CANCER & SAGITTARIUS: Let Sagittarius show you the logic of your situation, because Sagittarians usually don't let their moods affect their judgment. The hurdles and differ-ences of opinion that you encounter should have no ill effect if you remain flexible and willing to understand

Sagittarius's point of view. In this combination, you are usually the learner and Sagittarius is usually the teacher.

CANCER & CAPRICORN: Opposites sometimes show you more about yourself than you would like to acknowledge. So this time show your muscle and affirm yourself. At this moment, just as you are approaching things, the best thing to do is to rearrange your priorities. The rest will fall into place once you loosen up.

CANCER & AQUARIUS: Both of you are wizards at pointing out the uniqueness in everyday situations. But your point of view is colored by feelings while Aquarius is turned on by the unexplored. You would be the perfect combination in the next Mir spacecraft because when you're given the chance, you make a great team. Let Aquarius prod you out of being overly practical.

CANCER & PISCES: You two should have no communication errors unless there's a full moon. Be sure that you use quality paper, that all your documents are in place, and that the connections are functioning properly. If things don't seem to be working out, try again; it probably is just a document jam!

LEO

values

"Respect yourself in your purest emanation, your word."

—*S. R. Hirsch*

To take something into account in order to make a decision is to value it. Valuing something is a choice, and for you, Leo, it is always an illuminating one, because Leos are ruled by the sun. Even though everything that glitters is not necessarily gold, it does have a golden hue. You might pick something that has no value, but just by approaching it, you bestow value on it. I have to get you to agree. You have the cosmological insight to show everyone else the value of an approach, be it biological, logical, or literally explanatory. Instinctively, you recognize a fair return on any investment; you know how much service should be expected from it; and you understand why anyone would want to pass it on. Valuation is something you do objectively as well as intuitively. Leo, you must admit that you do this because you value yourself above all other things. Well, good for you. If you truly value something, it must be worthwhile.

You should have no qualms about prodding, showing, teaching, allowing, improving, developing, embracing, seeking, and finding the principal quality of something, because you can see the good in anything. You can therefore help others approach their goals by allowing them to soar. Leo, you should feel good about yourself first thing in the morning. If life were perfect, you would be able to stay in bed until you feel just right, because you deserve it! Your momentum is the most valuable thing around, and you are so generous that this is why you can help to fulfill everyone's needs. You are so good at understanding the hidden values of others that I would immediately put you on any panel, for all of these qualities make you a perfect judge. Who better than Leo to carry the burden pro bono publico—for the public good—especially since, as Tacitus (who was thought to be a Leo) said, "To everything its use." So, Leo, approach others and whisper the words of Tacitus in their ears. You will be doing them the great favor of illuminating the value of their choices.

LEO
values

LEO & ARIES: Aries won't let you get away with very much; in fact, Aries probably won't let you get away with anything, so always be careful about what and how you try. However, do keep in mind—and remind Aries—that perfection doesn't exist, even in science. Once you clear this up, most encounters between the two of you can be exhilarating, to say the least.

LEO & TAURUS: Your first impression of each other is probably not going to be the best. Before you approach a subject that brings you two together on a personal basis, you should try to do something for the same good cause or join a progressive volunteer program. Don't take extreme views. Wait a bit for things to work out—they will, in a funky way.

LEO & GEMINI: This combination could be pure hype of the best kind, even if both of you shun the idea of it. Get used to the attention you can generate, and use it to your advantage, for you may have only fifteen minutes' worth of fame. If the two of you are able to see the value in that attention, you could bedazzle, illuminate, and outshine everyone around you. Your best approach is to value each other as teammates.

LEO & CANCER: Floor Cancer! By this I mean you should find a way to get that Cancer person going. You will be doing him or her the favor, because Cancer needs to snap out of a lethargic dream world. You, of all the signs, can wake Cancer up. In order to prod Cancer into considering you worthy of interest, show off a bit. Your competence will do Cancer a lot of good, as he or she tries to catch up to you! By the way, you two are a great combination at dinner parties!

LEO & LEO: Two Leos either can be the best when they are together, or the worst for each other. Why? Because Leo is such a strong sign, when you multiply by two, sooner or later you will realize that you have met your match. So, please, be honest with each other at all times because no matter what happens between you, there will always be some kind of consequence. You two can make the decision about whether the outcome is good or bad.

LEO & VIRGO: If you don't show Virgo the value of getting rid of a lot of rubbish, he or she will show you. Virgo will not let you outshine him or her and might sometimes rub you the wrong way. But if you give Virgo time to settle down and tackle what he or she considers the right approach, you'll find out that any game with Virgo is well worth your time.

LEO & LIBRA: Imagine the sun shining for a couple of precise moments on something too beautiful for words. That image is what you can, under the best circumstances, get out of this combination. You probably will have to let go of something, possibly something material, but that short yet perfect moment will make up for any loss. The memories will last forever.

LEO & SCORPIO: You should see time spent in musing as a gain, not as a loss. You can get something worthwhile out of any situation, even if it doesn't turn out as well as you would like. You should approach Scorpio in a traditional way in large open spaces, enjoy each other, and then leave each other behind. Don't expect rationality from Scorpio here.

LEO & SAGITTARIUS: When these two very lucky signs get together, nothing should go wrong. With Sagittarius, you can make joint accounts, double deals, and bipartisan agreements. Things may seem chaotic at times, but try to hang in there. And do yourself a favor: throw common sense out the window—your approach will turn out better if you do.

LEO & CAPRICORN: If sex is—or is likely to be—an issue between the two of you, you should definitely talk about it. One of you could want more sex than the other. If you, Leo, admit your needs—sexual or otherwise—from the beginning, everything should work out, and I want to state clearly that this combination definitely can work out. I know a lot of good Leo-Capricorn marriages.

LEO & AQUARIUS: It won't be easy for you, Leo, to give in to Aquarius, and the other way around will be difficult as well. At any rate, the approach should have a direct relation to the value of the final outcome. The best thing you can do instead of pulling at straws is to find something to play at or with (it could even be each other!).

LEO & PISCES: Have you ever thought about recording your dreams in a journal? Pisces should, and you, Leo, could. If you aren't familiar with this process, read a book about dreams to show you how, and then use the wisdom from your subconscious to approach your subjects with your combined points of view. You'll be surprised how different things look when you see them in a new light. Please give it a try and you'll understand what I mean.

VIRGO
judging
"A moment's insight is sometimes worth a life's experience."
—*Oliver Wendell Holmes*

The nervous emotions that you Virgos carry within help you use your particularly imaginative "worry syndrome" to the hilt, so much so, that you take such good care of things that others don't even notice, but should! In fact, when my doctor reluctantly confessed to being a Virgo as I was wheeled into the operating room in 1995 for heart surgery, I felt safe, even though he thought it was strange of me to ask! He did such a magnificent job that to praise the outcome would be overkill. I will just keep relying on Virgo's good judgment when I need to approach something. Judge the best way for others to approach their needs until the end of time, Virgo.

Virgo, you are the most disarming of all cosmological interactive beings, which is good for you. Your unique inner rhythm allows you to tune in to important details on which you can base a fair and reliable judgment. Maybe you can do this because you have a deep-seated sense of fairness that has been preparing you, ever since your sign appeared in the sky, to handle frightening things. When you witness injustice, your heroic streak suddenly comes to the fore as you make decisions that arise out of your basic decency. Isn't that what judgment should be all about? Even when your critical, analytical, and restless self makes you keep your distance, you have the ability to teach all the other signs to learn from your example of being discerning. Even if a tumultuous situation is approaching, we can trust you.

Johann von Goethe, an excellent Virgo to examine seriously, actually touches upon astrology in his autobiography when he writes on the very first page about the "auspicious constellation" he was born under. He goes on to talk about good aspects and their "responsibility for his survival." I thank him profusely for writing these words, which move me so. Ever since I first found this extraordinary passage, I have relied on the judgment of all the Virgos I meet! Judge for yourself.

VIRGO
judging

VIRGO & ARIES: You shouldn't criticize each other unless you do so constructively. Find ways to diminish what Aries will judge as passivity in you and the end result will be greatly appreciated by Aries and his or her entourage. To advise you to "go for it" is almost an understatement.

VIRGO & TAURUS: Don't censure Taurus and never discuss the possibility of conflict, unless you are ready to face the consequences. If you pretend to let Taurus have his or her own way, rest assured that you should end up saving more than you imagined. By giving in a bit, Virgo, you will learn a lot from Taurus.

VIRGO & GEMINI: In order to get in sync with each other, you, Virgo, will probably have to help Gemini understand why he or she can't get away with as much as usual. Virgo, you are actually better than Gemini at using words, but Gemini is much quicker at coming up with answers. If things seem complicated between you two, wait awhile and try a different approach.

VIRGO & CANCER: Question everything, pay attention, and gather as much information as you can. There is no limit to how great your reward can be if you end up making a difference in Cancer's life. You don't have to worry about making commitments, because the fun here could be found within a "now or never" mode.

VIRGO & LEO: If Leo seems a bit off track, for heaven's sake don't let him or her know you think so. Leo values the face of things much more than you do. If you only knew how many approaches Leo has wiped off the screen because of slight discrepancies, you would do yourself the favor of using discretion instead of guile.

VIRGO & VIRGO: A crossword puzzle that has the word "emotional" as its main theme is an allegory of what you should be relating to when you are together. If you find yourself at a complete loss for words, take some time out and listen together to a symphony by one of my favorite Virgos, Felix Mendelssohn (his Symphony number 4 in A is a beauty). You may discover with wonder what a joy it is to soothe the soul.

VIRGO & LIBRA: Watch your finances. You are the best judge when it comes to proving that pennies do not always come from heaven when it rains. This approach needs your calculating eye so the pennies don't fall out of a hole in your pocket. Remove any bureaucratic hindrances and shun any nonsense that you may encounter. You can count on a Libra to say something nasty in a nice way.

VIRGO & SCORPIO: Juries comprising only Virgos and Scorpios would be conclusive and come to an immediate verdict. However, swiftness has nothing to do with making the right choice, which is something you must remember when you are pressed for time. When either of you worry, your health suffers. Together you can find the best way to get through any day.

VIRGO & SAGITTARIUS: You and Sagittarius are capable of having such a good time together that it would be easy to forget about the professional side of things. However, if you, Virgo, can somehow manage to maintain control of Sagittarius's wild side while still having some fun together,

APPR⊕ACHING   61

you will be doing a wise thing. Just be sure not to let little troubles become major hindrances.

VIRGO & CAPRICORN: Take a quiet stroll together in the country or on a tree-lined street to give yourselves time to discuss what your better judgment decides is right. You will do Capricorn a favor if you take the pressure off his or her shoulders. You are one of the only signs who can do it. If Capricorn doesn't seem to have the time, you could shorten the walk, but still try to do it in a pleasant place where you can hear the chirp of at least one bird.

VIRGO & AQUARIUS: In antiquity, Virgo represented the seven virtues: faith, hope, charity or love, prudence, justice, fortitude, and temperance. So, Virgo, try to convince Aquarius that this is still possible, perhaps by pointing out the kinder, gentler side of the matter. Aquarius loves to jump to conclusions, so it is up to you to show him or her another way to accept something traditional yet geared to our modern times.

VIRGO & PISCES: Whoops! Opposites. You two are very good at debating with each other. These discussions get more complicated the longer they last, but because you are opposites, this is a combination in which you should definitely not be judgmental. Apply all the knowledge you can in picking the right words. Have you ever heard of a thesaurus? Use it—both of you.

LIBRA

introspection

Defining "introspection" is much easier than most other brain-teasing activities: it means looking into one's own mind. But the real question is *how* does one actually do that? All kinds of questions are involved—in fact some scientists even ask themselves if the brain actually understands the mind, or ever will. No matter how you define the word, it is worth spending some time discussing it, especially in relation to Libra. Libra, you are the manager of the scale, consideration, finesse, tact, and harmony. You can show others the way into themselves, if they dare. All of us must learn how to scan our own selves with whatever tool we can get hold of: insight, rigorous and exhaustive self-study, a true mirror (a mirror that reflects you the way really you are, not reversed), by using some flair, hopefully a bit of taste, and artistic judgment. Doing so makes it possible to make more intelligent and informed approaches to the things that matter most to us.

But before you approach someone or something, Libra, you must take the time to balance the easygoing attitude that suits you so well, especially if, as you examine your thoughts and feelings, you don't lose your sense of humor. Once you have looked inside, you can then air yourself out. Then will you begin to understand what it is you actually need to approach and why. You might be reaching out toward a person, an idea, a feeling, a place, or a job. You even might be thinking of approaching the most banal thing. The mythical symbol of your sign corresponds to your ruling planet, Venus. Since the beginning of time, it has been believed to bring sensual pleasure to all things with which it comes into contact. The words also come directly down to you from *Splendor Solis*, a fifteenth-century manuscript. What could be more pleasantly introspective than that, and what could be more delightful than to imagine yourself approaching your wants in order to gain a deeper perceptual experience! Take it upon yourself, Libra, please, to help others improve the quality of their lives by showing them, even if in a nonchalant way, how to seek some solace within themselves. Then, they can take the plunge and decide how to make their first step toward self-awareness. Libra, yours is the sign that needs the comfort of others in order to be, to become, to enhance yourself. So take the first step toward approaching your illuminated self.

LIBRA

introspection

LIBRA & ARIES: Mention the word "tact" to Aries and see what happens. Your opposite sign, Aries, always brings a refreshing point of view into any situation, so let Aries express himself or herself as clearly as possible. You might find yourself less convinced than you would like to admit or even on less stable ground than you are willing to stand on, but it could be good for you to be a bit unsure once in a while!

LIBRA & TAURUS: Both of you follow lovely Venus in her unpredictable ways because both of your signs are ruled by this planet. Ever since the first astrological charts appeared on Babylonian tablets, this has been the case. You can lean on each other to see the visible as well as the invisible side of the world. Try it out by choosing the right colors or a comfortable space or by cooking an enticing meal that will loosen things up.

LIBRA & GEMINI: One of you—preferably you, Libra—can easily be the centerpiece for the other by dancing around an idea and not letting even a shadow of a bad mood approach you as you take time out to spend together. Also, you should try your best to completely ignore any nasty remarks or any difficult person who tries to spoil your picnic, even though this is not always easy to do.

LIBRA & CANCER: This combination could produce a first for either or both of you—the first jolt to your system that helps you realize that not all dreams come true because something called reality can sometimes get in the way. The process will do you more good than you would like to admit, even if you find yourself slightly embarrassed by one truth or another.

LIBRA & LEO: There is a unit of measurement called an angstrom, taken from the name of a Swedish physicist. It can measure the amount of water displaced by the landing of a fly on the water's surface of a swimming pool. This is, of course, a very outlandish way of measuring things. The two of you, however, connect so well, that any approach you take toward each other will be much more influential (in a good way) on both of your lives. Don't even bother weighing or measuring this influence, just go for it!

LIBRA & VIRGO: When you two get together, you can find common ground between Virgo's instant impression and your optical illusions. One thing is good for the other, even though you two don't share the same post of obser- vation. One of you should make the other keep on going—inward or outward. Thank goodness you have lee- way to decide.

LIBRA & LIBRA: "Every man takes the limits of his own field of vision for the limits of the world," said the German philosopher Arthur Schopenhauer (who was not a Libra), in some way anticipating psychoanalytical introspection. This idea is perfect for two Libras to dwell on as you approach yourselves.

LIBRA & SCORPIO: Have a quick look-see to measure how fast you can be when you are under pressure. Scrutinize. Look closely. After you have given yourself several oppor- tunities to approach the matter in a variety of ways, notice your own reaction while you back down. This relationship could be a marriage, divorce, and remarriage. And it also could work! Scorpio will always point out the right thing, and you will have to forgive him or her for doing so.

LIBRA & SAGITTARIUS: Keep the money in sight. Does this seem too straightforward? Nothing can be straightforward enough when you two combine forces, and you might make a bundle of money as well. So don't give in to things that can't be improved. It might even do you both a lot of good to strive for perfection.

LIBRA & CAPRICORN: Be careful of the defective-vision syndrome. By this I mean that, like one of the three monkeys, the one who covers his eyes, don't think that if you see no evil there is none around. It could be between you or just around. So don't ignore it and do try to figure out where anything two-faced or insincere is coming from, because it is not good for either of you.

LIBRA & AQUARIUS: You might think that this is the chance of a lifetime, the love of your life, or the best idea ever. Maybe it is; maybe it isn't. It is well worth your while to try things out and speak about all the things you could be doing if you had the time, the resources, and the stamina! Maybe you do, or maybe you will!

LIBRA & PISCES: You two should get together to find out what is not working, especially within your bodies. Don't overreact or get frightened, but the best thing to look into is how to improve yourselves physically before you go any further. Maybe you should join the same gym or go jogging together every morning.

SCORPIO

passion

"We may affirm absolutely that nothing great in the world has been accomplished without passion."

—*Georg Wilhelm Friedrich Hegel*

It has taken the terrestrial arthropods of the subphylum Chelicerata, of which the scorpion is a member, at least 20 million years to reach the present degree of perfection of their strange form. If the world were ever to blow up, the scorpion would be one of the few creatures to survive. The energy that Scorpio people carry within them has had all these years to develop. Perhaps that is why others may consider themselves lucky if they are caught up in a Scorpio's passionate wants or needs. Passion is a key to survival. All of us should hope that at least a couple of times in our lives, we will be as passionate about something as Scorpio can be about almost anything— if he or she deigns it important enough to approach.

Scorpio, you can present the word "passion" on a silver platter and serve it to others so their lives can seem more ful-filling. Passion is an extra something that kneads our souls in the same way bread dough is kneaded before baking. Without that kneading, the bread won't turn out right. And without passion in our lives, something will always be missing! Just look at any short list of famous Scorpios whose passionate endeavors speak for themselves: Pablo Picasso, Fyodor Dostoyevsky, Alain Delon, Grace Kelly, Carl Sagan, Indira Gandhi. The list of Scorpios could go on and on, but to be truthful, so could a list of passionate representatives of the other signs. However, Scorpios, more than any other sign, have the resolution to let their passion drive them forward.

You Scorpios usually have so much to say, as well as so much going for you, that you don't have to think about being passionate—it just pours out! It is little wonder that one of the largest known stars, Antares, has always been considered a reflection of Scorpio and of the sign's association with the eminence and activity of mankind. All the other signs might get passionately upset about these statements, but they would need to approach a Scorpio to understand how you, Scorpio, cope with so much passion in everyday situations. I hope that you, Scorpio, will take others under your wing and help them understand your intensity. Perhaps a bit of your passionate style of approaching will rub off on them. They should be so lucky!

SCORPIO
passion

SCORPIO & ARIES: When Scorpio and Aries combine their time and efforts, anything can happen. For instance, short tempers could flare and time could run out. It would be great if you, Scorpio, would take the time to ease Aries in or out of situations that he or she just might not be able to cope with. Easy does it as you move forward, please.

SCORPIO & TAURUS: Think of your relationship with Taurus as high and low tide at the shore. Taurus opposes your sun sign, Scorpio, so watch out for that rip tide, meaning that one moment you could be enjoying an embrace—literally or figuratively—that could be a passion-filled surge, and the next you could be alone on dry sand. Even if you never see Taurus again, once you fall for each other, heaven only knows what can happen.

SCORPIO & GEMINI: Fervor is a steadily glowing thing, something between passion and revelation. That's probably as far as you should go together, unless you try a newfangled approach to an old idea. Remind yourselves that even though many people have tried for the same thing, you two could work out a new approach.

SCORPIO & CANCER: You have found your match, Scorpio. It will take a longer time for you to admit it, but Cancer can be just as vehement about things as you can be—and Cancer has a protective shell! Besides, Cancers take things for granted, so your passion could become an everlasting connection.

SCORPIO & LEO: Try to whisper your approach to Leo so nobody else can hear. One of you will try to edge the other out of the way, even if love is in the air. Once again, I refuse to choose sides or sway any passionate feelings. Let ardor speak for itself and enjoy basking in it!

SCORPIO & VIRGO: May each and every Virgo get the opportunity to be induced by a Scorpio toward a passionate approach to something, no matter how small or simple. Virgo might turn out the material winner in the very long run. You, Scorpio, should be as discreet as possible and take things in your stride.

SCORPIO & LIBRA: When I hear tomorrow's news previewed on the radio the night before, I get really upset at the pretentious soothsaying of the radio announcers. I react by trying to find fault with what they say has happened. The same kind of thing can happen when you two get into any kind of escapade. No matter how hard you try not to, you end up listening anyway. Scorpio and Libra combined can sometimes predict what is going to happen without help from any other source.

SCORPIO & SCORPIO: The bottom line is either what can you do *to* me or what can you do *for* me. Once you have agreed on which of the two situations it will be, play around, but make sure you both have a passion for winning. Any kind of game is excellent to enhance your personal intensity, and the outcome will inspire your growth, even if it is sideways.

SCORPIO & SAGITTARIUS: Flaunt and display whatever you have that's worth showing and play it up to the hilt. If, while you are together, you dare to approach a passionate experience, just jump into it. It should be an excellent challenge to your mind and body, and almost everybody will notice you are glowing.

SCORPIO & CAPRICORN: Finding an object of desire usually awakens a new enthusiasm in Capricorn, which is an unusual sensation in Cap's carefully planned-out life. Sometimes Capricorn just can't deal with passion. This desire may or may not have to do with another person, plan, or idea. At best it will give Capricorn the ability to see a new way to approach many things.

SCORPIO & AQUARIUS: This combination might do better with some professional guidance or counseling, or by simply including a third party to watch over you. Be careful of the way you make things fall into place, Scorpio, because there is much too much energy between you and Aquarius, and the resulting sparks could easily set things on fire.

SCORPIO & PISCES: Approaching Pisces could be one of the most pleasurable experiences you have ever had—if you give in. If you don't, Pisces will leave you with a number of doubts about yourself that will hinder your next approach. But these doubts could very well turn out to be for your own good, so be thankful to Pisces before the passion dissipates.

SAGITTARIUS

to grow

"In order to act wisely it is not enough to be wise."

—*Fyodor Dostoyevsky*

Like a climbing vine, you, Sagittarius, change direction simply because there is always so much going on in your life
and your insatiable need to grow leaves you no alternative.
You add up forces, natural or artificial, which keep you
going and empower you to keep others going. Your growth
is directly connected to making any kind of approach. You
start things only if you instinctively know they can lead you
to what biologists call a growth substance, which your body
synthesizes to regulate physical and mental expansion. You
do things that take effect in uncanny ways because you are
so good at showing others "the way." And more often than
not, you end up on top of the heap. For instance, did you
know that many Sagittarians are valedictorians of their class
or role models for the masses, like Jane Austen, Voltaire,
Magritte, Flaubert, Noel Coward, Steven Spielberg, and
Emily Dickinson, among others.

The sign of Sagittarius is directly connected to the nine
muses by historical soothsayers (the muses of epic poetry,
history, love poetry, lyric poetry, tragedy, sacred poetry,
choral song and dance, comedy, and astronomy). If there is
a master or mistress of the universe, he or she is probably a
Sagittarian. Nothing can be better than for others to

embark on an adventure with one of these rather serendip-itous persons. You, Sagittarius, usually grow into your own chosen personality and take your pick, which is why you can show others the way to approach theirs!

Sagittarius, you happen by accident to get what other signs have to work very hard to achieve—making friends, for example. In general, you grow on others and help them approach mature choices. You are blessed with an everlast-ing optimism that allows you to be quite ambitious because you assure yourself—and rightly so—that you can achieve whatever you aspire to be or to have. Others should watch the way you approach things—it could even be used as a prototype for this whole chapter.

SAGITTARIUS
to grow

SAGITTARIUS & ARIES: You, Sagittarius, should be as elo-quent as Aries will allow you to be. The more impressive and unconventional words you use, the better. He or she will probably knock you off your high horse, anyway. And yet, the more daring you are with Aries, the better for both of you. You could even end up giving or taking lessons together!

SAGITTARIUS & TAURUS: Taurus needs some prodding from you to grow up within the context of approaching things the right way, without a chip-on-the-shoulder attitude. You will be doing Taurus a favor by using some guile to wean Taurus away from childishness and guardedness.

SAGITTARIUS & GEMINI: Be sure to use a good reference manual because no matter what you think you should try together, you will probably get lost in the details. Your steps are probably moving in opposite directions, as they should be, because you are opposite signs, but that doesn't mean that you can't help each other to grow up.

SAGITTARIUS & CANCER: My rough guess is that you could get Cancer to believe that whatever you propose is beneficial for him or her. Also, my cautious guess is that leaving well enough alone is the best way to grow in or out of this rather unusual situation—unusual because you probably do not have the same taste.

SAGITTARIUS & LEO: You are exactly what Leo needs to grow, even if he or she hates to admit it. You are exactly the right person to approach Leo and show him or her how much fun growing can be, even if Leo thinks he or she is already perfect. Be specific and let Leo be as loud as he or she wants to.

SAGITTARIUS & VIRGO: If Virgo complains, listen to him or her. If you feel like complaining, keep your thoughts to yourself for the time being. You have to agree on a one-sided arrangement for this combination to work out. You need to be the optimist here, otherwise Virgo will not see any light at the end of the tunnel.

SAGITTARIUS & LIBRA: Gently take Libra by the arm or hand, and direct him or her to move under a skylight or into a warm, sun-filled spot. Light and shadow can play a big part in the flow of your communicative efforts, so you should let yourselves be bathed in a very special glow that can also permeate what you are trying to do. Give magic a bit of a chance here.

SAGITTARIUS & SCORPIO: Together you should pledge to improve the world. If you, Sagittarius, without being too authoritative, could prod Scorpio into being a little bit more outgoing, you will have contrived a clever balancing act. One of you can convert the other.

SAGITTARIUS & SAGITTARIUS: Let go of your pride, then take a new approach. The growing part is in the bag anyway. You don't need any guidepost, unless one of you has a very nasty character, and if this is so, turn around and run because Sagittarians in general are usually bad at dealing with nastiness, even if it is within themselves.

SAGITTARIUS & CAPRICORN: You have already laid the groundwork, which is something you know but Capricorn probably doesn't. So give him or her a break and squander a bit of your time, since Capricorn will never admit to squandering his or her time—or anything else, for that matter. You can meet each other on the level of ambition, since both of you have enough of it and are wise enough to put it to good use.

SAGITTARIUS & AQUARIUS: You can approach any subject with candor when Aquarius is at your side. If you use force instead, you will probably get nothing done. Force has a funny way of working itself into places and feelings when it shouldn't be there, so watch out for it.

SAGITTARIUS & PISCES: Don't forget to use a good dose of humor, because if you get too serious together, you might find yourselves unable to stand each other for different reasons. Pisces might require something of you that you will be able to give only if you have grown enough. This could be a test for you, but it is one well worth watching for, Sagittarius.

CAPRICORN

power

"No one knows what he can do until he tries."

—*Syrus Publilius*

If you make a list of the most powerful people in any sphere of life—like the Fortune 500 or *People* magazine's fifty most beautiful people—an above-average percentage of those in power will probably be Capricorns or have a prominent Capricorn feature in their cosmological makeup.

Just as communication breakdowns can be blamed on sun storms, the power factor has been related to the planet Saturn, astrological ruler of Capricorn, ever since people started measuring time. The mythological Saturn carried a staff that represented solid principles as well as learning and deliberation. You, Capricorn, know that patience is power. You consider constructing as well as investing to be two compatible "majority leaders" in your privileged sky. These two entities may very well be the mortar that holds together the structure behind your throne, for no matter what stage of life you are in at this moment, your determination supports the power you hold on time, your ally. If you don't believe me, all you have to do is look at the history of famous Capricorns such as Joan of Arc, who represents the power of faith; Isaac Newton, the power of gravity; Aristotle Onassis, the power of wealth; and Albert Schweitzer, the power of kindness.

You, Capricorn, can and should construct your own affirmative action program that will lead you to the place where you want to be, even if it takes a while for you to get there. When you propose to approach something, life will dispose of whatever is in your way, mostly because of your powerful celestial hierarchy. You know how to make do with less, because you understand instinctively how to turn less into more. This instinct endows you with the power to fight for what you want, because you believe that not having it is an injustice. I do hope you eventually will have it your way and be financially secure because you have the power to set a good example by making the best of what you do have at the moment. You have the power to stretch, and all the other signs would benefit by learning from your approach. The power to endure could not have a better voice than Rudyard Kipling's poem, "If." Kipling was of course a Capricorn, and the ideas behind his words could inspire the best approach to life in general. In fact, the whole poem shows not only the best approach but also the finest questioning, the most excellent strategy, the most effective negotiating skills, and the value of bonding, and it leaves the path open to building a better life structure as each year passes. Read the poem and find your own inspiration as so many others have done.

CAPRICORN

power

CAPRICORN & ARIES: This is the best possible combination for the all-work-and-no-play syndrome from which you suffer, Capricorn. Both of you can feel that you have the strength of a leader—and you do. So you should keep in mind that if you can't beat 'em, join 'em, because judging by sheer force alone, it is not so clear who is the most powerful. It goes without saying, that the best way to make things work out is to approach them together.

CAPRICORN & TAURUS: This is a great combination for testing things out, although the two of you will have to figure out where or what to deal with. You can work out anything, and the more you try to make use of the power of numbers, the better for both of you. The final outcome might take longer than Taurus would like, but you can be confident about the positive nature of this robust alliance.

CAPRICORN & GEMINI: Don't let Gemini talk you into having a pessimistic outlook. In fact as far as your strong opinion is concerned, don't let Gemini talk you into anything. If Gemini accuses you of being inflexible, so much the better because you should be master of this game, Capricorn. You should keep the goods out of Gemini's reach.

CAPRICORN & CANCER: If you don't tone down your power, you could be too overbearing for Cancer. Capricorn, you should to take into account the excellent nurturing abilities that Cancer has and that you, believe it or not, do need. Let Cancer give the crabby approach a try and you just may find that others regard both of you as pillars of society.

CAPRICORN & LEO: On the one hand, this is the best combination for two people who have an open line of communication. On the other hand, it is the worst combination if one of you clams up, which you, Capricorn, could very well do, especially if you don't feel that you are on firm enough ground. I know it's not your style, Capricorn, but if you try some maneuvering, you may find yourself becoming one of the powers that be.

CAPRICORN & VIRGO: You both are conscientious enough to get the best out of a well thought out plan and its outcome. If you could also have a bit of fun or a good time, you would be strengthening the tie that could bind the two of you together. You might even give Virgo a break every now and then by spending money on him or her!

CAPRICORN & LIBRA: Perhaps "niceness" is not something that others can accuse you of, Capricorn, even if at times you mean well. However, niceness is a part of Libra's inner core. It would benefit you to try to figure Libra out, even if it means letting Libra's charms tease you a bit.

CAPRICORN & SCORPIO: There might be a powerful sexual feeling between you, regardless of which sex you are. Try to find out why this energy exists between you by doing some investigative reporting, even if you have to train the camera on yourself. Once you get over this phase, you will find yourself in a much more desirable position from which to work.

CAPRICORN & SAGITTARIUS: If you let Sagittarius have full rein, you will be doing yourself a favor, Capricorn. Besides, if together you create anything that seems to shine, it could really turn out to be as good as gold. If Sagittarius wants to take the lead, let him or her, Capricorn, even if it is against your better judgment.

CAPRICORN & CAPRICORN: The approach definitely will not come to the point of being "it's bigger than both of you." When first dealing with a fellow Capricorn, you will feel as if you could weather any storm. And if you are lucky, that is exactly what will happen. The power that you both exude as you try to overreach yourselves is one of the strongest.

CAPRICORN & AQUARIUS: Inconsistency usually rubs you the wrong way, but Aquarius might have a powerful reason to be inconsistent. From this moment on through the year 2001, all Aquarians should give full rein to their character so they can work things out of their system. This has nothing to do with you, Capricorn, except what you can get out of them. Aquarius can be a powerful ally to you.

CAPRICORN & PISCES: You two can teach each other all about status and achievement. Things will get complicated, however, if you let third parties get involved. So let Pisces deal with any outside aggravation at this time, while you take the easy way in or out of most situations. Whichever way you choose, herculean forces will stand behind you in the long run!

AQUARIUS

independence

"I ought, therefore I can."

—*Immanuel Kant, paraphrasing René Descartes:*

"Cogito ergo sum" (I think, therefore I am).

Independence plays such an important role in our country and on our continent that there is even a day set aside to celebrate it. Independence is by no means connected to Aquarians only, but when left to your own contemplative selves, you must admit, Aquarius, that you have this word imprinted in your "preferences" section. All other signs learn from the way you use your ability to think for yourself and make confident decisions in your life.

The methods you use to assert your independence are completely personal and can be delightfully or deliciously striking as well as unrestrainedly rebellious. For you, Aquarius, this venture will more often than not take its toll. This is as good a place as any to remind you of what Daniel Webster said about liberty, the first cousin to independence: "God grants liberty only to those who love it, and are always ready to guard and defend it." (Webster, by the way, was a Capricorn, which means that we can take his words very seriously.) You, Aquarius, with your ingenious mind, thrive on independence, which will usually become a big issue in all of your relationships and in life in general. You will, from an early age, make it quite clear to your parents that they need to bend more than they were counting on, for as an Aquarius, you are determined to get your way no matter what.

In a natural way and without too much pushing or shoving, Aquarians can pave the way for the other astrological signs to get as close as possible to finding their own "way" (as Buddhists dedicate their lives to doing). However, it is important for you to understand that your own love of freedom is not likely to please all those people with whom you come into contact. You must take this into account before you approach, bind, or commit yourself to other people or ideas. Remember what the Chinese sages say: when a butterfly flutters its wings, the effect may be felt on the other side of the world. In other words, there is always someone somewhere who will feel the consequences of your actions. You should always have respect for the opinions of others.

AQUARIUS
independence

AQUARIUS & ARIES: Aries needs to bask in the light of your freedom, which for an Aries goes deeper than independence. Aries will give in rather than share. So either it will be love at sight for both of you (I don't want to say "first sight" because that puts a limit on the possibility, and both of you do badly within the context of limitations) or you will feel that something is missing.

AQUARIUS & TAURUS: You should promise each other that you will enjoy yourselves. Otherwise the approaching situation might become unpleasant. If you find that you are accused of taking too much for granted and the outcome isn't what you expected, try to get other people involved so that you are not left to stick it out alone.

AQUARIUS & GEMINI: Don't hold anything back when you talk things over with Gemini, and make sure that Gemini doesn't keep things in for fear of thwarting your free-spirited self. Make sure to stand up for your rights, because Gemini can walk right over you if you allow it.

AQUARIUS & CANCER: You should try approaching the situation from different sides and do not forget that it will not be easy to vanquish Cancer's fears. Cancer needs more assurance than you can usually offer, while you, Aquarius, would not mind a healthy dose of nurturing yourself, although that is something you can't easily admit. When you make initial contact with a Cancer, it would be wise to tread softly.

AQUARIUS & LEO: Since opposites do attract, you need to find something that you both agree is liberating. Once you have found this possibly trivial common ground, you can approach any subject under the sun together. (Remember that Leos usually like the warmth of sunlight anyway!)

AQUARIUS & VIRGO: If you can get a Virgo to loosen up by getting him or her to chuckle, you will have a Virgo on your side! For the intellectually inclined, repeat the following from Epictetus out loud: "No man is free who is not master of himself." If that isn't independence, then what is?

AQUARIUS & LIBRA: You both need to get independent counsel to help you wise up. There is no need for either of you to worry about letting go, trying to stall, or submitting to captivity in any way. You just must be fair enough to let Libra take the better side of the bed, the nicer window, or the larger portion. Why? Because Libras are usually restricted by their personal needs, which are paramount for them. They loosen up when helped.

AQUARIUS & SCORPIO: Scorpio just might consider you a bit of a libertine, and Scorpio might be right! You will have to reconsider what you have acceded to and try to approach your plan without seeming oddly passionate. Do you need this aggravation?

AQUARIUS & SAGITTARIUS: Grant freedom to each other and you will find that independence has nothing to do with escaping when there is nothing to evade. Untie your apron strings, Aquarius. Untie your apron strings, Sagittarius. Then spend as much free time as you can doing things that help others rather than yourselves.

AQUARIUS & CAPRICORN: Serving doesn't necessarily have anything to do with being under someone's thumb, which is something you should be mature enough to understand, Aquarius. If you aren't, Capricorn will surely point it out to you. You'll benefit from listening to someone who, though he or she is restrained, is perhaps freer than you think!

AQUARIUS & AQUARIUS: Look for all possible alternatives to what others say cannot be done. Together you can find out which ones are right to use. If you feel bogged down, get some expert advice from a third Aquarius. There will always be one around who will welcome the opportunity to help.

AQUARIUS & PISCES: According to Mr. Webster's dictionary, "independent" is an adjective that means "not subject to control by others." When you approach something you are not trying to gain under unconditional circumstances, Aquarius, especially with a Pisces, you had better make it clear that your definition of "independent" is not just like Mr. Webster's. You're not the only one who needs his or her own space.

PISCES
self-esteem

"I am full of words."

—*Job* 32:18.

Self-esteem is one of the most subtle and yet perhaps one of the most important concepts in this whole book. I chose to put it in the first chapter with the first umbrella word because no one should start out on any quest, whatever its size or importance, without coming to terms with his or her own self-esteem. Pisces is the right conduit and could invent the perfect haiku to promote this word-feeling, because Pisces is the great supporter of the zodiac. If you have only one Pisces at your side, it is just as good as having a huge support group.

Pisces, you are above all a citizen of the world, meaning you put aside your own inner turmoil so you can help solve others' woes. You can sometimes be untrue to yourself but never to others. You have the capacity to become your own allegory, and by the time you have decided who you are and what you actually want out of life, you have taught those around you an important lesson. You can pick the best illuminated choice, if it is not your own. You sometimes lose your way, but you will never let those close to you get lost. You might find this a bit confusing, but it is important for you to know that your sign has mystical connections to complete chaos and to the last moments before the big bang! You are so good at finding out what makes others tick that you should be present in all the sessions of all the psychoanalysts of the world (even if they find this debatable). Since this is quite impossible, others should look to you as an example of how they can find the self-esteem to approach their own needs and find out what they actually have to offer. There is an excellent definition of "self" in the *Oxford Dictionary of Philosophy*: "self, the elusive I that shows

an alarming tendency to disappear when we try to intro-
spect it." Self-esteem is one thing you have of which you
have a healthy supply, Pisces, but you'd be hard-pressed to
explain to someone else how you got it.

This definition shows some humor as well, which you
must not forget to include as you approach others. Self-
esteem should never turn into self-deception, must be talked
out of self-defeating, can be an understatement when self-
fulfilling, and needs a lot of concern when it has to do with
self-respect. Self-esteem must be related in some way to
love, if only love of a certain kind and if inspired by imagination and warmed by creative ability. You usually don't
have to work on your own self-esteem because you have no
qualms about the way life presents itself to you on a very
intimate level (some might call this escapism), but since you
are so good at idealizing people, places, and things, if you
stick around others long enough, or if they stick around
you, their self-esteem will be boosted. One more thing: for
your own well-being and self-esteem, as you approach different moments in your life, take the time to follow your
dreams, or at least to write them down. They usually have
an introspective aspect that shows the way, even before the
illuminated choice appears.

PISCES

self-esteem

PISCES & ARIES: Aries' awareness of self is usually right up front, while your awareness of self, Pisces, is usually looking for something that is not there. You can form an endless chain of events that will finally lead to helpful insight, if Aries gives you time. Aries is usually in a hurry and he or she enjoys being so! Let Aries rush you.

PISCES & TAURUS: Taurus needs to feel strongly about feeling, seeing, thinking, and willing. Try to be as direct as possible when you ask if there is something you can do within this context. You might have to do a little detective work, for Taurus usually will not open up right away, but you are the perfect one to handle the job.

PISCES & GEMINI: This is a great combination of signs to delve into discussions about psychological issues—for example whether or not there is a difference between an ego and the subconscious. Don't let yourself be pushed and don't you try to shove; instead, approach the matter with a cautious eye so you will not take the blame just because of Gemini's unrequited feelings.

PISCES & CANCER: There is a self as an object and a self as a subject here. Let Cancer choose which is which, or how he or she plans to use either. Little by little things should fall delightfully into place. Experiencing a personal crisis can only help, because it will make you both see basic elements of doubt, which will clear things up.

PISCES & LEO: You should define clearly who's who and what's what. Then both of you will enjoy using your own self-determination. The self-esteem part will come in due time. Never you mind! If you can follow each other through what otherwise might be called a plethora of possibilities, you will come out with far more structure than you thought possible.

PISCES & VIRGO: Virgo might make you feel that there are a lot of difficulties between the two of you when in reality all you need is to let go a bit (both of you), smooth out the rough edges, and find a way to simplify. Since you are opposites, doing this should make you feel much better. Pisces, you might be confused by Virgo's stiffness, but if you can get over this hurdle, you will be doing yourselves a favor. This is the one combination in which, if things don't improve, you should see a shrink!

PISCES & LIBRA: Some people say that you can never pinpoint the exact problem with or about a Libra. Others, like Libras, just use a seduction theory that can work one way or the other to make an approach worthwhile. At any rate, if either of you can settle on a feeling of let's-get-what-we-can-out-of-it-while-we-can, you will both be treading on safe turf.

PISCES & SCORPIO: Find your selfish genes and use them for something productive. Once this is accomplished, self-esteem will appear. And by the way, the selfish gene in biological terms has to do with natural selection!

PISCES & SAGITTARIUS: Pisces, you will have to make amends so that Sagittarius can feel better about himself or herself. Since you, Pisces, are the chosen one of the zodiac to be helper, you'd better get used to letting Sagittarius have his or her way. Do not spend more than you can, but let Sagittarius spend more on you. The spending can be counted in money, time, or energy.

PISCES & CAPRICORN: If there is a moral to the story, it should be a personal one because you, Pisces, are so good at boosting the self-esteem of others. You two should find a moral part as a way to give in to what could become a very personal story. You also may take it more personally than Capricorn, who usually is not willing to show the need for introspection to other parties. However, if you build up Capricorn's self-esteem as best you can, it will be better for him or her than he or she would like to admit.

PISCES & AQUARIUS: Aquarius will need to shift his or her identity or, if worse comes to worst, pretend to do so. If you start pretending that all is well, it will not end as such. Do not exclude third parties or a novel approach. Perhaps a good dose of self-centeredness for either of you could magically transform imbalance into equanimity.

PISCES & PISCES: If you both indulge yourselves and find the right amount of self-respect to carry you through thick and thin (of which you should find plenty), it just might be the best of all possible choices. Do not bury your head in the sand. There is no need to question yourselves about taking the next step, for you probably are already in the middle of things!

CHAPTER 2

QUESTIONING

It goes without saying: the act of questioning is a quest in itself. By asking questions, you're directing your life, taking a chance, and hopefully setting yourself out on the right track. It makes little difference if you are a connoisseur, a dilettante, an amateur, or an expert in your job, at home, or while planning a vacation. By questioning, you are looking for something—it could be tangible or intangible. Your next step should be to understand what you have found. Even if you decide against it, you have chosen something that is an addition to your life (just by spending time on it). On one side of questioning, you have the interrogation, an expression, feeling, examination, or something that is subject to doubt. On the other side is a pause or a void. The effect of whatever you choose will add to your life history one way or another—like *Astrological Intelligence* itself!

Actually, the question is just as important, if not more so, than the answer, as when our elders would say, "Ask a silly question and you'll get a silly answer." The big difference for us in this chapter is that our great concern should not be with the answers but rather with our quest, for it is our search for the answers that matters, just as it's the journey, not the destination, that's important. In other words, you're unsure about something, so you must learn to form a question (preferably the right one). With these steps, you will begin to discover valuable information that will lead you to solutions. By making an illuminated choice, you can start to lead yourself. This is the time for you to ask as many questions as you like, as often as you feel you need to.

Of course, there is always another possibility or another choice to make. Even by making decisions about the most mundane things of everyday life, we are giving ourselves enough elbow room to swim, squirm, or float around in. Most of the time our decisions have little effect: which street to cross, which shirt to wear, or any of the thousands of things we decide every day almost without thinking. However, if you learn how each astrological sign, especially your own, can maneuver around, in, or out of situations (of the everyday variety as well as the extraordinary ones), it can be an advantage, like watching the weather report to figure out which of your five coats to wear that day. And if you find out about the little cosmological quirks of those around you, your personal quest will become more rewarding. When you start to relate to other people, you are tapping into their mythological selves, those beneath the surface, hooking yourself up to their questions. Using astrology in this way is like navigating the Internet to find the ultimate Web site! Asking the right question provides you with the correct data so you can find the most likely point of entry to what you were asking about in the first place.

There is no guarantee of finding quick and easy ways to perfect answers. But by asking questions, you give yourself a much clearer perspective and more options. You can blend your own astrological influences with the right timing—for instance, "Should I ask for that raise *today*?" Ultimately you may illuminate your own possible channels: "Should I take some time off to go trekking in the Himalayas or to sun myself at the beach?" If one thing doesn't work out, you can channel-surf until you find the one that does. You start training yourself to be more perceptive; perception is something that astrology claims you were born with anyway. And since this cosmological art also makes you—meaning all of us—the center of the universe, it is easier to scrutinize a project, even if it is the tiniest one in the world, and if you think it's important, you should still be proud of it. The question is at the center of your personal universe. You start figuring out how you fit into your own bigger picture. You should think of it this way: an astrological sign is no more than a pattern, and laying out the answers helps you see them from a better angle.

In philosophy there is something called the maximin principle, a principle of decision theory that points out that the right decision is the one that maximizes the minimum outcome—in other words, makes the worst outcome as good as it can be. The search for a question has much more to do with accumulating the right observations within your sign than you might imagine otherwise, like the best-out-of-the-worst or the worst-out-of-the-best theory described above. When you finally come to it, an answer should be much more a part of your fifth illuminated strategy—bonding—than anything else.

Questioning requires that you tap into your inner dialogue and find out about yourself before you sit down and do the puzzle! Asking has much to do with exploring your personal and natural history, so you should lay down the categories in which you are really interested *before* you take all those other steps. According to your sign, you do best when you lean toward potentials for Aries, hunches for Taurus, motivations for Gemini, support for Cancer, conceptions for Leo, skepticism for Virgo, influences for Libra, extremes for Scorpio, inclinations for Sagittarius, fundamentals for Capricorn, wonder for Aquarius, and instincts for Pisces. These are all parts of a larger process that has to do with the beginning of a good idea, which may start with this question: "Should I do it and is it worth worrying about?" This chapter will show you how to connect with your inner self while engaging others as a springboard to help you find your answers. It will help you reflect on the nature of your persona, and illuminate yourself within the context of a cosmological speculation—perhaps even an inquiry—but let it be one that comes from your very own source!

ARIES

to command

*". . . and of threads that connect the stars and of wombs of
the father stuff . . ."*

—*Walt Whitman*

While we would all like to be able to say, "I'm in charge"
some of the time, Aries would like to be able to say so all of
the time, especially when it comes to matters of the mind. It
is best for you, Aries, to be very specific when it comes to
time, space, reality, existence, necessity, substance, property, matter, states, facts, and events. To be in command is as
specific as you can get. I don't mean to say that if you are
not an Aries you cannot be in charge. What I do mean is
that when you question whether or not you should be in
charge, the part of you that is Aries is tuned in. If you are an
Aries, you were already tuned in when you took your first
breath.

If before you answer your question you can find an
opportunity to take a stand, you are on the right track. And
a good way to find out how others see you is by studying
the mixed reaction you are sure to get from friends, family,
and colleagues when you spell out your plan. They should
be enthusiastic, even if they don't agree. If your assumptions
can possibly lead you to the top of the heap or the head of
the class, then your question is taking you to the right place.
The question is your first message, which stems from your

inner core. You are receiving your own command. It's like starting your own art collection, but instead of hanging pictures on the wall, you are educating yourself to understand how to choose what is best for you in the first place: modern art, Renaissance art, or junkyard art. The important thing is that you do the choosing so that you can give yourself the chance to be your own commander. It doesn't even matter if, at this stage, nothing comes of your effort.

There should always be a path that leads you from your approach to your questions with some kind of authority. Henry Wadsworth Longfellow once said that "some must follow and some command." Aries, you are cut out to command, but you must remember that even if you feel that everybody would be better off if you were in charge, it won't always work out that way. However, if you start out your quest with the intention of ultimately gaining control, you are giving yourself the best of all possible chances.

ARIES
to command

ARIES & ARIES: One of you must be a bit careful not to turn on your combat mode, because you might just drive off the other Aries. Give each other a good chance to be a bit bossy and don't jump to any conclusions, because they just might not be the right ones. Lay claim to what you think is fair.

ARIES & TAURUS: You might be sending Taurus the wrong signal, so work a bit on improving your body language, which will definitely be the first impression for Taurus! You, Aries, need to let yourself be the project of Taurus, or at least let Taurus think that he or she is making the decisions here, which is something you don't like to do—but try it anyway.

ARIES & GEMINI: Sometimes a greater amount or more years of experience is not everything. Nowadays there are a zillion new ways to tackle projects, and both of you can do well by using innovative approaches to soar. It would be a pity not to let yourselves plan way ahead, even if others regard your plans as nothing but castles in the air. Take a chance on it!

ARIES & CANCER: You, Aries, can inflict much more pressure on Cancer's psyche than that Cancer person would like to admit. It might take much longer than you wish, and you have to be careful not to take the blame for something that has already gone wrong. Let Cancer work things out his or her way, because Cancer is wonderful at fixing intangibles.

ARIES & LEO: If you need an aphorism, Leo could be the helium and you, Aries, could be the balloon! Concentrate on using both your attributes to soar to the highest levels of achievement. You might reach your goals by doing this, at least until the balloon starts to leak—and unfortunately, the chances are good that will happen.

ARIES & VIRGO: If Virgo is out to entertain you, be careful, because that means Virgo is putting up a false front to get his or her wily way. Your question might be infringing on Virgo's wants, but it should be the other way around. You should be helping Virgo to see things clearly, because falseness is actually not Virgo's cup of tea. Virgo just might feel threatened by you, so half of the quest is getting Virgo to understand this.

ARIES & LIBRA: This is a command: let yourself be influenced by Libra's charm; you might learn something. Libra, your opposite, can at times show you the way to lighten one of your burdens, and your questioning should help you find out which one.

ARIES & SCORPIO: Select your words with care. Scorpio may weigh and measure your language for and against you. Don't jump into an argument for argument's sake only, because you could end up with a bad taste in your mouth. If you and Scorpio team up under the right circumstances, your involvement will be well worth your while.

ARIES & SAGITTARIUS: Imagine the Sag stark naked! Doing so will bring down any barrier, especially for your free-spirited nature, which enhances your charms and helps you to be more commanding. Then plan things far into the future when you have an innovative outcome in view.

ARIES & CAPRICORN: Whatever it is that you are going to be asking each other, make sure the question includes an industrial aspect, like choosing which vehicle to use to carry your loads, because if you can concentrate on the concrete aspects of your mutual quest, you will both benefit. Neither of your signs is a time-waster, but without caution, you could lose your way instead of creating a path.

ARIES & AQUARIUS: One of you is bolder than the other; the other is more of an explorer. When your two signs are put together, there is no telling which one of you will take on which of these two very important characteristics. Just make sure that you, Aries, don't take on both, because Aquarius will put up the most cunning of all possible fights!

ARIES & PISCES: Give Pisces a chance to talk things out, over, or through. Have you heard the expression, "He clammed up"? You might provoke Pisces to do that, so don't! You, Aries, need to command your heart to be warmer. You have more to learn than you would like to think.

TAURUS

strength

"We're all of us sentenced to solitary confinement inside our own skins, for life."

—*Tennessee Williams*

Taurus, if by any chance you find yourself lacking the strength you need to carry out a quest (and be sure you take things one at a time), don't be afraid to start again. When you admit that you need more time, you are taking the first step toward asking yourself the right question. You actually connect with your vital strength when you either bide your time or tune in to the right hunch. You really should be self-assured enough to make things happen. And you do. However, you must take into account that your strength swings up and down, from mortification to invincibility, from feeling overwhelmed to being absolutely tranquil. The question is an all-out cause for you, Taurus, meaning you should take care to put all your forces behind the right cause. When you don't find the right cause, you weaken yourself.

Taking all this into account seems like an easy enough way to work things out. However, as you are a person who considers each aspect of a plan slowly (and often surely), following this advice isn't as simple as it sounds. You can allow too many things to become personal quests for you, and at times you can become lost in an extremely personal labyrinth. For you, Taurus, when it seems easy, it means that your questioning has reached its deepest, most incisive point. Your strength lies in the ability to sort things out, and the strength of Aries, Gemini, Cancer, Leo, Virgo, Libra, Scorpio, Sagittarius, Capricorn, Aquarius, and Pisces lies in having a Taurus there to help sort things out. Your strength is in helping others discern the valor and the compassion of their questions.

It is extremely important that you do not confuse strength with toughness or energy. Neither has anything to do with the way you can and should question yourself. Leave quantity to the other signs, for it is the quality of what you think you can ask for that you, Taurus, can lean on and with which you find the true meaning of your strength. Your first step is to take the bull by the horns, but make sure that they are *your* horns. Of all signs, yours is the most specific, meaning that you, Taurus, can draw unbelievable strength from the 21,000 breaths you take each day. Does that sound far-fetched? It isn't, if it is seen from Taurus's perspective. This is a forceful cosmic connection, which is what Taurus is all about.

TAURUS
strength

TAURUS & ARIES: Aries can learn from your determination. You have the ability to stand your ground—and you should. Truthfully, Aries gets stronger by studying the ways and means with which you, Taurus, seem to strengthen yourself, so perhaps you should take the lead here, although getting Aries to be second-in-command will definitely take some time.

TAURUS & TAURUS: At the very center of our brains, there is a place called the nucleus accumbens, where pleasure is experienced. This precise spot will be at your disposal, Taurus, if you learn to push the correct buttons in yourself. When you do, you will realize that you knew how to feel pleasure all along; in fact you can teach all the other signs just how to find it! Both of you should realize that you are in this together.

TAURUS & GEMINI: You, Taurus, should learn a bit from Gemini's adaptability. I think it has been said before, but there is no way to emphasize it enough: loosen up a bit, stay cool, and show your strength in indecipherable ways! Wait a bit and don't be too pushy, unless you have to.

TAURUS & CANCER: If it is a full moon, cool off. If it isn't, take your time and sway, harmonize, get in the mood, fill the air with song, and tune in. In other words, use niceties and gentleness without having other appointments. Cancer is usually on a different circadian time zone from everyone else. If you connect, it can be just divine.

TAURUS & LEO: The "ohhh" could turn into an "oh-oh!" if you don't get your priorities straight. So work on a plan and keep an eye open for trouble that could arise, because Leo certainly won't. Leo will probably want the light to be in just the right place to be giving the right glow, while you are busy working on the plug. You should always try to beat Leo to it!

TAURUS & VIRGO: You could use some of Virgo's laid-back approach and Virgo could use some of your style. But don't let Virgo know that you are not completely comfortable with him or her, because Virgo will never forgive you if Virgo thinks that you think that he or she isn't hip enough! Sound complicated? It might be complicated with someone with this interesting sign, though it will be well worth it!

TAURUS & LIBRA: Both of you should be on the very same wavelength because you were blessed with Venus as a ruler. However, you possess the ability to stand your ground while Libra is happier when things go smoothly. To even things out, when in doubt, find a more comfortable or a lovelier place in which you can settle things. Let yourself be caught up in the possibility of splurging and the frequency of pleasure before asking a direct question.

TAURUS & SCORPIO: Since Scorpio is your opposite sign, no matter who he or she is in your life—colleague, neighbor, or lover—there is an undercurrent of sex in the matter. Once you accept this fact and get past it one way or another, you will be able to figure out how to measure any emotions that are involved.

TAURUS & SAGITTARIUS: "That is precisely what I wanted to know" is a response that Sagittarius is very good at giving, especially when questioned about something he or she is not too sure of. This is because truthfulness is usually part of Sag's own strength, so you shouldn't beat around the bush. Instead, be direct and forthright.

TAURUS & CAPRICORN: You might find that both of you are hunting for the same thing. Explain something in a different language—body language, sign language, or even pictures instead of words—and Capricorn will understand why you care so much about this crazy thing in the first place!

TAURUS & AQUARIUS: If you let Aquarius get tired out, you can make any question look like a springboard toward another goal. Once you've got Aquarius interested, be careful, for he or she just might slip away and move on to the next quest, which is what Aquarians are so good at doing. It would be great if you could get Aquarius to respect the fervor of your strength.

TAURUS & PISCES: If you let your spirits soar and get Pisces involved in the alarm system that just possibly could be triggered by the correct answer to whatever you are thinking about, you will be doing yourself a favor, and the general outcome could benefit a whole lot of people.

GEMINI

listening

*"We have two ears and one mouth that we may listen the
more and talk the less."*

—*Zeno*

Since you feel much safer when you are doing the talking,
Gemini, your quest is to learn how to listen. In fact, Gemini,
the "double sign," is only really double when you are deciding if you are in a listening mode or an influencing mode. Are
you talking or are you listening? Because you, Gemini, don't
have to be quiet when you are listening, although you do
need to heed what others have to say. And when you're the
one doing the talking, your extremely interesting and
volatile mind can turn almost anything around, changing it
into a completely different thing! To make it even more
quixotic, every question you ask should have a double meaning. In fact, you can make something out of nothing just by
listening to yourself. And even if you can't, you definitely
can convince people that you *can*. You need to make your
questions literally audible to others. From there things can
only get better.

"Know yourself," said Socrates, which comes down to
us like a quick-march from B.C. to A.D., perhaps with a little
help and illumination from the stars. If you allow yourself
the time for a heartfelt self-examination, the questions that
may stump others will enlighten you because by being a lis-

tener, you know how to increase, substitute, or duplicate the tricky questions. You "get" yourself so well.

Don't worry if you have doubts, because you are still on the right track. By doubting, you are tapping into the thing that gets you over the first hurdle, so you can continue down the right path because you have dared to defy your own double aspect. Your question should be double-edged, double-faced, have a double entendre (it could even have a rather risqué side), or be double-hearted. These duplicities will be best for everyone else as they listen to you, or, if worse comes to worst, as you listen to yourself.

The only possible downer is if you find yourself to be unintelligible—to yourself or to others. To be certain that this isn't the case, dare to ask the question, "Are you understanding me?" Or "Am I understanding myself?" Others should have no doubt that you, Gemini, can shed light on the answer simply by asking, "So what do you think?"— which is a great question no matter what sign you are.

GEMINI
listening

GEMINI & ARIES: Scrutinize. If you let Aries take the first step, you will be able to put future doubts where they belong—to rest. In other words, you can either forget the whole thing and find someone else or encourage Aries to follow your example by keeping still and quiet for once. You should cut out any in-betweens or go-betweens.

GEMINI & TAURUS: Be careful here. Don't assume that because the first step is easy the rest will be so, Gemini. You need to spend some quality time being introspective, and you would benefit from the advice of an Aries or a Leo. This is not true for Taurus, who could be more narcissistic than you expected. In this combination, especially if a question is involved, you should take the lead. Are you listening?

GEMINI & GEMINI: Whichever one of you figures out how to exchange listening for eavesdropping (which is much more subtle and requires more tact), or at the very least, just plain overhearing (which means you are in the right place at the right time), then that person will be the one to ask the right question first. So keep your ears open for the one thing you need to know and then sprint for the finish line. This combination should be filled with questions—the answers come when you take turns.

GEMINI & CANCER: You will have to learn to do two things at once, like walking and chewing gum. Learning to juggle can be difficult, but you'll realize that you get much more done when you deal with more than one feeling at a time. Try to pay attention to Cancer's mood before starting. And remember, if, on a whim, Cancer listens at the right time, he or she can be a wonderful transmitter of any question under all circumstances.

GEMINI & LEO: With Leo, try using any word-association game. The quicker Leo's reply, the better for both of you. Dwelling too long on a question or getting questionable responses can actually work against you because you are giving each other too much time to use your own strong pulling powers. This is the one combination in which listening is not as important as it is with other signs.

GEMINI & VIRGO: Virgo might feel that you, Gemini, are saying exactly the wrong thing or are being too demanding. To avoid exacerbating the misunderstanding, ask Virgo to make a list of his or her needs before you start calling Virgo's point of view some kind of nonsense. Each of you has a fifty-fifty chance of being right, so pay attention to your doubts because they could become a necessary tool.

GEMINI & LIBRA: Libra's easygoing yet headstrong power is just what you need to see straight and listen to the wind, the rain, and the world outside of yourself. There is so much going on that you haven't given yourself the time to see and listen to, that once you agree to ask the right question—at least one that Libra will agree with—you will change and you will be better off.

GEMINI & SCORPIO: If you are coworkers and there is in-house drama, it is just fine. If the question surpasses that situation, take time off to listen exclusively to Scorpio without being hindered by a third party who surely is getting in the way. You two will need more time than you think to work things out.

GEMINI & SAGITTARIUS: Sagittarius is a wonderful light-house for you, Gemini. Though Sag is your opposite sign, this is definitely a combination in which you should keep your mouth closed. Sagittarius is the best thing that can happen to you, if you follow these three simple rules: (1) find a Sagittarius; (2) let Sagittarius make the interpretations; (3) take inspiration from Sagittarius's words.

GEMINI & CAPRICORN: It might take some time, but try to encourage Capricorn to leave your first place of encounter and move on to a second. You can take this figuratively or not, meaning you can change rooms, cities, countries, or continents—what it is depends on you. The question could turn into a never-ending story, a quest in which you want to go on and on.

GEMINI & AQUARIUS: Some scientists say it's much more important to do something satisfying that includes hard work than only to have fun. They say that satisfying work leaves the mind more available for grown-up activities that require cognition. Both of you could come to this same conclusion if you put your minds to it by listening to the needs of the world and acknowledging the importance of a decent question. Try it out!

GEMINI & PISCES: I hear two people disagreeing. So try harder, Gemini, and entertain the deep-seated need to understand, which Pisces is born with, before you even ask whatever. Then try asking for something loftier than you thought you could get away with. You probably can't get away with it anyway, so give yourself a better start by listening to your conscience, and then maybe you will let Pisces pave the way.

CANCER

talking

"Behold, this dreamer cometh."

—*Genesis*

When you, Cancer, talk, you can illuminate those choices that make words light up memories or ideas in our heads. A tone or a gesture can change the meanings of the simplest words. When we talk, we deliver an expression of speech. Nothing else can imitate what the mind does when it interprets an idea by using one word. You, Cancer, hold the key to emotions, and everyone else should thank you for unlocking the door, or maybe we all should just blame it all on the moon, your fickle ruler.

A Cancer person, so connected over the ages to Mother Earth, should really talk things over—in any language—when questioning himself, herself, or others because Cancer is so good at giving other people a chance. If you are a Cancer person, record yourself talking and then listen to the sound of your own voice. You may be in for a surprise. If you hear something unpleasant, question others and work out a way to change it: modulate your voice, take voice lessons, or develop the musical ear that you were almost certainly born with.

You can play with a big percentage of the doubts that the rapid passing of the moon over your sign brings about, hopefully to your advantage, if you believe in your own personal language and in what you have to say to yourself. You need to be conscious of the way you can convince, console, or influence others by the sound of your voice. You should be able to use that unique sound as a device to charm others. When you are questioning, you are transmitting yourself in such a way that people enjoy talking to you, not just listening. You need their input and they certainly need yours. You do better when the vibes go back and forth and your asking turns into something compelling that is ultimately for someone's good.

You are the first of the three emotive astrological signs (the other two are Scorpio and Pisces), which means you should set aside some time each day to try to tune in to your own resonance, so you can learn to sort out the negative from the positive, the interesting from the boring, the healthy from the unhealthy. At times you might be at a loss for words, but that only means you should talk things over with others—as long as you don't gossip, for even though gossip is a way of telling a story, it brings out the worst in you. The ancient Chaldeans saw your sign, Cancer, as the path that led to the door where new souls could enter and understand the world. Open your door with words, let people in, and try to be as objective as the quest merits—or, perhaps, as you deserve.

CANCER

talking

CANCER & ARIES: Don't take it too much to heart if an Aries asks you to keep your mouth closed. It only means that you haven't been as precise as you should be, or perhaps as he or she thought you should have been. Instead of feeling hurt, let Aries show you a new way to work things out. Give in, but don't try too hard.

CANCER & TAURUS: You should "Let It Be," as a Beatles song said. If you can actually carry a tune and get the Taurus to enliven your song, both of you need no more than a breath of fresh air to get things rolling. The question doesn't even matter that much. You can show Taurus how to look better and vice versa.

CANCER & GEMINI: Don't give away your secret or anyone else's, for Gemini will not be able to keep from spilling it when there is a quest going on between your two signs. Gemini's untruthfulness could get you to take the blame for something you had no part in. So it's a bit of a Catch-22 situation between both of you. Wake up, Cancer, this is no time to sleep!

CANCER & CANCER: This might sound rather far out, but the way you talk things over will depend on the way you woke up this morning. When you are questioning yourself or talking about what might be coming with another Cancer, tune out for a moment and try to recall how you felt upon awakening. This first feeling of the day usually has a deeper meaning, and you would be wise to discuss it.

CANCER & LEO: You are going to have to put your best foot forward in order not to bore Leo. Propose something that has to do with fantasy—maybe not your own personal fantasy but what you suspect is Leo's. If you think that Leo is playing with your time, he or she probably is. Don't sulk about it; instead, give Leo a dose of his or her own medicine, so to speak.

CANCER & VIRGO: Virgo will hate to admit it, but you, Cancer, can flaunt your experience and you will be doing Virgo a favor by doing so. You will show Virgo that he or she has met his or her match, but it will take time for Virgo to agree. Ask Virgo why. It's just as good as a simple question as it is a whole conversation.

CANCER & LIBRA: Sometimes when the two of you get together, you might feel as if you started off on the wrong foot. You don't have much in common, but if you find something that you both agree is beautiful, you could have fun together. Talk yourselves out of dislikes and into likes. Doing this is comparable to tuning in to a radio station that a roomful of people call all enjoy.

CANCER & SCORPIO: "That Old Black Magic" should make you feel like "Here I Go Again," even if you don't seem to relate to Scorpio at all. The fact that a Scorpio is around means that "Something's in the Air" or something's gonna give! If you don't get this, you are not interacting as you should. In this combination, "Everything Old Is New Again," so recycle old feelings.

CANCER & SAGITTARIUS: Perhaps Cancer is more than a sign—it is a state of being. Well, Sagittarius couldn't care less and will think that is complete nonsense. So take what he or she has to give and make things better when you can, which may not be now, even if you would like it to be. The question is "Shall we give it a try?" Talk it over without going to extremes.

CANCER & CAPRICORN: One of you might show the other something rather unusual. If you get a little scared, it is only because you are dealing with a mirror image, since Capricorn is your opposite sign. This is a case in which you might be at a loss for words, which usually is not your fault, but which you can use as your forte. There is always a lesson to be learned here.

CANCER & AQUARIUS: Put any worries aside and try to work things out. The good part or the bad part may not last as long as you think, but if you get as far as talking about something you have in common, you might learn how to access genuine enthusiasm.

CANCER & PISCES: Here we go again. Emotions might get in the way of a simple conversation that doesn't have to be especially meaningful or important. Just take it easy and it should work out. And take into account that Pisces likes to tell others when to talk, because Pisces knows how to enjoy silence. And you need to learn to do the same.

LEO
spending
"Where there is no vision, the people perish."

—*Job.*

A Leo knows how to spend time with great pleasure, how to magnify his or her own powers, and how to enlarge any quest to everyone's benefit. Most Leos, however, need to curb their emotional spending to leave room to ask questions that fit their very specific, eventful selves as well as others. You are not alone out there, Leo, and if what I have to say offends you, please forgive me. You do not like to spend time on things you consider unimportant. When a Leo is involved, others should realize that nothing is very simple.

Leo, you can ask fascinating questions that lead to enthusiastic answers from other signs, and especially from those other signs lucky enough to spend time with you! Take a look around, if you dare, check out your surroundings, and then double-check them. You Leos are what I call multi-harmonious beings, which means you can make many people feel better, a few persons feel almost blessed, or one person feel assured—as long as they are on your good side. But woe to anyone who incurs your wrath. When you feel like it, you have the capacity to make others feel quite terrible at worst and "out of it" at best. You need to keep in mind that when you exclude people, they feel as if they are losing out on a good thing. Excluding people is one of your many weapons, though it can be part of your strength. Others should try to remember that it is always wise to have at least one Leo on their side, so when any question about expenditure comes up in their lives, they can ask you for advice. For you, Leo, helping others bring out your best—both for their benefit and for yours.

Leo, you are a great fix-it person, meaning you can usually help others find their way out of what may seem like gridlocked situations. Others may regard the time you spend on something as questionable or as a waste of energy, but you were born with the knowledge that whatever path you embark upon is a real illuminated choice toward finding the real, even naked, truth. While you are on this quest, the rest of us should spend more time leaning on you Leos who could, if you so desire, point out the most fruitful endeavors.

- LEO
spending

LEO & ARIES: This is an elite combination that can bring out the best in both of you and, once in a while, the worst— but that would be because Aries probably will not want to share responsibilities. This sharing is what you both need to work on so that when the time of reckoning comes, you both can be held accountable for the outcome, which could be okay.

LEO & TAURUS: This is the one combination in which Leo can set a real example by giving Taurus a break. Don't try to outshine Taurus in any way. Instead, let Taurus feel his or her way through the ensuing situation, and you'll see how far a simple thing like respect can go!

LEO & GEMINI: Both of you could talk a blue streak and thus restore a lot of confidence not only in each other but also in a third party. You are at your best when you are combining your knowledge about worth and money. At best, you will put enough aside to be able to spend a lot together in the future.

LEO & CANCER: If Cancer loosens up a bit—just a tiny bit—you can teach him or her a thing or two about spelling out feelings so that the time spent on oneself works out better. Once you put feelings in the right place, both of you will do just fine, even though Cancer will usually have more to lose.

LEO & LEO: If you are able to exaggerate a bit, by overspending, underspending, or even rejoicing in wasting some spent time, you will be doing yourself a real favor. If you can combine the three possibilities with another Leo, you might be on the right track toward making a better you. Question yourselves.

LEO & VIRGO: You might think it is easy to overrule a Virgo. It isn't—and it will do you no good to try. Focus is a big issue for you, Leo, so just use your magnanimous self to charm Virgo, and then listen to and learn from whatever Virgo has to say about how accountable you really are for your own spending.

LEO & LIBRA: When a Leo and a Libra get together, having a good time is what "being together" should be all about—neither of you should settle for anything less. You might have to work out a schedule to make time for each other and if you could fit in some kind of a shopping spree (literally!), each of you would be doing the other a huge favor. Your two signs can depend on each other for now, but Libra can depend on you, Leo, certainly through the next millennium.

LEO & SCORPIO: You should exercise caution here, Leo, because if you say the wrong thing, then you will be confronted with a person (your ever-quest-seeking Scorpio companion) who has completely shut down as if he or she were experiencing a real power failure because Scorpios don't like to be rubbed the wrong way. So, let Scorpio have his or her way, at least somewhat, or else there could be a real problem and you won't get too far.

LEO & SAGITTARIUS: This combination should either light up Leo's day or clarify Sagittarius's question. Remember never to be dishonest with each other, because there is not much forgiveness in this forceful combination. If either of you act on a whim, the result could be absolutely great. I think the word "supercallifragilisticexpialidocious" must have been invented by your combined effort.

LEO & CAPRICORN: Be sure not to let Capricorn wait around too long for your answers. Capricorn will never forgive you if you do this and could ruin your reputation by telling everyone about your faux pas. Some people claim that there is no such thing as a dumb question, so spend some time trying to convince Capricorn of that.

LEO & AQUARIUS: Curb your impatience with Aquarius, your opposite sign. Although you would like to spend time elsewhere, the affair in question will turn out to be educational for both of you. Take some time off, make Aquarius warm up, don't get mad, and don't get even!

LEO & PISCES: Anything that has to do with spending or with questioning why you are together has a deeper meaning than you might have expected. Assure Pisces that you are being truthful. Pisces is so intuitive that he or she can tell if what you present is outdated and soon will no longer be of use. Don't sweep anything under the carpet.

VIRGO
to win

"Victory often changes her side."

Homer, the Iliad

Winning is something that may still take you by surprise, even though you may have been waiting, planning, and preparing for its arrival. Winning is not solely Virgo's domain, but you, Virgo, do deserve to win, perhaps more than any other sign. Why? Because when you do win, others can learn from your reaction. When you win, it is because you have chosen the right thing, even if it took you longer than others would have liked and even if you picked on yourself without mercy in the process. No matter how you got to the finish line first, you should show others who were not born under this sign how you got there.

Virgo, you definitely know when to put your stake on something that is really worth winning. Only you can figure out what that is. The best question that you, Virgo, can ask yourself is this: "Does this triumph actually win me over to the side I wanted to be on?" If the answer is yes, the win will be an actual gain. Otherwise it could be risky or unwanted business on a small or large scale. Consider this: Ten lottery winners were once interviewed for a *New York Times Sunday Magazine* article. Only one of them felt that he had actually improved his life; the other nine almost wished that they had never won.

Winning does have to do with willpower, but as the old saying goes, "It's the way you play the game, not the winning, that counts." Virgo, since you work things out by asking the right questions, even at a very young age, you should know how to turn things around so that they become win-win situations; the rest is pure chance, not choice. The Chinese say that we actually choose the sign we want to be and that is why we are all born at certain times. Could it be that the baby's first cry is trying to say, "I made it! I won!"? By being born, we are all participating in this huge cosmological lottery.

Virgo, you can help others unfold within the risky business of winning because you know exactly how to pinpoint or match circumstance to experience. It is not that you will choose the right Lotto numbers for others, Virgo; it's that your instinct will help lead us to the store that is selling whatever it takes to make us feel like a winner.

VIRGO
to win

VIRGO & ARIES: The answer to this question will be a win-win situation if you put two great intellectual forces together: yours! However, you can't depend on intuition alone. Hard work and racking your brains can bring about a turn in the tide for a long-term difficult but worthwhile answer.

VIRGO & TAURUS: Even if you don't end up on the top of the pile, you should have a great time trying to get there. You two can be dynamite together, and you can, without causing harm, push and shove other people away so you can get to the front of the line. Are you asking a silly question? Not to worry; dealing with the answer will bring the winning streak.

VIRGO & GEMINI: Gemini thinks that by showing that he or she could be the boss, you will both win out over anything else. Not so. For you, Virgo to find a suitable gain, you definitely must not take the first step. The question here is this: Can you hold out long enough? If not, Gemini will try to trap you into doing something rash. Don't be afraid to practice caution.

VIRGO & CANCER: By teaming up, you two could become masters of any game. If you bend with the wind—that is, if you play a bit of that old game called *cadavre exquis,* in which you take turns doing your own thing, then put the bits and pieces together without a real plan—you will be doing yourselves and each other a favor. Go for it!

VIRGO & LEO: If it is absolutely necessary for you to win in this combination, make sure you win *with* Leo rather than making Leo lose. If you have caused Leo to be the loser, prepare yourself to accept Leo's fair revenge. If you, Virgo, can take being ignored by Leo, then go ahead and play any game, and may the best person win.

VIRGO & VIRGO: Together you two could surmount any difficulty and win almost any contest by being careful, precise, and thoughtful. So dare all the other signs to try to get you two on their side, for everyone's benefit. Your approach should be low-key, so others don't get frightened and consider you out of reach.

VIRGO & LIBRA: If either of you can enhance your own willpower, you will be able to convince the other that what you won is worth the price you paid. This is actually much better than just winning for the heck of it! Libra is such a good partner for you that it is always worthwhile to try again, try harder, try later, and certainly try over.

VIRGO & SCORPIO: Scorpio will probably be sure of winning because he or she has willed it to be so. Don't waste your time trying to convince Scorpio that he or she is wrong, because whether you win or lose, question or answer, you are probably in for a whopper of a surprise. The surprise will be Scorpio's response and should be to your advantage. You do make a good team.

VIRGO & SAGITTARIUS: Your quest might be a wild-goose chase that peters out into nothingness. But volumes have been written about nothingness both in philosophy and mathematics, which means that nothingness is actually something. You would do well to realize that Sagittarius has a very flexible viewpoint, from which you can learn a great deal. But keep in mind that neither one of you is likely to come out on top.

VIRGO & CAPRICORN: You could actually be stunned by Capricorn's insight, especially if you show Capricorn that acquiring honor is much more important to you than winning. Once you make this desire known, Virgo, the two of you can sit down and figure out how to acquire a reasonable triumph over unreasonable doubts. Basically you two make a good team.

VIRGO & AQUARIUS: This might be a wild ride that may not lead to much, but it should be fun, as long as it is safe. You shouldn't take any unnecessary chances unless you are sure they are worth your time. Forget about winning for a moment, and first deal with the question at hand: "Why are you here in the first place?" There is a first time for everything, and if Aquarius offers you a first time, Virgo, it should be a good thing.

VIRGO & PISCES: These opposites could turn a question into a no-win situation. However, sometimes Pisces can bring out the best in you, and the best in you despises failure. So you will have to obtain some of the bounty, whatever the price. An interesting challenge for both of you! In fact, maybe you two will prove that there is a pot of gold at the end of the rainbow.

LIBRA
loving
"Reason is the mistress and queen of all things."
                                        Marcus Tullius Cicero

It would be ludicrous of me to tie this illogical word—"loving"—to one sign only. From an astrological viewpoint, the world is divided into twelve parts, like chapters in a book. Leo, the fifth so-called chapter, has to do with love, luck, and the pursuit of happiness, while in the seventh chapter, Libra, marriage and associations are entwined with mystifying relationships. It is an interesting point of view, and well worth dwelling on. Love, in ancient Greek thought (and we haven't improved much there), was related to the word "eros" and was defined as having to do with desire, longing, imbalance, and more often than not, sexuality. Love causes people to gravitate toward strange things, which can dictate passionate pursuits and inspire irrational actions.

It would be very sad if any one illuminated choice could answer all questions dealing with love, because each question that has something to do with love is a unique creation, made by the person who asks it at a precise moment in time. There are not enough stars in the sky or neurons in the brain to pinpoint answers to all that our hearts desire. However, Libra, ruled by Venus, who is the doyenne or queen of love in most astrological books, has the talent to deal with the word in relation to others and the search that compels us to find some order in this balancing act. Libra, I bestow upon you the honor of being able to deliver the words "to love" or "loving" because you will be the gracious expediter of the words we need to decipher our love. Ask yourselves, "Why have I chosen to use these words: 'love,' 'to love,' or 'loving'?" Love is a challenge, an afterthought, a choice, a spark, a reminder, a transition, a cycle, a creation, a precise cosmological moment, a memory, a vocabulary, a language, a recognition, and a zillion other things that all of us can choose to name. Each sign carries certain faculties in its cosmological love chapter that can be used to view, feel, file, edit, and process the love factor.

So Libra is my choice to show us how to give ourselves and each other a break, loosen up, and illuminate a fraction of an instant during, while, or after you start asking yourself, "Is this love?" You could ask it many different ways: "*Is* this love?" "Is *this* love?" "Is this *love?*" Don't worry. If you ask yourself the question, it certainly is worth a moment in time to find some kind of answer, for love definitely is the most important of all quests.

LIBRA
loving

LIBRA & ARIES: Anything goes when opposites attract. Charles Dickens, the novelist and an Aquarian, once said that one never knows what one is capable of doing until one tries. Aries will try anything for love, even though that love may not last forever. Even so, in this case, it is well worth the attempt. Libra, embellish, perfect, and remember that Aries can always teach you something new about loving.

LIBRA & TAURUS: You two have a real link: your astrological ruler is Venus. Therefore the sensual side of your nature can carry you through thick or thin if you allow yourselves to accept it. Enjoy it, release it, and let it grow. Taurus needs a bit more assurance than you like to give away, Libra, so this could be a real crusade for either of you.

LIBRA & GEMINI: Subtlety is the right word for any loving situation that can be sought after, suggested, and sagaciously planned by either one of you. Gemini is at his or her best when allowed to choose, and you, Libra, can demonstrate without overdoing your cunning. You two should gravitate toward each other with ease!

LIBRA & CANCER: There might be some tension between you that can be worked out over a longer period of time than you two are willing to commit to. Cancer could get you, Libra, to double your efforts, but only if you relax. The mood here is like a mission straining to reach perfection, but remember, Libra, that perfection doesn't exist.

LIBRA & LEO: Love is in the air all the time for Leo, so don't dawdle and take whatever plunge is compatible with your feelings. If you don't forget Leo's telephone number or neglect to say thank-you, you might stir unused possibilities and kindle desires that only you can understand. One way or another, get in there and see what's doing.

LIBRA & VIRGO: Friendship and endearment should come first in this combination. After that, whatever follows has a slight chance to bring you good fortune or spirited poetry. Try to latch on to a questionable source that will add spice into the relationship. Does this sound rather complicated? Try to define love, and you'll see what complication really is. Always talk things over with a Virgo.

LIBRA & LIBRA: The two of you can either bore each other to tears or work yourselves into a frenzy. But the only thing you should really be working on is to make the relationship worth your while. You can take more from another Libra than you would from any other sign, for there is a real learning curve here: it's like seeing your reflection in a mirror for the first time.

LIBRA & SCORPIO: This combination may seem like one thing and turn out to be another. Both of you have to work within a me-myself-and-I mode without hiding your feelings or sparing words. Deep inside yourselves, which could be just as far as deep space, you need to figure out how to compromise. Remember that old song, "Taking a Chance on Love"—and do it!

LIBRA & SAGITTARIUS: It is important to be attuned to the time you are spending together as well as the way you are spending it. Try counting the moments, pleasures, promises, or whatever you can depend on for better or for worse. You may find that the pleasures outlast your attention span. What do you care? You need each other—no question about it!

LIBRA & CAPRICORN: Take your time with Capricorn and remember that it is completely irrelevant if you are not quite comfortable the first time around. Libra can work on idealism, and Capricorn can work on feeling comfortable, which is something he or she loves to question. If you find a loving interest that brings you together, your time together may be worth the search for that common bond.

LIBRA & AQUARIUS: Your relationship could be flashier than you are used to, but you might find yourselves enjoying things that you would not dare admit, especially when nobody is noticing. If you find yourself slightly bewildered, give in to a lurking desire behind the scenes. Just take into account that desire doesn't always have to be for physical intimacy; it can be a love for chocolate chip cookies, among other things.

LIBRA & PISCES: Look out: you could hurt Pisces by forgetting that you, Libra, sometimes get lost in personal journeys, which make you forget that others have feelings. Don't promise anything to Pisces unless you intend to deliver. This combination could turn into a very interesting friendship.

SCORPIO
mystery
"It is a riddle wrapped in a mystery inside an enigma."
—*Winston Churchill*

No one is as good as Scorpio at getting people to understand the enigmatic part of their own questions, if there is one. If there isn't, this special sign can turn the question into something more interesting. Because searching is part of your life's endeavor, Scorpio, it is easy for you to find the strongest and weakest points of any mysterious meanings in many situations since pinpointing is one of your gifts, Scorpio.

It is important to point out that the word "mysterious" has nothing to do with "vague" as far as Scorpio is concerned. If by chance you feel that you get confused by or because of vagueness, it is because you are not using the strong side of your sign. Mystery is knowledge, while vagueness for you is just a waste of time. You are the king or queen of alchemy and can exchange one thing for another by wishing for it, which is something very few people understand or are capable of doing. You have to remember that nothing comes easy to you. For example, even if you happen to have gotten your money the old-fashioned way, by inheriting it, for some mysterious cosmic reason, you will be unable to gain access to it as easily as others would. And another mystery is that you are a wonderful and enigmatic leader. People don't forget you because you are the only one who knows how to get in touch with the most difficult side of your immensely imaginative, spacious mind. You can usually express yourself in ways that reverberate in other people's ears. They want more, so you lead them. Sometimes, also in a rather mysterious way, you can scare people. Take heed: blockbuster movies earn millions by using scare tactics on their audiences. People let go of something when they are afraid, which brings us back to what you, Scorpio, can do for us.

Scorpio, you can help others by clarifying the importance of that which they have approached and now are questioning. Once the right question has been asked, the strategies for negotiating, bonding, and building are illuminated. You pick up the thread that is at one end of a ball of twine that will ultimately lead others through the labyrinth of themselves. You seem to help others unravel the mystery that sometimes makes them mumble and that can confuse them. Others should welcome you, Scorpio, to this part of their lives. You can to help others ask succinct questions so that they will have more time to understand themselves. In the end, others might have much more fun than they were counting on, and you can prepare all of us for the next pleasures with great expectations.

SCORPIO
mystery

SCORPIO & ARIES: Perhaps Aries will have trouble understanding you or will jump to the wrong conclusion because he or she might not give you the time to find out. Be prepared to change because of Aries. The change could be in scenery, in feelings, or in enigmas.

SCORPIO & TAURUS: Myrrh is a bitter fragrance, which is what you need to jolt Taurus out of his or her sophisticated conceit, which may be just as perplexing to Taurus as it is to you. Jostle his or her nature with an unexpected fragrance, as in medieval times when maidens and gentlemen used potent potions to capture souls.

SCORPIO & GEMINI: You are the one person who can usually restrain Gemini's tendency to be superficial. Gemini can get away with anything except when Scorpio is around. Take your time, Scorpio, and confuse Gemini with your profound observations.

SCORPIO & CANCER: You, Scorpio, could be the perfect alchemist for Cancer's deepest and most secret wish. All you have to do is ask. By the time Cancer understands what you really are up to, the question will have been redirected. There will have to be a spiritual side to the story you illuminate. Do try to work things out together, even if only a crossword puzzle.

SCORPIO & LEO: Leo never does anything with naïveté, so don't let him or her get away by confusing you with a vague answer. You could try being a little more sentimental, or you could remind Leo of any heroes in his or her family tree. If things still don't work out, give each other a break and look toward someone you both respect for better answers.

SCORPIO & VIRGO: Virgo can dignify anything you take upon yourself to do. To increase your perspective and to help Virgo, you will have to be productive and take some chances. Usually, Virgo's preoccupations are worth more than a glance. If you put your forces together, gambling might be an interesting thing to do together. Why not start by buying a lottery ticket?

SCORPIO & LIBRA: Both of you should measure the importance of each of your words and questions as if they actually
had weight and size. Things will fall into place by themselves, and the mixture of your two guided lights can turn
into incredible fairy tales that will benefit others. For inspiration, try reading a fairy tale to Libra or vice versa.

SCORPIO & SCORPIO: Luke Skywalker, Yoda, the High-
lander, King Arthur, and maybe even Delilah would be no
match for this combination. You could knock them out cold
with a mystic glance or a voiceless command. So do your
best when together and let bygones be bygones. No blows
below the belt, please.

SCORPIO & SAGITTARIUS: You can always count on a Sagittarius to clear the air, help you out, and show you an unclut-
tered way of answering something that could otherwise
confuse you. If the Sag's answer is no, don't try again. But do
listen to what the Sag has to say. It's good for you, or at least
it could be.

SCORPIO & CAPRICORN: If I had a difficult, mystical, magical question to ask I wouldn't think twice about asking the
two of you, together, to help me out. Put whatever other
things you are doing on hold and open a consulting business
together. Not only could it work out, but you might find
yourselves making some money!

SCORPIO & AQUARIUS: Silence could be golden—try it out. If it is a comfortable silence, continue your quest. If it is not, conceal any ensuing anguish and use an incomprehensible or perplexing restraining order. By this I mean try to confuse Aquarius into being quiet. Try going to a concert together and losing each other in the crowd. That way you won't have to face off.

SCORPIO & PISCES: You might discover that you and Pisces are soul mates. Or you might just have to promise to try understanding each other's karma and forget about relating to any question for your own good. You could get too intense and then confuse hoping with knowing. If this combination does seem to work out, you just might be doing yourselves a favor.

SAGITTARIUS

pleasure

"When you are sincerely pleased, you are nourished."
—*Ralph Waldo Emerson*

Sagittarius can be the best sign to point the way toward pleasure—and don't we all want some! Pleasure is such a wondrous surprise when it appears in our lives, and we spend much of our time waiting for it to do so. Can pleasure be categorized as a pure bodily sensation? We take pleasure in something, pleasure can complement things, and pleasure

can develop in our consciousness. It becomes such an intimate part of ourselves that it motivates many of our actions.
Whether the pleasure one experiences is social, economic,
physical, or emotional, the amount one gets out of something and its questionable measurement influences a person's judgment and character. It will certainly help with
problem-solving tasks if you figure out the most pleasurable
way to go toward or against something.

Perhaps you can find a way to carry pleasure around
with you or to activate it when you feel the urge, which is
underlined by Sagittarius even in its symbol. Sagittarius is
represented by a centaur sending an arrow into the air. The
centaur has probably seen the mark and is sure that he will
get the great pleasure of hitting it. Who doesn't want to hit
the bull's-eye, to shoot the ball in the basket, sink it in the
hole, or make the goal? Sagittarius has the talent to show
others that *now* is yesterday's tomorrow and today's yesterday, meaning that they might as well take pleasure in the
moment—this illuminated one.

By taking hold of the now, all of us should be able to
synchronize and harmonize with pleasure, just as you,
Sagittarius, do when you listen to your favorite music. You
add the beat to others' melody. Although there is no easy-
to-use guide to this ruse, you can unravel the little quirks of
your sign that make you attuned to your lucky star. If it can
be said that the sun influences the weather, why not add
that Jupiter can inspire pleasure? And why not, by Jove?

Jupiter rules Sagittarius, so let Sagittarius point the way. Of course, many other things also have an effect on pleasure—energy, casual or careful planning, and time—but why question the appearance of pleasure anyway, since it is always nearby? If you are a Sagittarius, enjoy yourself. If you are not, tune yourself in to their pleasurable vibes!

SAGITTARIUS
pleasure

SAGITTARIUS & ARIES: Things can fall easily into place because questioning Aries comes down to having something called good old-fashioned fun! Aries can sometimes forget that fun can lead to pleasure so you, Sagittarius, should plan for it, search for it, work toward it, grab it, and then use it as best you can. You could even forecast it, like the weather, if you think things out at the right time.

SAGITTARIUS & TAURUS: One thing should lead to another, so let Taurus help you discover pleasure in things you never dreamed you could achieve. You will do well by seeking pleasure when Taurus is at your side, for Tauruses are so good at it themselves—or at least they should be!

SAGITTARIUS & GEMINI: The synergy might be a little off here, so wiggle and waggle a bit, and if you must be precise, try to oscillate and expand. You could, you can, and you should be able to adapt easily, Sagittarius, for Gemini, your opposite, can teach you how to enjoy the little things even if you wish there were more pleasure to go around.

SAGITTARIUS & CANCER: Strive to satisfy your senses by giving Cancer a chance to be with you. The words "truly, madly, deeply," which have been used in many contexts, jump to mind when you are searching or questioning. Try to gratify Cancer's whims and ways. Do remember, though, that the full moon can make a Cancer do wild things!

SAGITTARIUS & LEO: You can actually light each other up like a switchboard and help one another find the most plea-surable parts of the day and of each other's bodies. You might even find a new way of enjoying life. But you and Leo must share this knowledge with each other and then with other signs, who would love to have some of your pleasure rub off on them.

SAGITTARIUS & VIRGO: The fewer questions you ask Virgo, the better. Try to arrange things in a novel way and don't let Virgo outdo you in personal matters. If you change your viewpoints a bit, this combination could be much more pleasurable than you were counting on. But don't put all your eggs in one basket—anything could happen.

SAGITTARIUS & LIBRA: "Delight," "delectability," and "fruition" are pleasurable incantations that you should repeat twice and enjoy many times when you and Libra are dealing with each other. There is no need to philosophize here; just have a good time.

SAGITTARIUS & SCORPIO: Try to be systematic; it works well with Scorpio and you. You two can be like a symphony orchestra in which all of the musicians play their own instruments and produce a wondrous, pleasurable sound that shows how good it can be when people cooperate to produce something pleasurable. And remember, every conductor needs an orchestra to show what he or she can do.

SAGITTARIUS & SAGITTARIUS: Make yourselves gracefully available to each other on a grand scale. You could show off or show how, in either words or ways, you can get pleasure out of your mutual accessibility. Team up, Sagittariuses, and you might make others understand that the more, the merrier.

SAGITTARIUS & CAPRICORN: You will have to rely on ambition to get Capricorn to admit that he or she actually wants more pleasure than he or she is getting. You might even help a Capricorn if you lighten him or her up and if you don't ask the Cap to show you how to save up something now for a more pleasurable time later.

SAGITTARIUS & AQUARIUS: Originality is one of Aquarius's pleasurable traits that could get you rolling and conquer your heart, even if love has nothing to do with it. Since Aquarius doesn't like to take the time to explain things, try to keep up and don't let yourself get confused. I am certain that one of your two signs invented the word "mind-boggling," so it probably will be up to you, Sagittarius, to spell things out. Don't forget to ask what Aquarius specifically has to offer.

SAGITTARIUS & PISCES: One of you will be the optimist and the other the pessimist. The best way to find out who is who is to flip a coin or draw straws. At any rate, Pisces has a secret side that you might not even guess about, and your enthusiasm might just get him or her going in a more plea-surable way. Think positive and try exchanging joy for plea-sure or try showing Pisces how to.

CAPRICORN

waiting

"Hold infinity in the palm of your hand."

—*William Blake*

When you are coping with difficulties, you are at your very best, Capricorn. Time is usually your ally, and although others may suffer because of the waiting game, you know how to deal with it. The biblical patriarch Methuselah could have been a Capricorn and the 969 years that he is said to have lived were probably not long enough. Any Capricorn would have no trouble waiting around that long. You realize what others may not, however: that waiting can be one of life's biggest lessons. Those who are not born under this sign and can't stand the anticipation should ask a Capricorn for advice. You sure like to keep others waiting around you, though, Capricorn, and others better have the right question ready. You don't like to make time for the unorthodox. Perhaps your sign reaches maturity before others. In fact, many astrologers state that Capricorns are born with a lot of grown-up knowledge. Capricorns are great at long-term plans, and they never mind the long wait.

Capricorn, waiting 187,000 light years doesn't faze you. Even though nobody likes to wait forever, you are at your best when showing all the other signs how to wait for what they wish would happen *now*. If you would give yourself the time, you could show Aries, Taurus, Gemini, Cancer, Leo, Virgo, Libra, Scorpio, Sagittarius, Aquarius, and Pisces how to endure with style and panache. You know how to weigh words and can teach others how to endure the wait.

If worse comes to worst and those around you just cannot stand waiting any longer, get yourself a good dream-interpretation dictionary and look up the meanings of the things they are dreaming about. After all, humans spend about one-third of their lives sleeping, and the question as to why we patiently await pleasant dreams is something that I know you can tackle. Even though you may be an unbelieving Capricorn, remember that playing the waiting game does you lots of good and answers a lot of all the other signs' questions—so thank you for at least another 187,000 light years so all other signs, too, will wait it out while you make your way from one end of the galaxy to the other using distance as well as time.

CAPRICORN
waiting

CAPRICORN & ARIES: Dream a little! When one of you dreams about crocodiles or something else that seems irrelevant but really has meaning, the two of you should discuss it because Aries usually has more insight than you do. If the relationship is such that it is not appropriate to talk about your dreams, then ask about Aries' aspirations. Do be prepared: some mischief might evolve from this volatile combination!

CAPRICORN & TAURUS: Whatever your expectation, Capricorn, this combination should show you all you need to know. As you and Taurus are deciphering things together, other extraordinary things can happen. Taurus is always a plus to you, Capricorn, so why not plan on taking a real break? Follow the stars, or a map, and let yourselves go.

CAPRICORN & GEMINI: The conservative side of you, Capricorn, is thrown into high gear when combined with a Gemini who is, most of the time, waiting for something better to come along. So above all, try to prove to yourself that your wait is well worth your while. Hold back your expectations until you are sure that you are getting more than you planned on getting.

CAPRICORN & CANCER: If something new is in the air, great, especially for Cancer. If not, it's a good thing that you are taking your time, because you need to give yourself space to adapt. Your opposite sign, Cancer, might take too long to feel as good as he or she wants to. Adding some zest to the relationship would be perfect!

CAPRICORN & LEO: The questioning process might die out before the waiting period is over. There might be a lot of hype from Leo, but not much delivery. Watch it, but don't erase it. Try counting minutes instead of hours, so the time you spend together won't be a time bomb!

CAPRICORN & VIRGO: Why doesn't one of you recognize the fact that you are good for each other without asking so many questions? Waiting is just part of a natural process, like growing. So stick with it; at best, instead of feeling as if you have been waiting for a long time, you will feel as if you have not had nearly enough time together! Capricorn, give Virgo the chance to show you how to loosen up.

CAPRICORN & LIBRA: A misunderstanding between you does not mean that the time you spent waiting for each other was wasted. The less the question has to do with emotions, the better chance it has to work out. Be careful not to let yourself get bogged down in a sticky situation. Libra can help you move on to the next thing as soon as possible.

CAPRICORN & SCORPIO: Include others in your quest while you wait it out in good faith. Resolve any hard feelings that will not get better as time passes. If things seem to take longer than expected, it is because one of you—probably Scorpio— is wisely considering all possibilities. Have you thought of having a third party time you with an actual stopwatch?

CAPRICORN & SAGITTARIUS: Time sometimes shows that yesterday's news is a boring subject today. So while you wait, keep up to date on today's issues and use the right search engine to bring to the screen all the alternatives that you consider worthwhile. If you need more time, work on getting it, even if Sagittarius asks you to hurry up.

CAPRICORN & CAPRICORN: Because you are so good at waiting, you should teach your fellow Capricorn the words of Sophocles: "Nobody loves life like an old man." Pause to give yourselves some respite as you call a truce and enjoy the passing of time.

CAPRICORN & AQUARIUS: It might be nice to steal some time from something that has nothing to do with whatever it is that you are thinking about. In this case, Aquarius can be a good teacher for you, Capricorn, even if the new idea sounds a bit far-out. Aquarius will be grateful if you allow him or her to stall for some more time and add a little eccentricity.

CAPRICORN & PISCES: A complex process that might take ages is just what you do not need. But if waiting means getting involved with Pisces in something that you are not quite sure about, wait and see how great it can be in its best form. You might go as far as writing a new chapter to the Bible.

AQUARIUS

guessing

"Things are always at their best in the beginning."

—*Blaise Pascal*

The verb "to guess" means to form an opinion based on insufficient evidence—unless you are talking to an Aquarius. You Aquarians probably believe that some achievements result from sheer luck, and perhaps other people, born under different signs, believe the same thing. It doesn't really matter who is right. Guessing is the "significant other" of chance, and both guessing and chance have to do with luck. Too many of the things we guess at are beyond our control, but you, Aquarius, are the human tracker of plausible guessing. Aquarius is the uncontrollable sign, the one others have to guess about. By aligning themselves with an Aquarius, others usually improve their luck. By doing so, they are using the Aquarius knack. And if they think that no Aquarian had anything to do with their question, their luck, or their answer, they are wrong, because Aquarius has everything to do with chaos and randomness, and thanks to those two states, everyone can dare to take the plunge.

Aquarius, luck is not harnessed to your personal stars. You just give yourself the chance to guess and luck comes your way. You have an illogical and very private language that usually only you truly understand. You are at your best when you are not quite sure, because then there is plenty of room for other adventures. Guessing should be fun, even if there is no definite answer to the immeasurable question (immeasurable because it can grow in either way, from perfection to chaos). When you guess, you are playing at odds, but with illuminated insight, you might just catch a glimmer of something that can improve your chance and help you work on the skill that will keep you out of harm's way.

AQUARIUS
guessing

AQUARIUS & ARIES: This combination has the brilliance of a crystal. If you leave things to chance, they should definitely work out with a bang and not a whimper, whether the outcome is positive or negative. Don't meditate on it too much. Either one of you can go with your first hunches and neither of you should fear reckless behavior.

AQUARIUS & TAURUS: There is too much energy between you for only simple things to happen. No matter how much luck you find, be wary of apparent uppers that could end up as downers and vice versa. It's a bumpy ride for both of you, but Taurus, always look for other options, even if you feel that you have answered some question.

AQUARIUS & GEMINI: Anything that can be conceived could happen. This is the best combination for science-fiction-like guesswork, meaning when planets are in these two signs, alien faces could appear on our TV screens and the stories on the "X-Files" are fact, not fiction. When Aquarius and Gemini link up, anything can happen!

AQUARIUS & CANCER: Ask yourselves or each other the basic who, why, where, when, how, so that people will think that premeditation was involved instead of a simple guess. Cancer should always involve other people in whatever he or she is trying out and Aquarius does well when you revise and expand other people's possibilities.

AQUARIUS & LEO: One of you is usually wrong. I would never dare guess which one, but when you punctuate a sentence with a question mark, you are leaving things open to possibilities. If you are counting on Lady Luck, Leo will probably end up winning. Since both of you can be overachievers, watch your step. Help your opposite sign stay calm.

AQUARIUS & VIRGO: You, Aquarius, should formally agree that instead of guessing, you will both be undecided. If you can't agree, guessing is better for this combination than going with off-base, biased assumptions. Virgo feels more comfortable proving things and protects himself or herself by doing so. You, Aquarius, love to vouch for yourself, too, but there is no way you can prove that your guess is a good one!

AQUARIUS & LIBRA: You two could literally join together in a great scheme to buy into what others never even thought would be possible to agree upon. Make a wild guess and force Libra to get involved. Just remember: Wherever there is chance, Libra does best when being wild. While Aquarius does best when guessing.

AQUARIUS & SCORPIO: If you mislead Scorpio, your two magnetic selves will be caught in a never-never land of unforgiveness. If you find out that one of you has made a mistake, leave. Leave well enough alone and don't let chance put you in the position of being called bad names.

AQUARIUS & SAGITTARIUS: Saint Augustine once said, "We believe in order to know." This statement can often take the place of a mad guess. Even if you are certain of the truth, Sagittarius will consider your self-assurance laughable. At any rate, you are cut out to do well together. That's not my guess—that's in the stars!

AQUARIUS & CAPRICORN: You need to prove to Capricorn that there are always other options. Capricorn is out for safety, not originality. The best you can do is to promise that you are not guessing at why the question is being posed in the first place. Say that you know why, and give Capricorn time to work things out in his or her own way.

AQUARIUS & AQUARIUS: "Riddle Yourself This" is an old limerick. There were also "gimmericks," whose meanings had to be guessed at. The time that you spend together could be dynamite if you play guessing games, but you must accept the fact that you could be too outlandish for others to understand. To be on the safe side, spell out your meaning to each other as well as to others.

AQUARIUS & PISCES: Guess whatever you like, but don't forget the ethics of whatever is in question. You need to care about the end product and profess an understanding of cooperation. Whatever project or question you are working on should benefit not only you but a lot of other people as well. Pisces should help you tone down, Aquarius, and you can help Pisces loosen up.

PISCES
assertion

"I think therefore I am."

—*René Descartes*

Pisces, you are a citizen of the world. As such, you should be comfortable anywhere, and you usually are. You know instinctively which things are true and which are not. You are like a sign used by philosophers that looks like a sideways T, which was put in front of sentences that were generally agreed on as being true, as opposed to those that needed reasoning and debate. If you believe it, then others probably should, too. This means that you, Pisces, will usually beat everyone by making the right assertion first. When you assert, you demonstrate the definite existence of something. For you, Pisces, asserting relates you to your inner idealism, which you cannot live without.

You relate your emotional state to your intellectual conviction, which is what makes you so tolerant of others' feelings because without knowing it, even if you can't read and write, you intellectualize them. When you say yes to something, it involves a conscious action. You have the voice that dismisses complacency. In fact, you could be the great provider of self-assurance for all other signs. To do this, you need to help others decide how to assert—to say yes or no; to associate themselves with questions they can answer and move them toward a person, an idea, a job, or a relationship; to help anyone and everyone accept ideals; to endure; to make an assertion that starts with "I" and goes on to fit in somewhere special.

One of the reasons why you make things so easy on others is because you usually make things so difficult for yourself. By the time you take a chance and make your own assertions, you have gone through a huge number of your own questions. You know how things can hurt but the one thing you are most sure of is that you don't want your hurt to fall on somebody else's shoulders. Instead, you are usually there so that somebody else can cry on your shoulder. And then, because you have given so much of yourself, they can return to questioning themselves, assured that at least they are not doing so in vain.

Pisces, you have the instinctive knowledge that can show others how to rejoice in choosing—just because. With your great intuition, you can help others double-click on their illuminated choices.

PISCES
assertion

PISCES & ARIES: Endure whatever occurs and make sure that Aries takes responsibility for his or her acts out into the open. By doing this, you will help not only others but also yourself in a roundabout way. Your emotions might get in the way of your acts, so take turns agreeing on things. Either one can assure the other.

PISCES & TAURUS: You, Pisces, would do well to try to show Taurus in what area he or she is lacking. But be careful, Pisces, because you just might awaken a dormant giant of insecurity with Taurus, which you will have to deal with. Nobody can nurture Taurus better than you.

PISCES & GEMINI: Don't let yourself be stumped by pettiness, Pisces. You can rise above common pettiness, but sometimes you can be at a loss for words because Gemini can be so thoughtless at times. You'll have to find an innovative way to beat Gemini at his or her own game. At times, things can be as clear as mud.

PISCES & CANCER: Because both of you can be so cautious, details might hold up agreements. Herman Hesse, a Cancer with a Pisces moon (which is a great combination), wrote that "A man's life is a path toward oneself, the sketch of a road." Pisces and Cancer can lean on each other with grace and still be assured of their own strength.

PISCES & LEO: Leo usually doesn't need help from others—Leo usually gives help and might be turned off by Pisces' deep-rooted knowledge about what an irrefutable assertion can do to Leo's ego. If this seems to be the case, just let Leo go his or her own way; otherwise one of you might become a pain in the neck to the other!

PISCES & VIRGO: The best thing that could happen to the two of you would be to find yourselves agreeing on what you know will not work out. If things are not crystal clear, Virgo, your cosmological opposite, might be overemphatic in legal actions—which is a nice way to say "lawsuits." Careful consideration is needed.

PISCES & LIBRA: Libra can be a wonderful reviewer of Pisces' sometimes confusing and at other times misinterpreted reality checks. If you, Pisces, become confused, the best thing you can do is look for a Libra to straighten you out—hopefully before you say yes!

PISCES & SCORPIO: If you, Pisces, can straighten Scorpio out, Scorpio can help you ripen. Yes, I mean ripen like a fruit or ripen within a situation. And it will do you good! Like a forecast of perfect weather, this is one of the greatest possible assertive connections!

PISCES & SAGITTARIUS: If you can, find a relative to act as a go-between before you agree, or even before you agree to agree, with Sagittarius. You should include a sense of duty in your choice or within the relationship. And remember, Pisces, that you are prone to count one glance as a full-fledged relationship.

PISCES & CAPRICORN: True knowledge, whatever it may be, is like true grit for Capricorn. You must be willing to accept this fact and not beat around the bush, because Capricorn will probably not stand for it. You'd better keep your promise, but don't ever try to get Capricorn to do the same.

PISCES & AQUARIUS: Have you included everyone? Have you taken the time, the date, and the weather into account?

Aquarius needs to include something that encompasses a larger scope than you might be counting on. So either corner him or her with your astuteness or beat him or her to it.

PISCES & PISCES: "Yes" can mean forever to another Pisces, and "no" can mean never. So take it easy and try to find a scale on which to weigh your words so neither of you will suffer any consequence or hold the other accountable for an unintended assertion.

CHAPTER 3

STRATEGIES

Someone once said to me, "I know what you mean by 'strategies'; it's like having the fire extinguisher hanging on the wall while you are remodeling your apartment." She was right. When you have decided to do something, the die has been cast. You reflect on the goals you would like to achieve and begin mapping out a plot or a plan. You need to make good use of your insight and your momentum. You compare and devise. You must take into account that things might not turn out exactly as you hoped they would, and before you start to negotiate, to bond, and to build your future alliances, you need to assemble your leverage kit. You have chosen to be the protagonist in what could turn out to be a wonderful or maybe just a normal daydream, a new quest, a hope, or an important deal that might change everything.

You are now starting to cover your bases. Should you be looking over your shoulder? You probably should—shouldn't we all? At this point in the process, we all have to

make an effort to maintain our focus so we don't let restless-
ness and distraction invade our space, making us unsure
about things that we were so convinced about just the
moment before. Always bear Murphy's law in mind: If something can go wrong, it will. But each astrological sign carries
so much information that by being able to use these so-
called tricks of the trade as part of your strategy, you will
connect to the heavens above. The words in this chapter
may worry you at first—and they are supposed to. At second glance as you start to relate, you will see how you can
be your own lightning rod, using the positive and the negative charges to harness your energy in order to build a strategy that will ensure your well-being.

In order to succeed, you need a design, a scheme, a
device, a compliance, or a consideration—all of the components of a good strategy. Your sign supplies the support.
According to *Webster's* dictionary, a strategy should come
from science or art so one can be able to handle the maximum strength of whatever he or she is facing. Great! That
happens also to be what astrology is all about. Astrology
depends on science and mathematics to calculate its
strength and gives every one of us a certain energy to work
with. It is also a form of art—in fact, I always call it an art—
because through astrology, we can search for new or different ways to interpret life and to observe the skills and
dexterities with which we all were born.

Before you begin strategizing, a word of explanation.
Many of the key words in this chapter have a shadow side to

them that might seem darker than the key words in any other chapter. I have made my own illuminated choice by picking these words on purpose. These twelve words should be used with caution because they can be seen in an optimistic or a pessimistic way. After you decide on your strategy, you interact with others. You are no longer alone. An illuminated strategy should help you deal with the world around you. Once you've thought things out, you should be able to predict what the consequences of the negative and positive might be.

You may be coming to these words because you want to change, to run away, to decide if you really want to stay on, to trip and fall if you would rather not push, to give in or to yield power, to fake or to give up. It might be wise to count your blessings before you really call it quits. Maybe you'll want to stop the world and wish another planetary entity would take responsibility for your actions. Contingency is perhaps the most important thing when deciding on a strategy. Any strategy you create must prepare you for the fact that, first of all, you are in the middle of something; second of all, that you want to continue; and third, that you must learn to acknowledge that time gives you not only your astrological sign but also your momentum. Time can do wonders for people, situations, and ideas. The passing of time reveals the true nature of things. Indulge yourself a little to decide on the right time frame within which you can devise and employ a strategy that is truly your own—an illuminated one.

If you feel at this point that you haven't been able to look over your shoulder as you should have, now is the time to recant, revise, or review. Your strategies should carry you forward while pointing out what you should be careful of along the way. After the strategy, you are no longer alone. You have worked things out. The plot is yours and you are relating to a part of something that is bigger than any of us. You have inherited the 69 trillion events that have made us what we are today. Now it is your turn to make your contribution to this ongoing chain of events that connects you to your own time. The sky could be the limit. Choose so you can make the most of your life and time on this planet. Tickle your fancy or illuminate your soul.

ARIES
fear
"The thing I fear most is fear."

—*Michele de Montaigne*

Of all the twelve astrological signs, the sign that has the smallest connection to fear is perhaps Aries, which is why I chose to make the connection between fear and strategies. Aries, you sometimes forget all about what could happen if things go wrong. Then, when they do, you are not prepared. Your energy has no bounds, and so you find it difficult to measure anything, let alone the consequences. Many other signs stall for time when they are frightened, but you, Aries, grab the sword and rush into the battle without giving yourself time to consider the danger. You can formulate a strategy in an instant because you are always ready to spring into action. When someone else asks you about fear, it is easy for you to say, "I don't know what you mean." The momentum in your actions usually doesn't allow fear to register on your radar screen.

And what is the right way to relate to fear? First of all, slow down and take time to consider your options. Calibrate yourself and your surroundings with a system of measurement that matches the situation. It could range from taking a couple of seconds to cool down to applying one of the principles of quantum mechanics: "The result of an action can only be expressed in terms of probability that a certain effect will occur." Few of you Aries need a certainty. By the time something is certain, you are on to the next thing anyway. Fear releases enough adrenaline in our bodies to make us stop or start doing whatever instinct requires, as in the fight-or-flight response. Stress, blood pressure, heart rate, metabolic rate, and blood sugar levels are all affected when we are afraid. Your lack of fear, Aries, is the only thing you have to be frightened of! Take a deep breath and give yourself the greatest gift: time. It is the best strategy for anybody born during the burst of spring. Since you usually get people so excited about things, they probably will not notice those few extra minutes that you should take for yourself and realize that fear could be your ally. The other eleven signs will be much too excited by being involved with you to notice the missing time.

ARIES
fear

ARIES & ARIES: Have you ever heard of the seven endocrine glands? If you haven't, look them up in a medical textbook so you can understand why they make you tick (they secrete the hormones into your system). If something feels out of sync between the two of you—perhaps one of you is tired while the other has a lot of energy—give each other a break. If you are out of time, which can often be the case for Aries, engage in a physical endeavor to balance out your energies.

ARIES & TAURUS: Aries, let Taurus indulge himself or herself in sensory impulses and sudden glances while you take a more passive role. Leave your connection with Taurus to pure instinct and first impressions. Try to remember that there is no pushing a Taurus, yet an encounter between you two could be regarded as a glorious accident.

ARIES & GEMINI: If this is the first time you and Gemini are interacting, the combination should be fun. If this is the second time around, you should give Gemini a chance to light up in some way the right road to fame, fortune, or just another good time. Your mutual strategy could enhance either of your track records and fear not, the time you spend together just might be exceptional.

ARIES & CANCER: Praising Cancer is a good way to start if you, Aries, can find the right time to schedule an appointment. You rarely think strategically about how to make others feel better about themselves, but do give it a try with Cancer, because you may have found a good, as well as a special, recipient.

ARIES & LEO: A lot of this combination's success will have to do with the height at which your eyes meet. One of you might find yourself wary of being observed by the other. Instead, pool your common fears by seeing as far as the horizon will allow you. You probably will end up on top of the world, but don't count on that feeling lasting forever.

ARIES & VIRGO: In case the number of possibilities between you seems overwhelming, you might be comforted to know that the largest number mentioned in the Bible is a thousand thousand (2 Chronicles 14:9), which is a million. Virgo could spend a lifetime counting while you, Aries, need to show that you can settle down every so often. There has be obvious trust as the two of you relate to each other.

ARIES & LIBRA: A metaphor for this combination can be found in the functions that appear on any word-processing program: word count, auto-correct, insert, and, most important, help mode. Libra can be your answer wizard. Once you two get over your fear of being astrological opposites, try merging. This procedure is definitely the best way to work together, for you two can learn something valuable from each other.

ARIES & SCORPIO: If you, Aries, can stun a Scorpio with a startling statement, the Scorpio's fear of being pushed into a strategy will be loosened up. In other words, before beginning, impress Scorpio with your know-how (even you are not too sure you have it). And remember that you always have to try harder with Scorpio than with any other sign.

ARIES & SAGITTARIUS: There are various ways to see things: normal human eyesight is one and X-ray vision is another. Keep in mind that a Sagittarius will notice every little thing and perhaps will be a bit judgmental. For starters, you'd better wear a color that suits the mood or an outfit that suits the day. Sagittarius usually doesn't forget a mismatched outfit or a fallible strategy.

ARIES & CAPRICORN: Capricorns need plenty of time to troubleshoot. Your impatience will succeed only in scaring Capricorn away, since neither of you are adept at the nitty-gritty side of planning. It may be beneficial to include a Taurus or Gemini in your strategic outline.

ARIES & AQUARIUS: If you wait until after the initial dynamic effect of your meeting dies down, you won't be able to count on your fearlessness. This is the one combination in which speed limits should not be imposed on what may seem to be the perfect plan. Things will fall into place on their own, even if in a rather eccentric, roundabout way!

ARIES & PISCES: Aries, do your very best to ease Pisces into a strategic situation that will allay most of his or her fears. This looks great on paper, but it can be overwhelming in action. Even if the odds of being struck by lightning are one in more than 600,000, you can actually work with Pisces to reach perfection—no matter what the odds or the stars say.

TAURUS

to possess

"Nothing is ours except time."

—*Lucius Annaeus Seneca*

By now you should be working through the fears that tend to incapacitate you and realizing that what strikes you as fearsome actually can be good for you. Taking your time helps. It also helps if you can make a friend of possessiveness and turn it into your playmate—something that should be part of any of your strategies. Although the word "possess" has as many definitions as there are astrological signs (to hold, to sit down, to own, to be located or situated at, to inhabit, to be master of, to adjunct, to have skill in, to have the patience for, to impart information to, to copulate with, to occupy the thoughts of), when "possess" spills out into possessiveness, it can become uncontrollable.

Taurus, you actually do well within the framework of uncontrollable acts, and perhaps this chapter will give you just the jolt you need to map out your whereabouts and your why-becauses. I will leave the meaning of possessiveness to each of you Tauruses to define for yourselves, because you need a bit of it to stay in focus, and you can best determine the degree that's right for you.

However, there are some things that you should watch out for. Try the following exercise and decide for yourself. During each day you should find only one situation in which you need to take control of yourself. If you are waiting for something, for instance, you can fill the time with a creative endeavor. If you need to curb your cravings, listen to some great music. If you are able to do this once a day within the context of one desire, then you are reaching an acceptable degree of self-possession, with which you will be able to accomplish anything you want.

It is also important to possess health and well-being before you start out on any strategic venture, because in order to feel strong on the inside, you must be physically comfortable. Wearing something that you feel good in will help you find a way to work things out. Your body temperature reacts to your feeling of ease or dis-ease almost more than it does to the external temperature. Feeling pleasure in what you have on your body optimizes whatever strategy you choose to use for anything else. You possess the strength to hold your own against the best and the worst, the easiest and the most difficult, and the strongest and the weakest. But this wondrous will with which most Tauruses are born needs to be kindled by external factors. You can conquer any fear by dealing with this. Once you have done so, lucky you! Many of your wishes can really come true.

TAURUS
to possess

TAURUS & ARIES: Stop for a minute, Taurus, and figure out what Aries would enjoy seeing or hearing. For instance, you could tone down colors and turn up sounds. You might need to maneuver a bit even if you do not feel quite up to it, but the results will be worth the effort. Understanding and anticipating Aries' wants and needs will serve you well and help you reach your own goals.

TAURUS & TAURUS: The chemistry that supposedly turns people on and off in split seconds has much more to do with your strategy than you would like to admit. This is very odd because underneath it all, feeling this sudden mood change is what you are so good at. So use a little spice to put yourself back on track.

TAURUS & GEMINI: Gemini can beat around the bush convincingly. If you are not too familiar with what Gemini is offering, don't let him or her knock you off your feet just because you think you are learning something new. Maybe Gemini actually wants what you don't even know you have. You will always measure up as far as a Gemini is concerned.

TAURUS & CANCER: If you and Cancer have a mutual interest or common values, you can set off together without fear. Be cautious, however. If you reveal the source of your power supply, Cancer might want more of the same thing. Caring for each other is in the best interest of both of you even if the end result doesn't seem overwhelming.

TAURUS & LEO: Taurus, make sure you are in possession of yourself, because Leo might very well try to bewitch you. Even if Leo doesn't dress up as a Magus and makes you comfortable as he or she disagrees, watch your step. Your conviction might be too sturdy for Leo to mess with. If you could get away together to a nice warm place, things would be much better.

TAURUS & VIRGO: Look at the title of Shakespeare's *Measure for Measure,* and you will find the best advice. Why? Because the Bard was a Taurus and the title of the play is a perfect motto for Virgo. Both of you should recognize when sudden and slightly magical inspiration appears—you can use it to put things into place.

TAURUS & LIBRA: Both of you are ruled by the same lovely Venus, who usually uses her wily ways to get what she wants, even if the outcome turns out to have masculine overtones. You two might be after the same thing, so watch what you use as a measuring stick and do not let Libra use you unless it betters your image.

TAURUS & SCORPIO: Are you listening carefully to yourself? Are you truly familiar with what you are trying to work out? Have you opened your mind to what an outcome might produce? Did you consider all probable possibilities? Will what you get be as good as the original, if there is an original? And does the information that Scorpio professes to possess come from a reliable source? If you doubt any of Scorpio's statements, watch out.

TAURUS & SAGITTARIUS: Before you two get together, take some time to think about how you could stimulate more than one of the five senses of Sagittarius. Practice your strategy beforehand, so that when it's time to use it, it will seem natural and not a ruse. If Sagittarius seems a little bossy, he or she has actually fallen for your ploy. And remember, these two signs interact very well.

TAURUS & CAPRICORN: Time can be measured in so many different ways that if each of you tried to explain the way each of you can fill a minute, you could be in for a rather scary surprise. Try to relate to each other on another scale, so that you can reduce the stress. Different opinions can do wonders because they open up new perspectives. Talk things over as much as you can. If you meet halfway, you can do a great deal for each other.

TAURUS & AQUARIUS: Be careful that you don't get into a pointless discussion—for instance, about whether the new century will begin in 2000 or 2001 or what year 2000 will do to our computers. One of you will certainly think that you possess the key to the absolute truth, so you'd better find a way to decide who really does, even if you have to flip a coin. And scarily enough, perhaps even that won't work out.

TAURUS & PISCES: There is something called Universal time (it replaced Greenwich mean time in 1972), which both astronomers and astrologers use and is a reference that helps pinpoint exactness, something that neither of you excel in doing. But you don't need to possess that skill to create a plan or to cover all the bases. You will need it, per-haps, to figure out at what point you really clicked, because by doing so you could fill up many voids or dispel each other's fears.

GEMINI
change
"'Twixt Tweedledum and Tweedledee."

—*John Byrom Byron*

You find the word "change" irresistible, Gemini, because your sign—with its double pillars—bounces you back and forth, even when your life is completely stable. The Bible says, "We shall be changed in a moment, in the twinkling of an eye." The millionth of a second before the Big Bang, which is being discussed by scientists, probably also belongs to your sign. Gemini, you have the power to change an idea, someone's life, or an outlook in heartbeat. For you, change is what life is all about.

Change is the driving force that enables you to keep others on their toes. Change doesn't let anyone get too complacent, and you, Gemini, can make things happen by sheer will. You can actually convince others that something is to their benefit when it is actually doing you more good than anyone else. If you don't stop to reflect on the possible outcomes of your influence on others, you may be short-changing yourself in the end. However, you do make people feel good about themselves.

In fact, Gemini, you are at your best whether you plan the change or the change simply happens. The millions of minute sparks that jump from neuron to neuron within all of our brains might even be Gemini in nature because of the profound influence they have on the human body.

When other signs need a change, you can give them good advice, but, Gemini, sometimes you are just not there when you are needed. Like the neurons, you jump from one side to the other, sometimes without doing anyone any favors. You must learn to change with care, Gemini. Life will call you to attention and remind you that everything you do, or cause others to do, should be for an unselfish cause. Others need to be around you so that they can benefit from your inventiveness and quickness of spirit, which will give them a boost so as to increase their self-confidence.

GEMINI
change

GEMINI & ARIES: Aries has much to offer you, Gemini. Your signs do well together when you focus on the task at hand and use your creative and innovative energies to map out a plan, while being careful not to let too much time go by. This combination can bring about great ideas.

GEMINI & TAURUS: In this strategic combination, you need to figure out the most comfortable way to ease in or out of needed change. As a matter of fact, if you use your inherent charm, intrinsic sympathy, and built-in skill, you will give yourself and Taurus a much better deal than either of you expected.

GEMINI & GEMINI: One of you will have to work at being sharper than the other. Decide together which of you has more to say. First, make a separate list of your needs. Next, ask the other Gemini to do the same. Then see whose list is longer—that is the person who should be in charge. If you can get into a pattern of being nice to each other, your strategy will probably fall into place on its own.

GEMINI & CANCER: Make sure you have the right day written down in your date book, Gemini. Cancer will not believe a word you say if you stand him or her up or even if you are late. And never forget that Cancer can change from one minute to the next in a rather vexing way when he or she feels slighted. Giving a special little gift to Cancer would work wonders.

GEMINI & LEO: Perhaps you could include an exchange of some kind of hard foreign currency in whatever you are working on because when it comes to dealing with global issues, Gemini and Leo are as good as a combination can get. This is actually an excellent pair for business-related enterprises, and you should convince Leo that the strategy is worth the try. Don't talk about this possibility right away, but do keep it in mind. (Keep a conversion table on hand in case you have to deal with yen.)

GEMINI & VIRGO: Virgo can endure whatever specific actions are necessary to wade through his or her own doubts, and this is something you should learn from, Gemini. If you are not careful, Virgo might regard you as someone whose ideas are as clear as mud, but you could find solace in investigating what makes Virgo tick.

GEMINI & LIBRA: The tools of Libra's trade could very well be something like what Native Americans called a dream catcher, which is a magic wand that catches bad dreams and makes you sleep in peace and joy. It is the silence, the pauses, and the things that are not said that count with Libra as you try to map out your strategies together. Libra is a good healer for you, Gemini. Try to keep the same pace at all times.

GEMINI & SCORPIO: Scorpios are at their very best when finding out how someone else's fear is born. But you, Gemini, must find a way to reach Scorpio on a deep enough level so as to make him or her respect your point of view. Use the best you've got and try to sustain, maintain, and prolong the strategy until you are certain that you are on track. In fact, the less change, the better here.

GEMINI & SAGITTARIUS: A scientific and precise agreement is best for you two opposite signs even if you are immersed in an extremely complicated relationship. At any rate, each of you is the best critic of the other so you could say anything but harsh words to each other. Don't try to be perfectionists because it won't work.

GEMINI & CAPRICORN: Finding a common cause might be just the right way out of dealing with the extremely complicated or intricate response that you can get from Capricorn, especially when Capricorn is not standing on firm ground (something Cap hates!). Whoever is older is actually wiser, believe it or not.

GEMINI & AQUARIUS: After a period of drought or doubt, you will probably find a quirky way to work things out. Aquarians, if they put their minds to it, can really pull the wool over your eyes, Gemini. At this point, it is best for you, Gemini, to let Aquarius have the upper hand because actually things are probably changing for the better.

GEMINI & PISCES: Don't claim a large gain. Grin and bear it rather than engage in a hidden power struggle that can only end in a standoff. Even though both of you should stick up for yourselves, with a bit of luck, you could emerge with a fear-proof strategy that gives you leeway to define your own individuality, which will bring out the best in both of you.

CANCER
leaving

"The butterfly counts not months but moments, and has time enough."

—*Rabindranath Tagore*

Cancer, when you are trying to accomplish something, whether it is an important project at work or the beginning of a new relationship, you leave a bit of yourself behind. This happens for two reasons: you have such a heavy presence while walking from one place to another that you have to lighten your load, or you are so adept at giving of yourself that you bestow little pieces on whomever you come in contact with. Cancer, you can sometimes make mountains out of moonbeams. If you are in a good mood, these moonbeams might turn into poetry; if you are in a bad mood, they might make you lose touch with reality. The irony of it all is that it might take you forever to realize that you have this ability. Maybe the other signs should be grateful for the piece of yourself that you give them as you move in and out of their lives. That certain something that makes kings and queens royal can be yours.

Representing Mother Earth, as Cancer has done through the ages, is no easy task. Your connection to the world around you could be imagined as either a stairway to the stars or, if things are not going well, a trapdoor into obscurity. Whether it is one or the other, or even the unknown in between, you always leave a tang of something behind. In fact, a Cancer will probably be chosen to make a trip through time on some kind of Cancerian starship into the future. You will be leaving, but everyone will know that you are on to something new. The moon will always be your ally, because it rules your sign. And just as the moon constantly waxes and wanes, you can come and go secure in the knowledge that it gives you a certain force that leaves others no choice but to give you another chance. Yours is the one sign that, throughout your life, should never leave well enough alone because you were born with an innate talent for improving whatever you come in contact with. Leave the sit-

uation to the other signs so that you can finally feel good
about the way things turn out.

CANCER
leaving

CANCER & ARIES: Aries can usually snap you out of any
unclear strategies that you might have been working on
together. I hope the Aries you are dealing with right now
will be kind. If not, please don't overreact. You might even
want to give in so things will go more smoothly.

CANCER & TAURUS: Whatever it is that is going on in
your brain may be mechanical, but there are so many different aspects of these mechanisms, that either of you
would do well to leave mechanics alone. Instead, work
together so you, Cancer, don't feel threatened about leaving anything, unless you are pressed for time and really
must leave, and Taurus doesn't fret about the time that has
been lost.

CANCER & GEMINI: Gemini could lighten you up and help
you feel better as well as safe as you leave on vacation, but
this is about the only kind of advice that Gemini can give
you. And if you are leaving a Gemini, or if Gemini is leaving
you, just replace him or her with another Gemini, which
should not be too difficult.

CANCER & CANCER: Both of you cherish your emotions to such an extent that you often end up feeling isolated and unable to focus on each other's feelings. Find somebody outside of all these moon signs about whom you can worry. That way you will get a clearer perspective on yourself and your situation, and you'll be able to leave your moodiness behind.

CANCER & LEO: You can learn from Leo only if you stop talking long enough to hear what he or she is saying. You might not like it, Cancer, but doing so will open up countless possibilities. When you are tuned in to Leo in the right way, you will discover how to accomplish your goals more efficiently. Leo can be a real time-saver for you if you listen, and don't leave before your time is up.

CANCER & VIRGO: Let Virgo do the worrying, and leave your money in Virgo's pocket. Virgos can be great when they are mapping things out. Maybe this particular Virgo can help you learn how not to leave in the wrong way. If by now you don't know what the right way is, leave it to time and it will become clear!

CANCER & LIBRA: Cancer, you should know by now that you keep leaving bits and pieces of your own psyche behind every time you interact with someone, whether it was for better or worse. Lucky for you Libra is just the right person to point out how to manage this tendency so it doesn't hurt you or leave you with less than you originally came to the table with. In this case, your best strategy is not to let Libra's direct words bother you.

CANCER & SCORPIO: If you can work out a way so that neither of you harbors a grudge towards the other because Scorpio usually wants something Cancer can't give, you will find that this actually could be a very dynamic relationship. Don't let first impressions count for everything. Each of you could be inspired by the other if you give yourselves the chance. You, Cancer, love the word "forever," but this notion doesn't fit into Scorpio's personal modus operandi. Try to schedule a regular time when you see each other so you can help each other develop.

CANCER & SAGITTARIUS: The dynamics between you and Sagittarius are fine, but there could be a real communications gap. Since it might be difficult to find someone to translate, why don't you try saying this to each other: "Let's just leave it at that and go on to something that feels better." After a while, things could fall into place beautifully. It's the long run that usually counts.

CANCER & CAPRICORN: Leave Capricorn, your opposite, to work out his or her own strategy in whatever you are doing together. Try to be understanding, Cancer. You two need each other, but you also need to leave well enough alone. Your experience has nothing to do with the way Capricorn sees things, but if you understand the difference between your points of view, you can both thrive.

CANCER & AQUARIUS: Musical harmony is the one thing you should never leave out of a deal when you are both trying to get some kind of strategy off the ground. Since there is so much intensity between you, a cool beat and the right Sinatra (definitely not "All of Me"!) could fan the wonderful possibilities of your chancy survival!

CANCER & PISCES: Be aware that the two of you might bore a lot of people. If you couldn't care less, so much the better and keep going. If you do care, solicit the opinions of those around you, but don't bristle at the things you don't like hearing. When you two are working at maximum capacity and cooperating with others, the Cancer-Pisces combination can yield excellent results.

LEO

yielding

"I was old till u came."

—*H.D. (Hilda Doolittle)*

When it comes to planning things out in a strategic mode, you, Leo, are the wild card of the cosmic deck. You always seem to have a joker under your hat, if not up your sleeve!

Responsible and far-fetched, your sometimes overwhelming personality can be the best around, but you also have the ability to become an absolute s.o.b. when you are rubbed the wrong way. Leo, you often have a hard time acknowledging that there is a right side to an argument that is not yours. As a result, others often feel that they are yielding to you. You work well under pressure and are perfect at showing others how to eliminate their bias. Like most Leos, you have a dynamic, creative energy that makes most other signs give in to your charm and force. Others consent, acknowledge, relinquish, bring in, or help manage, because when a Leo is involved, everyone else has to be flexible. And sometimes they learn a lesson that helps them get along with their lives. Even in strife, you can do good for other signs, even if the benefit comes about in a slightly unusual way. You sometimes see in an instant how to acquire what others have been seeking for ages.

To others, you may seem to be able to solve any problem, almost at will. They can always count on you to help them leave any predicament behind. But woe to them if they cross what you, Leo, consider to be your line of duty, for you will cross them out with the wrath of your royal constellation! You have a strong sense of yourself and how others should act. However, you always return the next day as if nothing has happened. For you, bygones are really bygones, and all the ire that others felt will have turned into gracious remembrances. Others will yield to your talent for persuasion as willing volunteers, and they will be doing themselves a favor, for as the old saying goes, "Where your will is ready, your feet are light."

LEO
yielding

LEO & ARIES: Where there is a will, there is definitely a way for both of you. If by any chance you and Aries feel a lack of incentive in the beginning, drop whatever you are thinking about and try something else. There is no use in striving to convince each other about the maybe, the perhaps, or the chance factor!

LEO & TAURUS: You probably will have to turn a deaf ear now and then, because you and Taurus are the most stubborn signs of the zodiac—you will do yourselves a favor if you play ignorant. Once you get on track, Taurus could become the wind that kicks up your fire. Or maybe, you, Leo, can show Taurus how to shine.

LEO & GEMINI: In bygone days, people spoke of noblesse oblige, the nobility's obligation to behave honorably. The only way you can get Gemini to see your light is to point out the nobler side of the plan. Gemini will stand for your regalness with difficulty. You will probably won't enjoy yielding, but if you don't, you might miss out on a very powerful interaction.

LEO & CANCER: Leo, try your best to show how very warm and understanding you can be, in the long or short term. Cancer might seem to be much more docile than you expected, and you might be caught off guard, for Cancers are good at hiding their feelings, like crabs scuttling away. Remember, Cancer can adapt beautifully to most situations and then whirl things up.

LEO & LEO: You probably would do best to make a final decision before you start thinking about working things out with another Leo, wondering what will happen if worse comes to worst, and deciding why you should even think about yielding. In this case, don't beat the other Leo to it!

LEO & VIRGO: Do not change strategies for lack of something better. Most probably, Virgo is already a couple of leagues ahead of you, so it would be wise to listen to Virgo's plan and adapt to it as best you can, even if it does take a bit of belt-tightening. In the long run, you probably will conclude that it was well worth whatever you left behind.

LEO & LIBRA: "Gladly" and "With pleasure" should be your response when Libra strategically identifies your Achilles' heel, especially if you are dealing with a Libra of the opposite sex. Remember that good manners and a pleasant disposition are your best armor when you are around Libra. You can outshine what Libra thinks he or she can rearrange. Try it!

LEO & SCORPIO: Try to give a bit of joy to each other instead of thinking about who has to give up what. And if push does come to shove, be careful of putting yourself in an unbecoming light. You should also watch your words, because they could hurt Scorpio more than you think. There is a lesson to be learned in that lovely old song, "Ain't misbehaving. . . . I'm saving"—work on rhyme and reason!

LEO & SAGITTARIUS: Do not forget to be courteous. Be respectful, and let Sagittarius understand why there is an escape route in your strategy. There should be no need for either of you to yield if you speak to Sagittarius with a honeyed tongue. An open-arms approach is the best way to put Sagittarius in his or her place, which probably will be necessary. Any irascibility is a sign of things gone wrong.

LEO & CAPRICORN: Try to make things as easy for each other as possible. Capricorn will probably want to have his or her way, and you can learn a lot from Capricorn's point of view, if you take the time to listen carefully. The best way for you to get things done would be not to plan too far ahead, even though that's exactly what Capricorn likes to do. You have the panache to show Capricorn how to have real fun.

LEO & AQUARIUS: Leo and Aquarius are opposites. Leo's strategic word is "yielding," while Aquarius's is "giving in." These two words are not opposites but your signs are. So, first you will have to work on understanding the basics. One of you must take the noble side and the other one the loyal one, meaning you, Leo, should yield only if loyalty permits and Aquarius should give in only if the time is ripe.

LEO & PISCES: You will have to find a way to buy out Pisces—literally or figuratively. Use your imagination and do not fear going overboard on offering compliments to Pisces. Pisces will understand how good you are at whatever you set your mind to, and you just might find time to congratulate each other because you ended up picking the perfect strategy.

VIRGO

worrying

"How many things I can do without!"

—*Socrates*

"What are you worried about?" Is this a question that you have asked yourself once too often? If it is, you must be a Virgo. When you, Virgo, start out on any quest, you often slip into a Chaucer-like way of thinking (he wrote, "For ever the latter end of joy is woe.") Virgo, let me be blunt: sometimes you dive right into overkill and spoil things by worrying too much. If you work on it, you could turn your worry into a literary allusion and end up "unexpectedly and surprisingly worrying about the arrivals and departures of pleasure," as Chaucer also wrote. Might this idea sum up your spirit? It would be a perfect strategy.

As my mother used to say to me, "May nothing worse ever happen to you," meaning that you should comfort yourself with the knowledge that most events in your life are not as bad as they seem. You are the perfect sign to illuminate for others what they should be worrying about, but you often dwell too long on what might go awry.

You have ability to help others peacefully accept what is happening in their lives, and you can help them affirm their inner strength and confidence so their worries do not become overwhelming. Your best personal strategy would be to find allegories to play around with a bit and help you loosen up for a change. Why not give others the chance to worry about you? Yours is the sign that can turn worrying into something quite creative, productive, or artistic. You instinctively can sum up what could go wrong and save everyone a lot of time. I would trust you with anything!

VIRGO
worrying

VIRGO & ARIES: The only thing to worry about with this combination is the possibility of losing your focus. Aries needs to take the time to understand fully what you are trying to lay out, turn on, or plan ahead. You, Virgo, probably will have to take that extra time on your own, but just in case, remember to give Aries a break.

VIRGO & TAURUS: You two can be so supportive of each other that you need to take more into consideration than usual. Taurus can actually turn you, Virgo, on to being more cheerful, which you usually forget about as soon as you start to worry—which could be as soon as you get up in the morning! By the way, try working things out by having some enjoyable music in the background.

VIRGO & GEMINI: Low spirits and a sinking heart can become a games-people-play syndrome, meaning that you and Gemini will talk each other out of anything if you don't watch out! Be careful not to tread on each other's heels.

VIRGO & CANCER: Listen to what Cancer has to say, Virgo. Cancer has an instinct for nurturing the truth that most other signs would do well to try to emulate! You, Virgo, can benefit from Cancer's spontaneity, and then you both can rise above any worry, to the point of implementing a spectacular "rose-colored glasses" strategy, which means that all will end well.

VIRGO & LEO: When or if you find yourself worrying about this partnership, use any kind of strategy as long as depth, investigation, and challenge are part of it. The outcome needs to have a comforting therapeutic side to make you feel as good as you should, could, or will allow yourselves to!

VIRGO & VIRGO: Take it easy on yourselves. Inhale and exhale in a great, enjoyable environment. Otherwise, you might find yourselves lost in an ocean of criticisms that could be witticisms if you let yourselves go a bit. Relax. You should turn whatever you do into a win-win situation.

VIRGO & LIBRA: The solution to a worrying thought could very well be to leave it very much alone. Never try to work things out if you don't feel physically up to it. Try improving your health before you get down to business. Libras work things out better when someone else is putting forth the most effort. Before you know it, you may be celebrating.

VIRGO & SCORPIO: Find out what Scorpio's idea of a good time is. Then get ready for sparks to fly. You could end up finding delight in the process, so whatever worry is left over will be well worth the fun.

VIRGO & SAGITTARIUS: Be careful with Sagittarius, because you are probably right about whatever is worrying you. In the meantime, you can do each other a lot of good if you do not get obsessed with the possible outcomes. There is a popular saying, "Let sleeping dogs lie," which you would do well to remember.

VIRGO & CAPRICORN: There shouldn't be a worry in the air between you two, but since we all carry bits and pieces of the other signs within us, it is possible that you two are trying for completely different things. So if you and Capricorn find yourselves at a stalemate, get a Scorpio or a Taurus to help you work things out.

VIRGO & AQUARIUS: Are you both being truthful about your ultimate goals or have you missed out on an important point—not willingly, but perhaps you have both been misguided about the truth of the matter. Look at facts and figures and don't get bogged down with emotions or hunches.

VIRGO & PISCES: You are opposites and your dynamics will always be interesting. The intention of your strategy should never worry you when you are with Pisces. Pisces has so much insight that for once, you should take the time and figure it out. It is all about "aboutness," silly.

LIBRA

to pretend

"Two men look out through the same bars: One sees the mud, and one the stars."

—F. Langbridge

Are you changing when you pretend? Or are you pretending to change? This double value is actually what the pretending mode is all about. It might be an excuse, it could be stretching the truth a bit, it can be a claim, it definitely is a holdout, it usually is an extension of time, and without the proper knowledge it could be devastating. Libra is represented by a sign that historically has almost as much of a double value as Gemini, but your double-sidedness, Libra, has to do with an outside vision: you are continuously watching for something new to appear on the horizon. Since you instinctively know that you are a lucky and posi-tive sign, you are easily able to keep pretending that what is coming will be for the best.

For you, Libra, "to pretend" is really a commitment "to aspire," which is an excellent way to approach a strategy. You probably have the skill to put things in place; if not, you have the skill to pretend that they are already in place. Since you are so adept at disguises, you will find yourself playing follow-the-leader with yourself, because you can convince yourself that you are capable of anything. The trouble is that the next step is to pretend that you are sure.

Pretending is what makes childhood a rehearsal for life; it strengthens our nature and stretches our imagination. You, Libra, may sometimes seem to others to be off-course or unfocused. You may even be accused of acting childish. But none of these things are so. When Shakespeare said, "Life is but a stage," he was perhaps explaining to those of us who are not Libras that a little pretending is an important part of our everyday lives. But, Libra, you knew that already. Like others born under your sign, you effortlessly employ pretense as you move in and out of the best strategies. May the world of make-believe live on through you in our imaginations.

LIBRA
to pretend

LIBRA & ARIES: Libra, the voice of your opposite sign brings a no-nonsense approach to a unconvincing subject, which is most likely what you are trying to achieve. Aries finds it difficult to acknowledge the fact that pretense even exists! Libra, you are around to prove the contrary, and you can do so by pretending not to be resentful, even if you are. Watch it!

LIBRA & TAURUS: You must not show guilt in any way. If you do, you must make a promise and endorse your pledge. Both of you are ruled by the same planet, Venus. If you keep your cool, Venus can always help you to get hold of the easier side of any argument that surely will come up. So get your act together and don't appear slovenly.

LIBRA & GEMINI: In this combination, Gemini is pretending too, but you can use his or her disguise to your own advantage. If you work things out without getting sidetracked or distracted, you will grow into whatever you want to be. Pretense can work its way into any imaginable corner, but you and Gemini need to lean on each other to make things work.

LIBRA & CANCER: You need to be careful, because Cancer is apt to find your pretensions unappealing. Such sentiments would definitely not be the best thing for future strategic possibilities. Cancers feel their way through situations with care.

You, Libra, might not even be pretending when you show Cancer how little interest you have. Work on yourself a bit before undertaking a serious commitment with this sign.

LIBRA & LEO: Libra, you could very well outshine Leo. A Leo might pretend not to care a bit if you do this, but in reality he or she does. Try to find a way to accomplish your goal while leaving enough room for others to shine. The strategy might turn out to be a bargain if you take a second look.

LIBRA & VIRGO: I can only take a rough guess at a guideline for this combination. Libra, you can pretend all you want with a Virgo, but you cannot be pretentious. You should let yourself be taught by Virgo, even if in a roundabout way, because it is Virgo who should carry the stick. If you follow this advice, your strategy can't go wrong.

LIBRA & LIBRA: There might be a mutual gruffness between you that is a cover-up for fear! You know that "I don't mean to sound harsh but I have to tell the truth" syndrome? Maybe you should keep the truth to yourself. In this case, the truth could hurt, and that won't help the cause. Your best bet is to proceed with caution.

LIBRA & SCORPIO: I recommend that you let Scorpio take the lead in proposing a strategy that could morph or shape-shift at any moment. Libra, you will not accept that the truth of the matter is really possible. So don't. But be assured that if you are pretending with Scorpio, he or she is doing the same. One more word of advice: touch is important here—not the finishing kind, but rather the physical kind.

LIBRA & SAGITTARIUS: The key to this combination is to add some spice to your strategy. You could even pretend to be more outlandish than you actually are. Sagittarius might ask you to spend some money, and it will probably be well spent, even if it is on something frivolous. Good times should be in the bag.

LIBRA & CAPRICORN: Even if you come from different continents, if you both return to your respective family trees, you will find a strategic connection that you were completely unaware of. You will probably have to try hard to make things work with Capricorn. But learning more about yourself is always a good thing.

LIBRA & AQUARIUS: Of all the possible relationships, this one gets the astrological thumbs-up as a match made in heaven. If it isn't working out this way, an external force is probably getting in the way. Could you possibly pretend that everything is just right until it really is? Aquarius is always ready for a surprise anyway.

LIBRA & PISCES: The three words "healthy, wealthy, and wise" are what you have to take to heart and live by in order to put things on track with Pisces. Make sure the pretense of the times doesn't make you get lost in ridiculous fashions or meaningless trends. Pisces usually knows how to catch you when you are unprepared, and complications actually lighten things up, which might do you some good!

SCORPIO
to fall

"The great business of life is to be, to do, to do without, and to depart."

—*John Viscount Morely*

Robert Musil, author of *The Man Without Qualities*, is a Scorpio whom I will never tire of quoting. He once wrote that "everything one can think of is either affection or aversion," which is a perfect description of Scorpio's modus operandi. In a way, you fall into what should happen to you. When you, Scorpio, trip, fall, stumble, or download, it somehow usually works to your benefit. Most of the time the results transform, liquidate, surprise, assimilate, convert, benefit, sometimes usurp, and certainly re-form strategies, quests, and choices as well. The only condition that can make you hit rock bottom is getting fatigue—mental or physical. Any other fall, even if it seems that the descent has nothing to do with gravity, has a far deeper meaning than you or I could suppose. Why? Because you, Scorpio, fall into deeper meanings as you extend yourself constantly and carefully, in a way that all other signs could learn from.

Scorpio, you have the strength to astound and astonish others under any circumstance. Your biological clock is cosmologically set to do so. In some earlier astrological books, there is even a reference to the fact that the falling of comets and meteors, building or destroying one thing or another, has much to do with Scorpio.

You Scorpios are also at your significant best when you are pointing out the right way to others so they do not fall into traps set by their own unreasonable doubt, undiscriminating praise, or alluring seduction. One of these three or all at the same time can impede their progress. But guess what? You can magically, mysteriously, and masterfully turn these three traps into something that works for you. You, Scorpio, can tell us, point out to us, and awaken our ire in such a way that we forget that we need you at our side to point out what we are talking about: how to avoid that silly stumble or that stupid fall.

SCORPIO
to fall

SCORPIO & ARIES: You might blame each other for being tempted to make someone else stumble. You just might go so far as to think that one of you is a snake, while the other provides the grass! And then again, if you do manage to sort things out, a perfect temporary calm could ensue, like the eye of a hurricane.

SCORPIO & TAURUS: When a Scorpio and Taurus work together, neither believes that the slightest stumble is possible. The outcome of this relationship could be so fantastic that any obstacles will eventually be forgotten. This bliss might not last, but then, absolute delights never do. Instead, they stay in your mind and help you over future hurdles. Opposite perfection!

SCORPIO & GEMINI: Gemini can quite easily fall from your grace. But take heed: there is something for you to learn even if you secretly classify Gemini as superficial. Double your effort to find new skills that will help both of you stumble onto the right path.

SCORPIO & CANCER: You might find something seductive in Cancer's demeanor, and Cancer will certainly be charmed by the way you seem to fall into the right situations, but be careful. If you fall from Cancer's grace, the outcome could be mediocre. Plan your strategy with more care than you thought necessary.

SCORPIO & LEO: When I was in the third grade, we used to say, "Sticks and stones may break my bones, but words will never hurt me." Translate this idea into any situation and pay attention to the way words fall your way. Leo might say something that he or she doesn't really mean so you both would be wise to let someone else in on the deal so you won't get stuck in a dead end. Any strategy you can employ to guard either of your tempers is well worth your while.

SCORPIO & VIRGO: Here is a stern warning for those of you who belong to this possible combination and experience a fallout: stick together, keep at it, and ignore your feelings if things are not working perfectly. Your combination is the perfect strategic antidote, so much so that you should be able to bottle it and sell it to others.

SCORPIO & LIBRA: Scorpio, the best thing for you to do is fall right into a vociferous conversation with Libra that could be the beginning of a great idea. And if the right idea doesn't seem to fall into place, you will have had an enlightening time anyway. You could be great critics of each other's strategies.

SCORPIO & SCORPIO: Here are some words with which both of you could do well (you don't have to use them in their given order; simply let them fall into place as you try for your own dream team): rough, oddly, fantasy, receive, obdurate, myth, idealism, accurately, really, power, racy, and facts. These are all words that apply to the energy of your ruling planet, Mars. If you don't get your words crossed, they will all fall into the right place.

SCORPIO & SAGITTARIUS: You need to let Sagittarius have enough access to you because you might think you have explained yourself when in reality you haven't. You need to be clear about what you want to be given to whom, so decide what you really care about.

SCORPIO & CAPRICORN: Hey, hey! Fall into step here! You should have no doubt about the future or what you two can, could, would, or may plan together. If you are out of step, you have fallen out of sync with yourselves, because this combination is supposed to be perfection, especially if you hope for pennies from heaven!

SCORPIO & AQUARIUS: It is quite amazing what a difference a day makes. Aquarius, who comes just after Capricorn, can muddle things up for you, Scorpio, unless one of you tries some smooth-talking or fancy footwork, like a perfect tango. Why don't you try giving in?

SCORPIO & PISCES: The more care you take in helping Pisces fall into place, the better the outcome of your strategic dreams. Play out your fantasies and see how far you can go. Both of you can land on your feet again, especially if you do not fall back on your word!

SAGITTARIUS

continue

"To be a man is to feel that one's own stone contributes to building the edifice of the world."

—Antoine de Saint-Exupéry

There is no way that you, Sagittarius, can move ahead with your strategy without having a continuous contingency plan. If something goes wrong, you always have a backup. The point is that since things usually come easily to you, Sagittarius, you need complicated subjects and hard facts to keep you interested in what you are doing so you don't stop in the middle. It's not that you don't have a good attention span, it is just that you get bored when things come too easily. Be careful. Your ups and downs are like the stock market, but wouldn't it be great if the stock market would be on a continuous rise? When your interest is piqued, you don't even bother to ask yourself what the thing you are doing is all about. Your inherent curiosity keeps you going. Alas, you may jump off one bandwagon and right onto another one. So when others are dealing with a Sagittarius, they have to keep an eye on you, and as a Sagittarius, you'd better continue to be interested in the heart of the matter so you won't leave the project behind before it is done!

You are great at getting other people to feel good about themselves. Please remember to keep up the good work, because you are quite capable of leaving a sentence in the middle while somebody is hanging on your every word.

Remember this idea when you are trying to convince your-self that something is worthwhile. When you continue this strategy, you are doing more than just a favor. Sagittarius, you can be the great teacher of astrological empowerment, and you can help others find the mode by which they can better themselves and cope. Helping others to live up to their potential is your strongest connection to the world around you.

Don't excuse your wondrous, spontaneous self from the table before the game is over, even when it looks as if you might lose. Your being there will make others want to con-tinue to play, and isn't playing supposed to be the best part of a game? Even if it isn't, your continuing presence can make anybody feel like a winner.

SAGITTARIUS
continue

SAGITTARIUS & ARIES: There should be no doubt about what you and Aries can accomplish together. No matter what stage you two are in, keep at it. Your strategy is built on the best possible foundation, especially to keep going, to run for it, and to make a final grab.

SAGITTARIUS & TAURUS: By not cutting corners you will be doing Taurus a great favor. You're the best one to show him or her how to continue whatever it is you are doing. If you are able to give Taurus a slight push with a loving nudge on the side, anything can be done. "Pleasurable" should be the bottom line.

SAGITTARIUS & GEMINI: If you and Gemini are part of a group effort, things will work fine. If you are working one-to-one, the fact that you are opposites might be too much of a burden for things to continue to go smoothly. On a one-to-one basis, you might find each other too glib. The more people you involve, the merrier it will seem.

SAGITTARIUS & CANCER: Shorten the amount of time you spend on this strategy and you will do better. The more you tarry, the less chance there is that things will work out your way. You need flexibility to work things out. Uncertainty can actually pave the way for expectations because the element of surprise does Cancer a lot of good. Be careful not to choose the wrong words.

SAGITTARIUS & LEO: Once you've got the right words in place, you can see where you stand with a Leo. And if this sounds like the advice above for strategizing with a Cancer, rest assured it isn't. Uncertainty is just what Leo does not need. Have you ever heard of the saying "to pack a wallop"? Well, that is what Leo can do to you if you don't continue on what he or she considers to be the right track.

SAGITTARIUS & VIRGO: Everything will eventually have a long-term effect. So consider yourself within an extended time frame when you look over your shoulder with or because of Virgo. Virgo will need to know where he or she stands with you. Otherwise Virgo might leave you alone with half a strategy.

SAGITTARIUS & LIBRA: Each of you should take your own side and proceed as if you were working on a scenario for a movie or a play. Keep going and transform your ideas into a safe reality. The end product could be deserving of an Academy Award or an everlasting continuous bond that has no specific terms but lots of interesting results.

SAGITTARIUS & SCORPIO: Pull a clever trick out of your hat to astound Scorpio into wanting to continue to stick around. Your let's-get-on-with-it attitude might make Scorpio feel that things are not really worthwhile. Never plagiarize from Scorpio, and keep up the good work.

SAGITTARIUS & SAGITTARIUS: One of you had better have your feet on the ground while the other points the way. Otherwise you might get your priorities confused and find yourselves just battling windmills like Don Quixote and his sidekick, Sancho Panza. Of course, who's to say that this isn't the best of all possible ways to keep on going? So if you must, continue. . . .

SAGITTARIUS & CAPRICORN: I call this combination the perfect association for a comic strip. You could jump from scene to scene like a doodle on a piece of paper. You do need to give yourself a chance to figure out if other people are interested. Once this is clear, Capricorn will have more faith in you and will continue to listen to you.

SAGITTARIUS & AQUARIUS: There should be a straight line to a real pot of gold here; otherwise, discontinue! (Yes, this is all!)

SAGITTARIUS & PISCES: I would change the last letter in the word and use "continuo," which is the Spanish word for a flute-like instrument and paves the way for you two to get together in harmony. Instead of trying forever to figure things out, find something that is as good as music in your ears and gets you to enjoy togetherness.

CAPRICORN

counting

"One man with courage makes a majority."

—*Andrew Jackson*

You carry within yourself, Capricorn, tremendous strength for everlasting endurance. Longevity in all arenas is yours for the taking. You usually endure longer, take more, and wait around for the right opportunity without counting the passing of time. This is one reason why you can work so hard and people are relieved that you are there doing so. You also know how to count on yourself, as aloneness is something you can describe in countless ways and are very knowledgeable about. You understand so well that we are born alone even if so many of us count on not being out there on our own.

Capricorn, you are tuned in to practical questions that pave the way for conceptual ones, once you start counting. Perhaps it is thanks to you that we have sequence, because you also have a cognitive knowledge that brings about the need for numbers to fill our time and space. Possibly, you, Capricorn, are convinced that things come our way because we are tuned in to the right number. So many mathematicians and scientists, including Stephen Hawking and Isaac Newton, were born under your watchful sign that even when you disagree with one strategy or another, those of us who belong to all the other signs need to count on your support.

You count everything, whether it has to do with love or not. But it is not the accumulation of things, ideas, or affection that you are interested in; rather it is the coherence of why things stay put as they forge ahead at the same time, just like the movement of our solar system, our galaxy, and ultimately our whole universe. Perhaps one could even say that you measure your strength in numbers. Why? Because your specific accountability can be everlasting (other signs had better take this into account). When the numbers don't add up, you wean yourself off counting on others like Scrooge, who was probably a Capricorn.

CAPRICORN
counting

CAPRICORN & ARIES: Capricorn, you are up against an astrological sign that usually doesn't like to wait. Yet many really good couples are made up of this combo. So make your decision as to whether you are in or out and take it from there. If you can, make the first move; otherwise you will be giving Aries too much of an advantage!

CAPRICORN & TAURUS: Unless whatever you are planning to count has to do with a bank account, accountability can be a turnoff for a Taurus. Instead find something tangible that could heighten Taurus's pleasure. You might have to relearn the meaning of "giving in." You may be a master or mistress of time, but Taurus is an expert at packing an emotional wallop.

CAPRICORN & GEMINI: Try to avoid a standoff, and you can do so without too much effort, as long as you and Gemini try to outwit others and not each other. Count on the possibility that you might deserve the couple of dirty tricks that Gemini tries to play on you. Actually, you could learn a whole new way of seeing the world through Gemini's eyes, and this might be just what you need.

CAPRICORN & CANCER: Capricorn, you need to feign what should have been a calculated move. Cancer will probably feel that you have broken your promise. Even if you win, Capricorn, believe it or not, you lose. Remember that opposites should usually work things out by counting your blessings.

CAPRICORN & LEO: If the flow seems to be going in opposite directions, leave well enough alone. It is better to find a novel approach and not jump to conclusions without counting the challenges. Availability means something very different to each of you. It is more than probable that one of you is just not comprehending what the other one has to say.

CAPRICORN & VIRGO: You, Capricorn, should be able to find a way to cut through any of Virgo's perplexing counterattacks if you prepare yourself well in advance. You both will have to take time out to get ready for little upheavals. You should study, use, and apply the old saying, "less is more," when you are dealing with a Virgo.

CAPRICORN & LIBRA: Capricorn, you relate to numbers in a more intricate way than Libra does. Consequently, Libra could (although he or she shouldn't) drive you crazy by ignoring all the rules. Before you give up trying, try to get help from some an instruction manual that actually spells things out in black and white, whether it be a practical business book, a cookbook, or the Kama Sutra.

CAPRICORN & SCORPIO: To make things work between yourself and a Scorpio, you must take into account the psychological side of the why's and the how's of what you are trying to strategize. The situation between you needs the human side of the story to develop into something accountable. So look a little deeper beneath the surface and try to understand Scorpio. Perhaps reading the sections in this book about Scorpio will help.

CAPRICORN & SAGITTARIUS: You will need to show Sagittarius what you mean by taking things step by step, because Sagittarius likes to throw everything into one large bag and just go for it without taking anything into account. Maybe you can make Sagittarius understand that obstacles can crop up, but you surely will overcome them.

CAPRICORN & CAPRICORN: A euonym is a well-chosen name. Before counting whatever it is you are strategizing together, you have to find that specific word, like a great nickname, a perfect code, or even the mysterious password to identify the core of the strategy within its own context. Finding the right name could then be a magic key.

CAPRICORN & AQUARIUS: If Aquarius can actually make you, Capricorn, feel as though you are trying to cut through a lot of red tape, it is because Aquarius is being too extravagant. Don't let Aquarius count his or her blessings too soon. Watch out and maybe you will catch a falling star.

CAPRICORN & PISCES: Even though my grandmother always said there are no free lunches in this world, you, Capricorn, can actually figure out a way to get one from a Pisces. Even if things don't seem to work out right away, by working together you are giving each other the best of all possible chances to reach a satisfactory conclusion.

AQUARIUS
giving in

"Remember that happiness is a way of travel, not a destination."

—*R. M. Goodman*

Aquarius, you are renowned for standing your ground and not giving in. When you do, it has absolutely nothing to do with yielding. That is not only because Leo, who holds the key to the word "yielding," is Aquarius's opposite, but also because if recent studies in neurology are valid, we are still not sure if the mind can fully understand the brain. As far as I can see, your Aquarian mind has established a very firm link with the consequences of *not* giving in. You see straight through to cause and effect: your own. So you will change a personal pattern only if you feel that either the cause or the effect of your strategy can be liberating for you. You give in only if a leap toward inner freedom is your goal.

Aquarius, you are around so other signs can realize how much they need to lessen or intensify whatever it is they are not quite sure they need. You show others why they should give in to the urge to let go of what is not very interesting. You know how to leave something undone and pretend that you have given in by doing so. When you discard something that everyone else thinks is needed (and is never missed), it is another way of showing others how to give in. Galileo Galilei, who was an Aquarius, never gave in, even though it took hundreds of years to prove him right.

Aquarius, yours is the only one of the twelve signs that can feel for, understand, and represent many different points of view at the same time. You can't be pinned down, and it is no use for others to try to persuade you to give in if you don't want to. "Fortuna fortunatum" is a point in any astrological chart that is connected to the good luck factor that was once directly linked to Aquarius. Perhaps that is why it does all other signs so much good to listen to what you, Aquarius, suggest, for it just may help everyone else ride on the tail of that lucky star!

AQUARIUS
giving in

AQUARIUS & ARIES: Personally, I think you should just take one big guess at the strategy because Aries won't be a big help picking just one. If it works, great; if it doesn't, make a run for it. So many different vibes are possible in this

tremendously eclectic combination, that to plan out a strategy that requires either one of you to leave each other alone
is a real bummer.

AQUARIUS & TAURUS: Take it easy. Then make a decision.
Take a break. Then try to talk Taurus into making a break for
it. Then have a drink. Try to shove Taurus into the do-over
mode. It might not be too much fun, but creating strategies
with Taurus is well worth the try. (Giving in is something
that may be extremely difficult for you to do together.)

AQUARIUS & GEMINI: Aquarius, you know instinctively
that we all have a shared heart. You can teach Gemini how
to get a good hold on his or her heart by delivering the right
words at the right time, without having to give in to any
pressure. Gemini will do best by leaving it all up to you,
Aquarius, and if there is a common denominator to happiness, you can find it together.

AQUARIUS & CANCER: One of you, preferably Aquarius,
can certainly bestow a new meaning on the other's acts. If
that isn't giving over an illuminated possibility to someone
or something, what is? Cancer can be taught a lesson in forgiveness that will last for a long time.

AQUARIUS & LEO: Leo yields. Aquarius gives in to change.
Perhaps the two of you would do well to leave both the
strategy and the outcome to chance. Doing anything else

might be a waste of time because your viewpoints are so far apart. Don't forget that both of you have more to give to the world around you than you would like to admit. A big thank-you from everybody!

AQUARIUS & VIRGO: Submit to Virgo with a formal touch and you may be blessed with a growing pain that has an immediate effect. Don't act up if Virgo tells you off. Instead, give in, for once, to good advice. If this seems too terrible for you, Aquarius, look for a new astrological sign. And if you choose to be a Leo, yield.

AQUARIUS & LIBRA: Try for a philosophical point of view, whatever you think that means. If you can persuade Libra to give in to words, your duty is done. By joining forces, both of you can strengthen other ties in addition to your own. Language does count a lot in the way you strategize.

AQUARIUS & SCORPIO: What if one of you (and it proba- bly will be Aquarius) showed up in the wrong place at the wrong time? Would one of you give in? Probably not. So keep your cool and hope that this will not happen. In other words, "Let sleeping dogs lie."

AQUARIUS & SAGITTARIUS: Both of you should step into the limelight, accept any adulation or praise, and let others consider you for a well-deserved prize. Give yourselves the opportunity to cry out a heartfelt "Hallelujah!" so others can see what happens when you give in to what you hope is the winning strategy.

AQUARIUS & CAPRICORN: Be careful not to give in to gruffness, something that Capricorn will find uncouth and won't deal with. You can alter the future if you dare, even if time machines exist only in science-fiction novels. Try to show Capricorn how to avoid giving in to bigotry or dogmatism.

AQUARIUS & AQUARIUS: Forget all strategies, any questions, and most approaches except the need to give in to a celebration. Find out when both of you observe your birthdays and throw a great party between the two dates. Invite as many Aquarians as you can and have a good time! Chances are, things will work out.

AQUARIUS & PISCES: Circumvent a quibble and amass as much information as you can before letting Pisces give way to his or her feelings, which can become a roadblock to productivity. Pisces needs prodding to commit to a timetable, and unfortunately you are not the perfect person to do the prodding. If you were both astrologers, it would be perfect because you would know enough about each other and yourselves.

PISCES

escape

"Those pleasures so lightly called physical."

—*Sidonie-Gabrielle Colette*

The strategy in this section is meant to show you, Pisces, that your responsibility toward others has so much to do with helping people escape in or out of situations that you know how to deal with and have already worked out, even if only in your dreams. Dealing with dreams is another thing you are very good at; in fact, some people claim that any Pisces can transform dreams into strategies by instinct!

The most advantageous thing that can happen to any sign is to escape into your fold because you, Pisces, show others the strategic way down the long and winding road, paved with many colors—even if it isn't really there. But you should be careful, Pisces: if, as an adult, you are relying too much on escapism, you might be on the wrong track, and then everyone else is, too. As a matter of defense, you might be counting on your id, your ego, or your superego. It is okay if you use one of the three as a scapegoat—take your pick—but don't get everybody else involved. Keep your choice to yourself so you can fortify your own defense mechanism. Pile up whatever you can, strive toward perfection, and let others share your philosophy of "carpe diem," or "seize the day."

You are so good at escaping into joy while driving everyone else to distraction. Sometimes without knowing, sometimes as an act of contrition, and sometimes because of your extremely mystic soul, you show others how to trade in a bad feeling for a good one, which is the perfect escape. Usually, you do so "just because." Because you are a Pisces. Because you are a Pisces, you can motivate and manipulate others into eluding whatever unpleasant or difficult things arise, which consequently you can turn into either a temporary escape or a long-term avoidance. The only thing you cannot do (actually, no one can) is to help others escape from their own destiny, because destiny is where you are at this very moment, as a result of the choices you have made.

PISCES
escape

PISCES & ARIES: There should be a flow without hesitation as you move from one mode to the next. Even if you find that you need to break down barriers and Aries needs to start from scratch, it could be like love at first sight, with no possible escape, even if you exchange the word "love" for "healing tool" (yours).

PISCES & TAURUS: An adventure or an escape to new horizons is in store for you both. This is not a prediction; it is a fact. If things are not working as well as they should, show Taurus the way toward a brand-new strategy that will send

Taurus on a chase. Even if it is a wild-goose chase, it will be well worth the trouble.

PISCES & GEMINI: The conclusion of your strategy might not be as acceptable as you would like and quite certainly not as plausible as Gemini expects. So try to leave an escape hatch open for yourself, without drawing Gemini's attention to the fact that you are doing so. Don't bog yourselves down with words. "Light and easy" should be your motto here.

PISCES & CANCER: Don't limit yourselves. You can find extremely pleasurable distractions, even if they are of the virtual reality kind. Any situation that you jump into—even if it seems impossible to escape from—will be the right one. Lucky you. Lucky Cancer. Lucky both of you if you are in it together.

PISCES & LEO: "Your people" should explain the different escape plans to "Leo's people." Otherwise you will end up at the end of the same route, vying for the same strategic microcosmic feeling, which will diminish your chances instead of giving them room to grow. Confrontation is not the answer here.

PISCES & VIRGO: When these two opposite signs are trying to work things out, silence is the absolute worst way to get out of a difficult situation. Be sure that you are not escaping from yourselves by clamming up. Instead, try talking as much as you can, or tape your message and let Virgo listen to what you have to say.

PISCES & LIBRA: This combination could be the perfect one to write a new kind of dream book. Compare your dreams so that you and Libra can see how to enlighten each other, even if the end product is a sorry excuse for a great idea. There is no need for you to travel; you two could create a time machine that would send HAL, from 2001: A Space Odyssey, into a tailspin!

PISCES & SCORPIO: You will have to destroy something to make things work again or to get things back to normal. But you could be the perfect escape artist for Scorpio's need to express himself or herself in a new way. Let your spark light Scorpio's fire.

PISCES & SAGITTARIUS: Sagittarius can escape from almost anything you prepare, and Sagittarius is probably much faster than you think. You need to get things on a solid social standing, so go outside and try to arrange things while you both are in a nice green setting, breathing fresh air.

PISCES & CAPRICORN: There should be no disadvantage here for either of you. In fact, if something disappointing does crop up, it is either because there is bad weather in the making or because there is a heavy full moon. Others might try to escape from your combined strength but even if they do, you and Capricorn will come out as winners.

PISCES & AQUARIUS: You, Pisces, will have an opportunity to show Aquarius your true mettle—and it better be good. Otherwise, Aquarius will call you on the carpet for escaping through breach of contract, either because Aquarius feels a lack of freedom or because he or she is in an emotional predicament. Before any of the previous situations appear or after you clear them up, use unorthodox ways, which are the best strategies here.

PISCES & PISCES: Escape from disagreeableness, disreputability, unfeeling actions, and unwillingness to cooperate by being forthright. It seems evident that you should shun these destructive possibilities, but there may be times when you have escaped into unreality and don't see what is going on around you. Get someone to act as mediator between you and the other Pisces, and use the extra time to indulge in clear-sightedness without pulling a disappearing act.

CHAPTER 4

NEGOTIATING

We all have to negotiate at some point in our lives. In fact, many of us have to do it every day, if not a few times a day, in all kinds of situations. We negotiate with ourselves and with others, with or without intuition. Some people use therapy, some use financial advisors, some use friends, and others just wish on the stars, because negotiating is not simply a business technique. It is a necessary part of successful living. We negotiate with parents, mates, children, friends, siblings, grocers, plumbers—just about anyone with whom we come in contact. We negotiate our point of view, our leisure, our learning, our working, and our loving possibilities. We even negotiate how ignorant we choose to be and how individual we are. We also negotiate those things in our daily lives that we take for granted, such as how much time we spend working, whether or not we exercise, and what we should have for breakfast. Sometimes we negotiate without even realizing it! We negotiate when we smile, say yes, no, even maybe. And we definitely negotiate the path we take in order to achieve our successes—and, unfortunately, our failures as well.

The word "negotiate" is a combination of the Latin prefix *neg-* and the word *otium*—"not leisure." By definition, the act of negotiating is not necessarily meant to be a leisurely, relaxing, stress-free practice. It is one of the most challenging and complex interactions people have with each other, because each person involved has a desired outcome or goal in mind. But the good news is that this doesn't mean negotiating can't be fun.

There is an art to negotiating and every sign goes about it in his or her own way. Each sign brings its own style and rhythm to the negotiating table. Happily, there is no limit to the wonderful things you can negotiate for yourself! In Zen, there is a saying that "everything flows from your own heart." With the help of this next chapter, you will learn how to tap into your personal negotiating mode—the one you were born with under one of the twelve astrological signs—to create the right flow for yourself and then to figure out the flow that others are using according to their own cosmic strength.

While there are no proven ways to conduct negotiations, you'll do much better if you know something about the way other signs negotiate. The three previous umbrella words represented activities that you could do on your own. Moving to the negotiating stage is like getting a wake-up call to interact with other people. You know how to take into consideration all kinds of external factors, such as other people's emotions, levels of confidence, and beliefs. Having this information will enhance your own personal negotiating skills. As you cruise through the negotiable possibilities using the wisdom of astrology, your relationships—both professional and personal—will become building blocks that help you take that first step into a better future that *you* choose.

ARIES

to begin

"In my beginning is my end."

—*T. S. Eliot*

You'll have an idea of what Aries is about if you know that David—the young man in the Bible whose stone felled Goliath—is supposed to have been an astrological prototype of Aries. David was an instigator—no doubt about it. Aries carry their courage with the same strength that they carry their own name. Any negotiation is great at the start for you, Aries, because you flourish during those important "firsts." Spontaneous answers and quests of any kind are a must for you—and a must for anyone else contemplating getting together with you. Just as the saying, "You never get a second chance to make a first impression" rings true, the first step of the negotiation sets the tone no matter what sign you are. But if you, as an Aries, feel that this interaction may be the beginning of something that has more to offer than meets the eye, those involved have it made! Others shouldn't worry about what comes next with an Aries. They should just do it! If you feel that you can jump right into things because the negotiation has begun propitiously, then others should jump right in after you.

The right timing is important in this world, especially now that everything moves so quickly, and for Aries, most beginnings *are* the right time. I could go on forever about Aries. My mother was one, and she married six times! For her, each new marriage at the start was to be better than the last, and each marriage was a joy that was a wonder to behold. In fact, there never was a man who met my mother and didn't remember her with awe and admiration. (As a marvelous example of her sign, I can assure you that she did not regard the ends of her marriages as failures; they were preparations for new beginnings!) She was able to convince these extremely intelligent men that wanting things to work out ruled everything in the right way. That goes for all of you Aries: the joy, the wonder, and the exuberance of all beginnings is the hallmark of your sign. However, you (and others) must be cautioned: sometimes you get bored before the negotiation is over, and then you want to move on to the beginning of something new. . . . Speed is of the essence. So make sure you finish what you've started before you decide you've had enough.

ARIES
to begin

ARIES & ARIES: For an Aries negotiating with an Aries, there is one rule: only one of you can be the leader. Otherwise aggression will spring up from one of you. Before you undertake something with another Aries, decide who will adapt and who will defer—but be careful never to let go of your spontaneity.

ARIES & TAURUS: As long as you, Aries, feel or think that you are at the helm of the negotiation, all is well for you. Keep in mind, however, that Taurus is skilled at seeing the light at the end of most tunnels. If you let him or her lead the way during the latter half of the negotiation, you will have a better chance of accomplishing your goal and coming to a mutually satisfying conclusion.

ARIES & GEMINI: Everything will be fine between you two if you, Aries, can make Gemini immediately understand that, as it says in the Tao Te Ching, "That which we look at and cannot see is called plainness. That which we listen to and cannot hear is called rareness. That which we hope for and cannot get is called minuteness." Aries is the one sign that could get Gemini to stop and ponder true meanings before you two begin something together. Take your time, Aries, for otherwise you could stumble into the gap of misunderstanding.

ARIES & CANCER: An Aries negotiates with reason, while a Cancer negotiates with emotion. This attention to emotion enables Cancers to have a better sense of rhythm and reality—two important aspects of negotiating. Take the time to listen, and if what Cancer says sounds unclear, it will make more sense if you wait for the moon to change signs, which never takes more than three days and will certainly make a difference in Cancer's mood.

ARIES & LEO: Try to show the best side of yourself when you negotiate with a Leo. Anything can be negotiated between you, even if it seems complicated, although, it might take someone who is neither Aries nor Leo to really get you going because of your strong egos. Once you do get going, everyone else will follow!

ARIES & VIRGO: The enemy of both of your signs can be the word "procrastination." Please change or adapt your schedule to move more quickly because it's all in the timing. Since you and Virgo both have great imaginations, don't criticize each other for what may seem like a stupid idea, for it might actually be "such stuff as dreams are made on."

ARIES & LIBRA: This combination is pure yin-yang—one gives, the other takes, depending on which one of you is up and which is down. Meanwhile, don't be shy about saying exactly what you think. Never underestimate the farsightedness of a Libra, whether or not you understand what he or she is saying.

ARIES & SCORPIO: It doesn't matter at what level you start the negotiation, for Scorpio's insight reaches far enough beneath the surface to see the inevitable outcomes. Remember to pay attention to the details, though, so you don't keep tripping over the same cracks, because Scorpio will not hesitate to remind you of even your tiniest mistakes.

ARIES & SAGITTARIUS: There can be boundless enthusiasm here, and if you can get your negotiations off to a fast start, you two should become a powerful force. However, Aries, you might forget what you were so excited about in the first place if you get too carried away while Sagittarius has already gotten everybody on his or her side. So keep a datebook and stick to the schedule.

ARIES & CAPRICORN: Capricorn will weigh and measure every word, so be certain that there can be no misunderstanding of terms once you two come to anything close to a conclusion. Capricorn is usually in for the long haul and will quickly find any mistakes or inconsistencies. So, Aries, never give up! You and Capricorn have much to learn from each other.

ARIES & AQUARIUS: Aquarians can work with things that seem to have no rhyme or reason but which turn out to be stepping-stones toward something incredibly interesting. There is no rule to getting into sync with them—you just jump in at any time like double Dutch jump rope. If there's no pleasure involved, forget it—or try to find the pleasure! Wait, watch, and listen. There's always something in it for you.

ARIES & PISCES: Pisces are great at holding back and waiting to start any negotiation. They think they know the outcome, but they do sometimes make mistakes. If you can push or shove them forward, they can respond by providing just the kind of insight that Aries needs.

TAURUS
endurance
"It is surely harmful to souls to make it a heresy to believe what is proved."

—*Galileo Galilei*

Taurus knows that to be is to withstand. Nobody endures things better than you, Taurus, for you can actually wait forever. Once you understand this about yourself, negotiation is possible, so long as no one is telling you to hurry up. You must give yourself the time to decide if what you are negotiating for now will be temporary or permanent. For you, Taurus, the most important thing is to take the time to negotiate with yourself to find your own inner equilibrium. If perchance this process takes longer than others expected, that's just tough luck for all the other signs. Let them endure the spirit of Taurus, so filled with emotion, and while they wait for you, let them spend their time trying to relax. You, on the other hand, once you have negotiated with yourself will be able to control any situation with tremendous skill.

Your personal strengths are the five senses. The more you satiate them, the more powerful you will become. The sweetest scent stimulates you, the greatest taste enables you to dream, the gentlest touch activates your brain, the most beautiful sight gives you energy, and the most melodious sound gets you into sync. You, Taurus, have a marvelously strong nature that can get the best out of anyone by playing with the five senses—your own or those of others.

Those who deal with Taurus should know that they are going to learn more about themselves than they expected, no matter what the negotiation is about. In other words, the reasons behind the negotiations are the important thing to Taurus. Others can negotiate to their hearts' content, because if they endure long enough, then all will be well, even if there is no apparent immediate benefit. And remember: some astrological sources say that Taurus is the only sign that can keep a dog from biting by sheer willpower. If that isn't negotiating, what is?

A word of caution to Taurus: you do need to give others the benefit of the doubt. Before you negotiate, take a deep breath, sit down in a comfortable place that pleases yours senses. If you can endure sitting there for a longer time than you expected, then you can work out anything!

TAURUS
endurance

TAURUS & ARIES: It is in your nature, Taurus, to save things and to rescue ideas. Thus you can teach Aries all about enduring so they can see for themselves that time is not being lost, and perhaps they can even loosen up a bit. It doesn't matter if you are not too practical with Aries; when you are together, nothing is a waste of time.

TAURUS & TAURUS: The world-renowned psychoanalyst Sigmund Freud was a Taurus, and it goes without saying that he negotiated with other people's psyches! Two Tauruses together need to rely on their treasured ability to endure: the longer you can keep at it, the better for both of you. The outcome might involve more yielding than you think.

TAURUS & GEMINI: Adaptability, though it is not your strongest trait, is important for any interaction between the two of you. You may have to stretch to accommodate Gemini. If you can surprise Gemini by teaching him or her something new, you will be doing yourself a favor because Gemini is best when combining forces.

TAURUS & CANCER: You'd better keep track of the time; otherwise the two of you will spend forever in the preliminaries and never get to the actual negotiation! Cancer needs to feel that he or she is really sharing something, so if you exclude Cancer from the process, you might lose Cancer's attention and therefore interest. Staying in the right rhythm will keep things moving forward.

TAURUS & LEO: Both of you have such strong characters that if you don't try to be more gracious, Taurus, you could make Leo lose confidence. Now you have to figure out which one of you will use daring and which one courage. Remember the thorn in the lion's paw? Taurus, why don't you dare to pull it out?

TAURUS & VIRGO: Taurus, you should never forget that spending time with a Virgo is good for both of you but better for you. Virgos are great at pinpointing the best way to find quality time, and quality is something that you revel in. Most Virgos will help you ask yourself the right questions. Try some innocent physical contact—maybe a hug or a vigorous handshake.

TAURUS & LIBRA: Before spending even a minute of Libra's time, be sure that you look as good as you can; then a negotiation could be sheer delight. Invest a bit of time or money in sprucing yourself up, which, as far as Libra is concerned, induces a pleasant atmosphere and is never a waste of time.

TAURUS & SCORPIO: If charm doesn't work between you and Scorpio, your opposite, your sensitivities are being thwarted by the moon. You absolutely must find the right biological timing. This has to do with new moons, full moons, and the time in between. You do not have to be an astronomer or an astrologer—just wait a couple of days. Reschedule your appointments and sweat it out.

TAURUS & SAGITTARIUS: When Sagittarius feels that there is a higher cause, he or she always does better. So slip a philanthropic ideal into whatever the two of you need to work out, and both of you will definitely benefit. Place no head above your own, for one of you is the real optimist, and usually it is not Taurus. So, Taurus, let it be . . .

TAURUS & CAPRICORN: Work on the possibility of a real, personal Magna Carta in which Capricorn leads the way. Then you will have it made. Always put things in writing. Capricorn needs to be able to see if something is good and, if so, good for whom? Unless that's clearly spelled out, you could be caught in a never-ending discussion because both signs dislike giving in!

TAURUS & AQUARIUS: A third party could add spice to your negotiation since Aquarius usually doesn't have all the time to give that Taurus needs anyway. Aquarians can wreak havoc on the negotiation because they exist in their own time frame, not yours, so why don't you just flip a coin, take a wild guess, or let yourself be taken advantage of? It could be fun!

TAURUS & PISCES: Take twenty-four hours to think things out before you begin the negotiation, and then anything can be accomplished, endured, and worked on, because you will find that the time you spent together was worthwhile. This is actually more important than any outcome.

GEMINI

risk

"Freedom is not worth having if it does not connote freedom to err."

—*Mohandas Gandhi*

You, Gemini, are at your very best when negotiating. You take the plunge and risk your word at least once a day. You relish the power that your negotiations can bring you. When you take a risk, you influence people to see you as *you* want them to, because you are actually able to project your lucky stars onto yourself!

Hardly anyone likes listening to your nattering as much as you do because you know that you are at your best when you're the one doing the talking. In negotiations, however, you need to understand and accept that less talking is more. You may think you are a strong negotiator because you can pinpoint all the risks, but never forget that this ability could ultimately be your downfall, just because it is a cinch for you to convince anyone of anything— remember the story "The Emperor's New Clothes"? The worst thing you can do is to take an anything-goes attitude:

it might just work, and you might just get used to it, and then what would you do?

You might find yourself moving on and taking another risk, and before you know it, there you are, lost in a labyrinth of your own decisions! Just because you don't see situations like everyone else doesn't mean you can afford to take so many chances in a row. For some people, winning or losing is everything, but for you, even those terms are negotiable. The excitement of the process of negotiating is your high.

Gemini, your strength should be your own flexibility. By reading this book, you are proving it. Take another risk and believe in yourself while you negotiate, but don't lose track.

GEMINI
risk

GEMINI & ARIES: If you repeat three times to Aries, "What you are distracts me from what you are saying," you will definitely make good use of all the energy that you have to give to each other as you negotiate, even if you are blindfolded. Maybe by the third time you say this, Aries will begin to understand what you are all about and enjoy you.

GEMINI & TAURUS: For a Gemini, ideas, like grapes, come in bunches. This is not so for Taurus, who likes to take time to think things out. Even the shortest story in the world has as an everlasting meaning: it is written, read, and then can be quoted forever after. You should be so lucky!

GEMINI & GEMINI: You can't do better than to use imagination and speed as far as risk is concerned. When two Geminis negotiate, one of the two will always find the right thing to say, even if the timing is not quite perfect. Try using an old-fashioned tactic or tool, such as a quill pen, to present your case. And if that does not work perfectly, take the risk of giving up.

GEMINI & CANCER: Cancer will never forgive you if he or she loses out because you encouraged Cancer to take a risk or at least some risk. You should know that Cancer needs more nurturing than you think. Try to find new ways to present your case in a playful way, without acting coy, because Cancer will see right through you.

GEMINI & LEO: Goethe, who blamed his astrological chart for his personal character, said that "excessive virtue is only hidden pride." This should be taken into account for both Gemini and Leo because you are capable of hurting each other's pride. Let a Virgo, like Goethe, intervene and help sort things out. What seemed to be an impossible situation may turn out to be magically negotiable.

GEMINI & VIRGO: Try saying "oy vey" to each other to clear the air before beginning any negotiation. If you, Gemini, admit to a little bit of guilt about your advantage in this combination, you'll have it made. And if you let Virgo complain a bit, you will be doing more for him or her than you can imagine.

GEMINI & LIBRA: In this combination, Gemini, don't give in, even if all Libra wants is peace and quiet. One of you might be a drag for the other, so figure out how to give Libra a little boost by risking a serious negotiation. Libra might find out that you are a lot of fun and that the serious negotiation was a bit of a bore.

GEMINI & SCORPIO: You two could rub each other the wrong way if you take too long and are not careful about clearly divvying up responsibilities. If things do fall into place, however, you might find yourselves enjoying each other more than you counted on. And if by chance you are of the opposite sex, try a little seduction act, no matter what your sexual preference is. It doesn't have to be sexual in nature; mental seduction works, too.

GEMINI & SAGITTARIUS: Sagittarius is your opposite, and opposites attract, so this combination is good for both of you and could encourage a productive flow. There could be a lot of thrills in this negotiation. Why not let the other ten signs do the worrying, as long as one of you has the right connections and uses them?

GEMINI & CAPRICORN: If you both manage to keep your eyes on the prize, the negotiation is well worth the risk.

Gemini should always remember to stop, look, and listen to whatever Capricorn has to say; then the song "We Can Work It Out" will prove itself true. After that you can go for whatever is popular or trendy at the moment, and you will do no wrong.

GEMINI & AQUARIUS: Aquarius can be the spark that ignites Gemini's fire. To work things out, you must be certain that one of you kindles the other. A lucky charm, the right color, or a quick plea will always help, for both of you are tuned in to the stars even if you have never glanced upward! It doesn't matter if your roles are not quite clear—this is an equal match!

GEMINI & PISCES: If you let Pisces believe that he or she has the negotiation in the bag, you will be strengthening a possible karmic bond, even if you, Gemini, have never counted on anything related to karma! Play it cool with Pisces, and neither push nor pull. Remember, Pisces can irk you, but you will blossom if given time within a negotiation.

CANCER
reality check
"Science is for those who learn; poetry for those who know."
—*Joseph Roux*

Getting things together, doing things with others, and mediating have everything to do with your sign when you negotiate. Why? Because the concept of closeness is so strong for most people born under this sign that you need to endure a reality check in order to give yourself some distance. You could also think of a reality check as insight. You might think you are a good negotiator but you need to push your emotions aside and focus on what is really happening in front of you. For you, this may sometimes seem impossible, but it isn't. When you are free from your emotional bonds, your reality check is better than almost anyone else's. Complete objectivity will help you find the way.

You can fascinate, charm, or amuse anyone into believing that you hold the magic wand that chooses what's right. But you must also take into account that you have perfected your ability to keep people at a distance, so much so that others sometimes don't even realize they're actually negotiating something! Being a go-between can seem so easy, and yet emotion plays such a large part in your life that the more you use your negotiating skills so you can give to others, the better for everyone around and, most of all, the better for you. If a thing is real, if it persists at times when it is not even perceived, the practical part takes place when you least expect it, even though connections are what Cancer people are all about. Antoine de Saint-Exupéry, a Cancer and the author of *The Little Prince*, negotiated with readers' imaginations all over the world by enabling people to imagine elephants walking on the moon.

Aloneness is actually not such a bad thing to feel. At times, it can help illuminate a person's choice, and it might help you turn on your charm and increase your creativity. Have a new idea ready in case the one you are working on now is out of sync with the time and the mood. Once in a while, try to erase everything and start over from scratch, like pressing the delete key on your computer. Instead of sidestepping like a crab, face problematic situations head-on. Take time out for that much-needed reality check. Let your ego press you forward and then lean back, for you usually get more than you bargained for anyway.

You are born under the sign that gets the best out of change, which, given the speed of things these days and of your ever-changing moods, can occur once each second, which makes it about 74,400 times a day. Whatever it is that you are negotiating at this precise moment is much more important for you than what came before or what is coming after. You can actually change your reality to fit the moment, and thereby make many others happy!

CANCER
reality check

CANCER & ARIES: Sometimes Aries might feel that he or she doesn't have the time to deal with whatever the negotiation is about. This is a problem for you, Cancer, since you can be oversensitive. One of you—and it will probably not be you, Cancer—will have to get down to business and make your time productive. Of course, you can always pretend that Aries' intelligent skepticism doesn't rub you the wrong way. At any rate, giving in would help.

CANCER & TAURUS: Taurus might try to overwhelm, over-power, or outdo you. If you give Taurus the time he or she needs, things can fall smoothly into place all by themselves. This combination is perfect to find out what the best side of any story may be, because optimism abounds between the two of you. But—oops!—if there is a full moon, wait until tomorrow.

CANCER & GEMINI: Geminis will always show you another side to any story—their side, of course—but allow them to do so, because with them, your side does not really count. You will just have to find a way to get your own foot squarely and surely in the door. Once you do this, it will be like looking at yourself in an exact reflection rather than an reversed one. Can you relate?

CANCER & CANCER: To be able to use that absolutely superb sharp edge that brought you together in the first place, you may need a middleman, because two crabs need a double dose of assurance from someone else who is not involved in the negotiation. Remember that the moon makes your energy wax and wane and a mediator can help both of you produce delights, arrange things to perfection, and animate the world!

CANCER & LEO: Leos like to get to the point—too much so for you, Cancer. Why don't you lean on one, just for now, and perhaps you'll see that what was once confusing becomes as clear as the big beautiful sky. Don't worry if the course of the negotiation emulates that of a roller coaster; these ups and downs can be good—and productive.

CANCER & VIRGO: Teaming up with Virgo magnifies your strengths, Cancer, especially if you dare to use the word "instead" as part of your basic equation of negotiating with Virgo. Try not to bear testimony immediately by stretching out the negotiation; don't bother yourselves with nitty-gritty specifics, which Virgo adores. Try to agree on one thing "instead" of another.

CANCER & LIBRA: If you and Libra both stop, look, and listen to what you say about each other, you can avoid a titanic clash, but just remember that the negotiation could go either way. If it doesn't, then the resulting negotiation can be a very positive learning process. You are both at your best during negotiations because both of your signs thrive on combinations. So get real, and give yourself a chance!

CANCER & SCORPIO: You have to admit, Cancer, that your style may trouble Scorpio. But if you get past that first hurdle, you can do really well together. Try first talking everything over as well as through, and then wait patiently to see what happens. Don't lose an opportunity just because a first impression makes one of you miss out on the other's true value. Take a second, and a deeper, look.

CANCER & SAGITTARIUS: A Zen master wrote, "The knife does not cut itself, the finger does not touch itself, the mind does not know itself, the eye does not see itself." The basic instinct of each sign is so different that the finger of Cancer could be an eye for Sagittarius, meaning that to see things in the same light can be very difficult. But if you keep this in mind, you and Sagittarius can negotiate something better than absolutely fabulous!

CANCER & CAPRICORN: Team spirit is good for both of you, especially since you are opposites. Cancer needs to accept the fact that to commit doesn't mean forever. Once you get going, you could work out long-term plans, especially if you, Cancer, can cut through the B.S. and if each of you can take a good dose of constructive criticism—in fact, any criticism is okay. Don't blame anything on circumstances; both of you know how to make things happen.

CANCER & AQUARIUS: Recalcitrance could abound here. You and Aquarius could really have fun if you can agree on how to disobey, when to withstand, with whom to be firm, and how to repel authority. That reality check of yours, Cancer, comes in very handy here, so if the negotiation works out, the result could be one of the very best.

CANCER & PISCES: A myriad of ideas plus all kinds of variations could and should be produced here, if both of you give yourselves a good chance by letting go. While the two of you are negotiating, you, Cancer, need to forget about reality checks, unless there's really no light at the end of the tunnel. Be careful never to lose respect for Pisces, and remember that it really does take two to tango. Cancer and Pisces need each other.

LEO

vulnerability

"The opposite of talking is not listening. The opposite of talking is waiting."

—*Fran Lebowitz*

Don't panic, Leo. It isn't that *you* are vulnerable; it's that when you are near other people, *they* become vulnerable because of your presence. Your sheer presence makes them feel open and unsure of themselves. If you don't already know this, learn it by heart, because this power is one of your greatest assets.

The only two things that can threaten your prowess are a lack of harmony and an absence of order—the two things that are absolutely vital to your well-being. The more you learn to dominate and control disharmony and disorder, the better for you. Your negotiating prowess diminishes when you aren't in charge; but to be in charge you need inner calm, which most people believe you have anyway. If only you would remember to really look at yourself in the mirror at least once a day, you'd be doing yourself the biggest possible favor, because your sign makes you shine, glow, and reflect back exactly what you need to be in control of. Usually, with one glance, you give yourself the chance to actually see things clearly for yourself. Once you feel more secure, everbody else will feel as safe as you wish they would be, or as you think they should be. (You never think; you know.) Alas, this harmonious security isn't always possible, and *that* is where the vulnerable part sneaks in—the best of cases for others and in the worst of cases for you. Sometimes, even if you are present, you just don't seem to be able to put things in the right place, but only because you don't dare use that wonderful, stately, and magnanimous pride you were born with, which should make you a winner in any situation.

Your exuberant strength can also turn into your softest spot by becoming the thorn in the lion's paw. Remember, you are prone to overdo, although personally I would love to have a Leo at my side whenever I negotiate, for you are someone who can create anything for others to benefit from, and everybody is better for it. I call this Leo's negotiable generosity, and if you take a minute to recite to yourself, "We are what we think" (an ancient Buddist saying), you will realize how lucky you are to have been born under this sign, and you'll understand why you never give up—nor should you.

LEO
vulnerability

LEO & ARIES: If there isn't a spark of enjoyment in the interaction, forget it, because this can be a funky combination. It
could get complicated, since the right or wrong moment
could make the silence comfortable or uncomfortable, or
the power of a handshake trustworthy or untrustworthy.
The silence can disable, confuse, or conceal whatever Leo
wants; on the other hand, it could make the negotiation
work out with a double advantage—for both Leo and Aries.

LEO & TAURUS: As long as you don't try to negotiate with
a superior point of view or curl your upper lip, Taurus will
not feel cornered—something a Taurus usually cannot
stand. Keeping some precariousness is recommended when
negotiating with Taurus, but any storm that might result is
well worth the calm that might follow. Tauruses usually
want to have the last word, anyway . . . so let them.

LEO & GEMINI: Gemini can charm Leo into giving in, giving up, or even believing a little white lie, so if one of you
catches the other in an unorthodox practice, you should get
a kick out of discovering the other's Achilles' heel. If you
lack trust, you might want to start over with a clean slate.
You might find that you enjoy airing each other's dirty laun-
dry instead of negotiating anyway. Good luck.

LEO & CANCER: Leo, if you think that Cancer's vulnerability is too obvious, you are wrong. Cancer knows how to beat the tide and swim around most obstacles even if the reality is a virtual one. Careful here Leo, you might be the one taken for a ride (although, if the negotiation works, it could turn out to be a moveable feast!). (By the way, Hemingway was a Cancer.)

LEO & LEO: You both relate so well to changing relationships that any negotiation can be done in many contexts— so many, actually, that you should probably be on the lecture circuit together instead of each pushing for your own side of the story. There can't be two kings in one pride, but there can be two kings in one jungle. For Leo, winning is a must but sometimes it takes longer than you might think.

LEO & VIRGO: Virgo needs the benefit of Leo's diplomacy to be able to loosen up. You, Leo, should show Virgo how to follow the beaten path, why you should patch things up, or how to start an interesting negotiation. You cannot assume that everything Virgo says will be done, so get as much as you can in writing. Always keep your guard up, because Virgos know what they are talking about.

LEO & LIBRA: The outcome of your negotiations could be a master class for all the other signs because of the strong differences that you both carry as your cosmic baggage and the empathy that you can project when these differences fuse. The more the merrier: always be sure that there are a lot of people around you, because this combined energy will bring out the best in both of you.

LEO & SCORPIO: Negotiating with Scorpio could be like opening up Pandora's box. There might be a push, there might be a shove, and there definitely will be more than you were expecting! Scorpios are wonderful at searching for meanings—words and/or replacements for the same. Let Scorpio be the one to get to the heart of the matter. There is no easy way out unless you happen to be in love.

LEO & SAGITTARIUS: Sagittarians usually need outside motivation (they themselves might call it insight), and you, Leo, can find out which is the first button to press to get them rolling. Why not try a good dose of humor? If the humor falls flat, it could be a potential nightmare, but if you press the right button, it will be as good as a miracle solution.

LEO & CAPRICORN: Leo must remember the motto "Live and learn." You and Capricorn can lean on each other's strengths and weaknesses without losing the characteristic elements of yourselves. The challenge for you, Leo, is to understand a point of view that is not your own but is perhaps worthwhile. Capricorns know how to be farsighted. So let them.

LEO & AQUARIUS: Staring each other down might be an effective measure. Because you are astrological opposites, you should be able to see the exact reflection of yourself in each other's eyes. But do not stereotype each other—you both are much too eclectic and unique to stand for it. Don't let emotions mix things up. Leo, think twice and use your head, not your great big heart.

LEO & PISCES: I suggest that you don't give each other time limits for any negotiation, for you can always find a way to bridge large gaps as long as you can take forever. Creative expression is the best way in or out of any negotiation between you two. Creativity doesn't mean that you have to become an artist; why not invent a great new drink? Use your creativity as a tool for getting where and what you want. So hit the local coffeehouse or watering hole.

VIRGO
bargain

"Time eases all things."

—*Sophocles*

Bargaining means negotiating a better deal without ruling out other people's winnings. And this word fits Virgo better than anything even Goethe could have said about you and your sign. In his autobiography, Johann Wolfgang von Goethe, born into Virgo in 1749, relates his birth to his character, to his life, and to the stars. Like Goethe, people born under the sign of Virgo usually take on life with an inner strength that all the other signs don't see for a long time— sometimes, unfortunately, even centuries! The ancient sages believed Virgo represented all seven virtues: faith, hope, charity or love, prudence, justice, fortitude, and temperance.

The sentence, "I've got you under my skin," could have been written about Virgo, because you get there, you stay there, and most people will end up thanking you for being there. Virgo's strength is in negotiating a better deal for all of the other signs. You might have to strike a bargain with yourself to become more accessible to them.

Too many people worry about your meticulous eye, but they should give you a break! You, Virgo, were born to analyze, and you are so good at it that you can drive everyone absolutely crazy with your constant synthesis, analysis, and reasoning. Sometimes, by the time you've decided which side of the negotiating table you want to sit on, everyone else has already left the room! When you finally do get down to negotiating, you do so in your own individual freethinking way. All other mortals should just thank you (once in a while) and have at least one Virgo on hand to read the fine print and figure out the smallest details. And if *you* stand by someone's side, that person has it made.

You, Virgo, will always know just what word to use at precisely the right time, and with this great talent, you can either make or break people. It is up to others to decide if your best of times are their worst of times, or vice versa. You can learn a lot about yourself by testing your articulateness:

if your words spill out, you are on the right track, but if you have difficulty finding what to say, you need to backtrack and do a bit of bargaining and negotiating with yourself!

VIRGO
bargain

VIRGO & ARIES: There is a lot of nervous energy between you that needs outlets. So open up the window to let in fresh air—literally and figuratively. Take a deep breath, talk things over, and follow your instincts down what may be a bumpy road. If you keep going you will get to the end of a tunnel, and if you can get Aries to work on the real details, you will end up agreeing on more than you were counting on.

VIRGO & TAURUS: Tauruses have a way of getting whatever they want from you, Virgo, because they know how to soften you up. And you do a lot of good for them if they lend you their ear. The setting of your negotiation is very important to Taurus, so work on creating the right atmosphere and don't balk if Taurus touches you on the arm, pats your back, or even asks for a hug. Just settle down and prepare yourself for a long haul—it should be a great one.

VIRGO & GEMINI: Once you have taken Gemini in with a furtive, but not futile, glance (which comes naturally to you), try to be easier on him or her. Let time do most of the talking, and use your life-knowledge so that Gemini doesn't think that he or she knows all the best stories. Geminis can be flippant and impatient, but you can see through their blunders, as they can see through your fears. So try to act courageous, even if you don't feel it.

VIRGO & CANCER: Relying on your intelligence is best when you are negotiating for bargains, given all your talents. You can actually assure Cancer that anything he or she doubts is right, except when it comes to doubting you. This might make Cancer back down at the last minute. Not to worry—the moon, Cancer's ally, does change signs every two or three days, and Cancer can be much more flexible than you think.

VIRGO & LEO: If you, Virgo, cannot find the exact word, then shut up already! Don't interfere as much as you would like when a Leo is around, or you might find yourself without anyone to negotiate with. Leo does not like to bargain with anyone about time. Come to the negotiating table free of any old or outdated ideas, and even if it hurts, be a bit humble in front of Leo.

VIRGO & VIRGO: Look out—for there is much more here than you are bargaining for. If you feel that you have the upper hand, so does the other Virgo. In all probability, if you both promise to contemplate the matter first, then you can negotiate full steam ahead. Sound complicated? It is. It would be much easier if one of you were not a Virgo! But hang in there, because if the two of you manage to conclude your negotiations, a true bargain will ensue.

VIRGO & LIBRA: Lily Tomlin, a wonderful Virgo, said a very pertinent thing that can apply to this combination: "We're all in this together—by ourselves." If this were an equation, the "ourselves" part would be you, Virgo, and the "together" part would be Libra. After all, Libra is the astrological sign that follows yours, and because of this, Libra can often open doors for you.

VIRGO & SCORPIO: If Scorpio feels that the going is a bit on the bumpy side, it's okay. Scorpios can get feelings for or about Virgos that are usually valid. Scorpios often lie in wait, because they have patience on their side and know just how fabulous the outcome of this deal eventually will be. On the other hand, if they have no feeling about it at all, just let go.

VIRGO & SAGITTARIUS: If you could negotiate everything with Sagittarius by E-mail instead of face to face, so much the better. The more technology you use, the easier it will be for you, Virgo, to get the upper hand. Why? Because this combination is ruled by "first come, first served" and heaven only knows which of you is the first. When you use telecommunications, it's all a matter of pushing mechanical buttons instead of each other's.

VIRGO & CAPRICORN: Your ambition should sweep Capricorns off their feet. That might be harder than it sounds, however, because Capricorns usually do not get swept off their feet by anything, since they plan far ahead. So get out your schedules and lists of ideas and help Capricorn visualize the realistic possibilities of your negotiation.

VIRGO & AQUARIUS: Aquarians know all about control, even if they are not so great at controlling themselves. And you, Virgo, know a lot about inspiration. If you put control and inspiration together, you two can beat most others in any negotiation. As a team, you can work; solo, Aquarius could churn out something you never even heard of, so come prepared to learn something new.

VIRGO & PISCES: If your palms start sweating and your heart starts pounding, you're ill. It's not nerves. You're facing your opposite, and opposites attract. The inner workings of bargains, negotiations, transfers, compromises, and coming-to-terms have nothing to do with having your own way, opposites, or attractions. Count your blessings and then help each other, or ask others for help. Virgo should ask, and Pisces can show how to help.

LIBRA

conquer

"If I have seen further . . . it is by standing upon the shoulders of giants."

—*Isaac Newton*

To say that Libras conquer their negotiations might seem like too strong a statement, but you, Libra, are nourished by making a go of—and conquering—anything you set your mind to. The word "conquer" comes from a root that means "to query, quest, and seek." You are the seventh sign of the zodiac, the one that starts the zodiac's togetherness cycle. This is a wonderful position, but it also carries a heavy weight, for so much depends on your own personality and what you can conquer with it.

Your search for the self is never-ending. Your intricate nature usually can work itself through obstacles when you dare to be a little more egotistical than others would like. And the balance that comes with your sign lets you tune in to the delicate goings-on of all eleven other signs. They would love to possess your charm, for sometimes, just by smiling, you win the competition. Fate, fortune, or bad luck has nothing to do with it, because your astrological sign somehow helps you disarm those around you while giving you an upper hand by making them feel at ease. You should always give out the booby prize.

And a word of caution: don't think that you are better than others. You have a good dose of narcissism, and if you do not acknowledge the value of sharing, appreciation, and generosity, you may lose out. If you are comfortable within your sign, people are comfortable with you, and you can shine while you stealthily conquer.

At times, you may find yourself in the middle of a negotiation that has gone further than you expected. You are in the middle of a crowd, and they are calling out for you. Use this to your advantage. Your ability to convince, conquer, and negotiate on the spot gives you a leg up on your unsuspecting competition.

LIBRA

conquer

LIBRA & ARIES: You know, Libra, that your opposite is Aries, and Aries knows that perfection is almost nonexistent. You also should know, Libra, that Aries never let their guard down, so if you can conquer an Aries, it is almost like taking yourself by surprise, which is hard to do. You're in a spot. Charming as you may be, perhaps you need to find out more about quantities and qualities instead of just smiling.

LIBRA & TAURUS: Take your time when you are negotiating with Taurus; you're in it for the long haul. Remember, both of you are ruled by the same delightful planet, Venus, which means that negotiations might get a little emotional, so prepare yourselves to accept what you were not actually counting on.

LIBRA & GEMINI: Persuade Geminis to be truthful to themselves. Then they will have to admit that being conquered is actually their cup of tea! So try to have fun together. If you want the upper hand, find out what kind of music Gemini enjoys, and nonchalantly come in whistling the right tune. Gemini will be knocked off his or her feet!

LIBRA & CANCER: Getting conquered does not bring out the best in Cancer, unless he or she feels that the negotiating process comes from a worthwhile lunar effect. In other words, you must convince Cancer that someone else is going to get something good out of the process. You've got to lighten Cancer up—just like a moonbeam. And never think it's over without reminding yourself of what Yogi Berra said: "It isn't over until it's over."

LIBRA & LEO: Leos may see themselves as great conquerors, but communication isn't their strength when Libra crosses their path. So, Libra, turn on your communication skills. A good dose of cooperation is needed here and nobody knows how to yield more graciously than you two. Once you've found it, the fruits of your negotiation will grow and grow and grow by themselves.

LIBRA & VIRGO: If you carry a little banner that says "Live and learn," you'll charm Virgos right out of their seat. Try to remind yourself of the details or the meticulousness of everything involved, even though Virgo will always remind you. Take criticism with a grain of salt, and let a Virgo boss you around (for a while).

LIBRA & LIBRA: If things get too confusing or a little mixed up, just hang up a little sign that says, "This is happening somewhere else." If this doesn't sound completely right, you haven't gotten it! Get yourselves a good dictionary, for otherwise you could use the right word but send out the wrong meaning. And for now the "somewhere else" is actually here, so get real.

LIBRA & SCORPIO: The vibes between you should be jumping around like the electrical currents in your brains. You should connect easily, unless Scorpio judges you too flighty and makes you lose your self-confidence. When Scorpios lose ground, they back away and you might be missing out on a good thing. There's nothing better than having a Scorpio at your beck and call, so be ready to give each other another chance.

LIBRA & SAGITTARIUS: There's a children's song whose chorus is the perfect phrase for this combination and it goes: "the moral of the story is never to lie." Write this on the wall, because it might seem a bit too easy for either of you to sneak in a little fib, but you definitely should not tell either a big one or a little one. Make sure you have the facts in order and then truthfully cheer each other on.

LIBRA & CAPRICORN: This is the one sign with which you, Libra, cannot be sure that your charm will always work. First of all, Capricorns don't like to be charmed. Second of all, you should always take into account what they want to explore because they see all kinds of circumstances that you probably aren't aware of. Don't put things off for too long, for you might find yourself out of the picture.

LIBRA & AQUARIUS: Remember that word "spontaneity"? Charm yourself into really understanding it even if you don't think you can. Spontaneity should help things fall into place easily without too much effort. You should know that Aquarians carry some heavy-duty influences within their sign all the way into the year 2000. Listen and learn.

LIBRA & PISCES: The two of you can arrange bits and pieces to fit neatly together, like one of those huge 3,000-piece jigsaw puzzles, and as long as you do not shut each other out—which might occur because of a minor misunderstanding—big things can happen. Intricacy and refinement of details, as well as a bit of magic, will help you find the perfect way to a perfect solution.

SCORPIO

imagination

"Space isn't remote at all. It's only an hour's drive away if your car could go straight upwards."

—*Fred Hoyle*

There's nothing incompatible between negotiating an extremely serious matter and exploring anything you can imagine! Imagination is so much a part of your secret language that perhaps this is why any Scorpio could take to heart what the author of *The Man Without Qualities*, Robert Musil (born smack in the middle of Scorpio time), wrote with his soul: "Everything one can think about stems from affection or aversion."

For you, Scorpio, the connection between negotiation and imagination comes directly from your incredible perception. When you read "Rose is a rose is a rose," you immediately compare it with a rose you once saw in a specific place at a specific time that had a specific meaning that, unfortunately, usually only you connect to. Yet your built-in knowledge comes from the most imaginative of all cosmic minds. Experience, which is what we all need while negotiating anything, is intricately related to the vast imagery you carry within yourself. Waking up is already a form of negotiation. With your Scorpio intuition, you know what side of the bed to get out of, what to put on, and how to present yourself so that the day will be on your side. While you sleep, your brain is communicating with your psyche trying to put things in an agreeable perspective. The rest of us, poor souls, who weren't born Scorpios, need to have one of you nearby to remind us of our daily follies. Life is a challenge, as are the roller-coaster possibilities of negotiating through it. You, Scorpio, know that this true even if nobody ever told you. And you should spread around your personal resilience to the other signs, for you are the one who bounces back in the best of all ways. Time is no object, not even from millennium to millennium!

Unfortunately, you usually connect with others on quite a different level, so all the other signs must learn to live vicariously through your imagination. You would love it if people would act with more certainty, but you'll just have to live with the fact that this is not usually the case. Keep this in mind when you start doing deals, shifting positions, counting possibilities, rearranging thoughts, and marking out pathways. Do remember, please, that still waters run deep—and your waters will run even deeper if you give yourself room. Your time has always been there, is always here, and will always be coming. Wasn't Merlin the Magician a Scorpio?

SCORPIO
imagination

SCORPIO & ARIES: There is always a better way to ask a question, and Aries, although perhaps sure of his or her position, will be grateful if you point out the possibility of change. Of course if Aries beats you to it (which he or she is very likely to do), try some sort of tongue twister that could turn into a mind twister to confuse Aries and thereby prepare both of you for new challenges. Try to keep things interesting.

SCORPIO & TAURUS: For once, don't let your imagination get carried away and don't try to carry Taurus away with your imaginative self, even if it is your opposite sign. Courtesy should be paramount; otherwise Taurus could bury his or her head in the sand. With Taurus, there might be some rough edges to circumvent, so maybe you could be a little nicer. Taurus will certainly appreciate it.

SCORPIO & GEMINI: Map out your territory, because whatever you do, Gemini will try to do it better and might even try to corner you. If you really know what you are negotiating and all its pitfalls, nobody can accuse you of superficiality. Gemini will feel safer, and your negotiations will prosper by leaps and bounds. You take the leaps, and let Gemini scrutinize the bounds.

SCORPIO & CANCER: If you believe that it takes two to tango, you'll believe in the huge possibilities of negotiating in this doubly intuitive context. Once you've determined how long it may take you to actually learn the steps, you may just be the ones to find life on Mars! Two water signs can invent anything at any time!

SCORPIO & LEO: With this combination, one of you will end up being stubborn. So draw straws to decide who has to give in. Now that this decision is out of the way, why don't you plan some fun on the side (as long as neither of you acts like a curmudgeon)? Once you begin negotiating, you, Scorpio, can operate with wit while Leo operates with insight.

SCORPIO & VIRGO: You might have to just think positive here and leave things alone, because what might seem to be a lack of understanding or a misconception is actually a product of somebody's bad taste (it could be yours, Scorpio). You can do wonders by opening Virgo up, and then Virgo can show Scorpio how to see real silver linings, so try boosting each other's egos by carrying the negotiation all the way through.

SCORPIO & LIBRA: Libra can be the best possible audience for Scorpio because of the magnetism that should be felt on both sides. That doesn't mean that everything will go well. Things can go well, though, if you respect each other's imagination as well as your imaginative selves . . . and then get a third party to put things in place.

SCORPIO & SCORPIO: Scorpio and Scorpio? There is such a strong urge in both of you to merge with others (yes, on all levels) that when you aren't negotiating something, usually you're imagining yourself doing so! Good for you. Just keep in mind that you are better off when negotiating a personal response than a general case. So don't lock yourselves in; just dare to go for it.

SCORPIO & SAGITTARIUS: The salient traits of Sagittarius are energy, method, sensitivity, excitability, and bravura. If you, Scorpio, can tame one or all of these characteristics, you've got it made, even if the negotiations turn into something you were certain you never would have thought of or felt an interest in. You can always count on Sagittarius to help you see yourself in a different light.

SCORPIO & CAPRICORN: Philosophically you two were made for each other, but the world doesn't always need the philosophical side of a story. So try to actually *see* what the other is talking about, and try physically to *show* what worries you. Less is more here.

SCORPIO & AQUARIUS: You need to use moderation because you should probably curtail some of your actions. If, after this analysis, you decide there is something within the negotiation that isn't needed, then you have found the right path. Don't forget to take eventualities into account, especially around an Aquarius. Your partnership could turn mishaps into something good. In fact, why not make a plausible mistake and see what happens?

SCORPIO & PISCES: Scorpio is instinctive, Pisces is intuitive, and the whole negotiation depends on finding the subtle difference between these two very important sides to your contemplative imagination, which you both carry in excess. Count on luck more than you would normally, and remember that whoever is in the middle, between the two of you, is perhaps the luckiest of all!

SAGITTARIUS
to simplify

"$E = mc^2$" (*energy equals mass times the speed of light squared*).

—*Albert Einstein*

Sagittarius can be the great teacher for all the other signs. The only thing you have to do is ask yourself: "How can I get this done and negotiate without wasting time?" Sagittarians are usually so focused that the fact that others can't see what's really in the air seems unbelievable to them. Sagittarians can't wait to finish, because in the middle of this very important negotiation, you see another one coming up right behind. You believe that time is never on your side. For instance, if you could make everyone else understand that there is always one step too many, things would be so much easier. So you spend time sorting out what is really useful, and thus, almost without knowing it, you simplify things. It is not so easy for you to live with a sign that is related to the seven muses and most of the prophets, as yours is supposed to be.

Sagittarius should be objective and subjective in the right balance at the same time. With your enthusiasm, you can usually wow others, and, whatever the outcome, they should thank you over and over. You, Sagittarius, can see the details and the whole picture at the same time, and you usually know exactly what everyone else needs in order to negotiate a simple path to a perfect solution.

The only thing that you cannot stand is defeat, so you need to find your own simple way to keep the other signs on your side. Doing that makes you negotiate for yourself, however, and that's another story because you usually thrive when working for others but lose a bit of perspective when working for your own dear self. When you say, "Trust me," people usually do. Alas, when you work alone, you sometimes oversimplify and just forget what the bottom line of the negotiation is. "Be careful" is a warning that you should always keep in mind. There are usually so many people around who like you or, more probably, love you that you lose sight of the big picture. To get around this, imagine that you're representing someone other than yourself. This isn't difficult, and the rewards can be incredibly inspirational for you as well as others. You could even end most negotiations by being everybody else's role model!

SAGITTARIUS
to simplify

SAGITTARIUS & ARIES: Both of you are actually on the same quest, but you are traveling down different paths. Find one specific action that simplifies everything, and you will let each other see that wonderful inner glow that you can produce together. Jane Austen, the early-nineteenth-century novelist (a Sagittarian), wrote, "One half of the world cannot understand the pleasures of the other." She knew it, and you know it, but does Aries know it?

SAGITTARIUS & TAURUS: You could make this negotiation so much easier for Taurus because you can point the way to better feelings and easier ways. Sudden breakthroughs can occur when you spend time together, but one of you will have to dare to cut things out. If you get rid of a lot of junk, you both will have time to enjoy things. And you both are so good at enjoying!

SAGITTARIUS & GEMINI: Since you are opposites, if you don't impose your schedule or let Gemini impose his or her schedule on you, there can be a real mix-up. Try pushing each other around and see who gives up first. You, Sagittarius, can always call giving up flexibility.

SAGITTARIUS & CANCER: "Live the question now," said one of the greatest German poets, Rainer Maria Rilke, a Sagittarian, and this sums up the best course of action that Cancer and Sagittarius can take without feeling repressed. This saying also means the more you think about your negotiation, the more complicated it gets. Neither of you should let the situation get to that point.

SAGITTARIUS & LEO: Give Leos special outlets so they can use their energy to shine: let them be the first to talk, give them the best microphone and, of course, the best possible lighting. The world is their stage, Leos are happy when they shine and glow, and you are good at putting them in the right light. Once they are happy, you can do your own thing, negotiate to the hilt—and end up having a lot of fun.

SAGITTARIUS & VIRGO: You two might rub each other the wrong way, but only for a moment, like a little cold wind blowing into the room. So adapt to the current conditions and if things still feel difficult, distract yourself with a lot of noise (turning on a boom box would be fine for a start). You and Virgo might connect with a secret language that has nothing to do with sound.

SAGITTARIUS & LIBRA: There are two sides to every story, and if "btw" can mean "by the way" on the Internet, "lgs" can means "let's get serious" in the illuminated language of the stars where Sagittarius and Libra are concerned. So stop, look, and listen before crossing any road or signing any papers. As the intensity of the negotiation increases, more flow and glow will appear.

SAGITTARIUS & SCORPIO: Specifically, don't waste any time with Scorpio. Put your noses to the grindstone. Instead of losing yourselves in euphoria, labyrinths of words, and misinterpretations, get completely informed about what you need to do together, and make up your mind that things will work out—and they will.

SAGITTARIUS & SAGITTARIUS: Two peas from the same pod can oversimplify and mess things up if both of you are not careful. If you get yourselves on the same wavelength, you can amaze one and all with whatever kind of negotiating you decide to do. Letting yourself go is the best thing you can do for yourselves, but not while you are together. It will get too crowded.

SAGITTARIUS & CAPRICORN: Sagittarius, you must be absolutely true to yourself when negotiating with a Capricorn; otherwise forget it. Capricorn can see right through you, and he or she had better be seeing a good thing. Don't let this frighten you, though, because your truthfulness can be extremely beneficial if Capricorn decides that you are worth listening to.

SAGITTARIUS & AQUARIUS: Sagittarius needs to focus on the "how," while Aquarius should be prodded into focusing on the "why." Then you can easily put two and two together. Give yourselves a break, though, because the answer is not always four; the outcome depends on perspective and convergence, not simple math. A good tip: if things don't seem to be working out, change rooms or locations.

SAGITTARIUS & PISCES: As long as neither of you gets hot-headed and you both keep your presence of mind, even if things get icky, the negotiation probably can be worked out. If you can, use plays on words or stoke the ensuing competition. Nastiness is something that neither of you are good at handling so keep everything aboveboard by choosing your words carefully.

CAPRICORN

to invest

"Behold, I do not give lectures or a little charity, when I give I give myself."

—*Walt Whitman*

People around you could learn so much if they would just invest the time and watch as you get actual returns from your negotiating powers and prowess. You're at your best when you negotiate, especially when teaching others how to feel endowed and when creating long-term outlooks. By the way, if these outlooks have to do with markets, stocks, and bonds, nobody can do it better than you. You are able to show the other eleven signs, in no feeble terms, the value of situations and agreements and why one should invest in them. Everyone who is not a Capricorn should listen to your advice because you see what can or cannot be an ever-lasting valued object. You usually relate to what counts in a logical way, and in the long run, your intuitive sense of what one should invest in can be counted on during many a negotiation and you can teach a thing or two about ambition to whoever crosses your path.

Everything under the sun is related to investing and nobody can see that connection more clearly than you. But you could work on yourself to help others by showing, telling, or hinting that you're available, because too often people who would like to include you in their negotiations think that you are not interested. If you loosen up a bit, you can be helpful to those who come close enough. If something doesn't makes sense at first, think about it for a while and see where it goes; don't waste your precious time telling people that they are mistaken. Your practicality works for you, so let others do the running around—just don't thwart their curiosity. You tend to see things in terms of responsibility, keeping track of which can be very therapeutic for you, but responsibility isn't everyone's style. Come full circle by investing in other people's personal values, and nobody will ever forget the time you gave them or the insight you provided.

You're excellent at sizing people up, and that makes you a good judge of just how far you can go. If you're waiting for something in return, good for you: you usually get what you ask for, because you would accept no less. Summing up, when you invest, you are luckier than when you don't, as long as your terms are negotiable.

CAPRICORN

to invest

CAPRICORN & ARIES: Sorry, but you two will just have to learn to cope, even though this combination can sometimes rub you both in the wrong direction. Remember, when you size people up during a negotiation, they look smaller when they're far away and bigger when they're closer. This is called perspective. I know how you hate to be told what to do, but you should use the right planes and accept other people's patterns.

CAPRICORN & TAURUS: A Catch-22 negotiation is not usually delightful, but in this case it could be. Let yourself feel your way through things instead of deciding in your usual calculating way how things should be. Size 'em up, and see what this particular Taurus has to offer, then take him or her up on it. If you do this, your imagination will surprise you.

CAPRICORN & GEMINI: You can probably see in an instant what Gemini has missed out on, but you will probably be forced to admit that he or she can be spunkier than you, so let Gemini present his or her negotiation before you balk. You need to pressure Gemini, and Gemini might find you glib. The Spanish say that it is not the same to talk of bulls as to be in the bullring—so teach that to a twin!

CAPRICORN & CANCER: You, Capricorn, are an antidote to your exact opposite, Cancer. This may not sound quite logical, but it is true. You tend to be stingy with your time when Cancer's spirit exasperates you. Avoid doing this, and try to negotiate with Cancer even if there are emotional ties. You might think you don't need it, but a little emotion would actually do you some good.

CAPRICORN & LEO: Do not start anything without being absolutely sure of what you are *supposed* to know. Leos might make Capricorn squirm, but don't let them push you off track. You can teach them about the better side of materialism (the more the merrier), and they will never forget the favor. Anything that has a golden hue (gold, a great sunset, or an autumn leaf) is just right.

CAPRICORN & VIRGO: If you are not a bit choosy with your words, you could really get hurt. Virgo can wipe you out with a rubber stamp, which would be a shame, because this combination can be a lifetime negotiation that works out for everyone's best interest. You two can really come up with a cause célèbre, so why not congratulate each other before the deal is done?

CAPRICORN & LIBRA: When negotiating something together, you two need a constant reminder that time is money, so don't waste either. One of you could bring something from another country into the pact, like stocks and bonds from the European common market. To improve your chances of working things out, the best thing for you to do would be to communicate, if not from different time zones, at least from different locations.

CAPRICORN & SCORPIO: Be cautious and don't overestimate yourself, Capricorn, because you may promise something and then be unable to deliver. Scorpio has a great eye for the bottom line when you don't even know there is one. So listen to Scorpio's upside or downside advice, and let Scorpio choose the direction.

CAPRICORN & SAGITTARIUS: The inherent extravagance that usually comes with being a Sagittarian could actually do you some good, Capricorn. This is the one sign with which it is not dangerous for you to be disarmed. Though you are usually reluctant to trust someone else, it is important for you and Sagittarius to trust each other. Whoever dares to say "Trust me" first will come out the winner.

CAPRICORN & CAPRICORN: If you don't let your feelings intervene, two Capricorns together could conquer the world. Take care to give yourselves the chance to size up the situation with the right perspective, and do not act curmudgeonly, or you will not do anyone any good. Why not try to show all the other signs how well you do when you invest in yourselves? Then let them follow your example!

CAPRICORN & AQUARIUS: Aquarians can point out the meaninglessness of unnecessary acts with an exuberant phrase that seems to come from their gut. Capricorns might really do themselves some good by listening before negotiating and by acting on whatever seems related to self-growth. Say to yourself, "This time I'll give myself a break."

CAPRICORN & PISCES: You two may intimidate each other, and if the situation gets too intense, loosen up. The will in both of your psyches is so strong that it can point out the right way, even if you leave things to chance—which might be the right thing to do. You even could team up and win a game together, if you, Capricorn, tap in on your practical constancy and let Pisces use his or her ever-ready caring reception. Have you ever been to Las Vegas?

AQUARIUS
exploring
"A few observations and much reasoning lead to error; many observations and a little reasoning to truth."
—*Alexis Carrel*

A bird sings to protect its territory and attract a mate, a cat purrs as a sign of contentment, and Aquarians explore as part of their nature. You are at your best when you are exploring. There is no limit to the endless possibilities in your natural quest, so you will just have to settle for a number between a femtosecond (one quadrillionth of a second) and decillion (a number with thirty-three zeros) to try to count the extreme reach of your negotiating talent. The other eleven astrological signs must learn to coexist with your daily negotiative extravaganzas, and they can learn from watching you, since at this moment two important planets—Uranus and Neptune—are moving through Aquarius, and will continue to do so into the next millennium. You Aquarians spend so much of your time helping others that you actually negotiate for others what you could be negotiating for yourselves. And then you have to explore whatever possibilities are left over. Strangely enough, you end up with new ideas, and people begin to understand how much of a plus you can be when things need to be put together. Did you know that at one time in history your sign was called "fortuna fortunatum," which means that you're always an asset?

Aquarius, you will do yourself a favor if you sing a tune, whistle a song, or have a great sound system around, especially while you are exploring the possibility of a negotiation. Music—that special chord in nature that may be a property of our minds, perceived by sound waves—brings us back to sequences and frequencies, Aquarius's opus! Music is your astrological vitamin. So just as the bird sings and the cat purrs, you, too, need music to express what you are feeling and to enhance your talents.

You, Aquarius, are born with the knowledge that no two people have the same faculty for sensing, and you are on this earth to prove this truth. You are very good at picking up and sorting out other people's vibes, but you need to give yourself a specific time frame before you step into any situation so that you can adjust your personal energy field. Be careful when others schedule your time; that can thwart your strength. Even though it is impossible, pretend that you are walking on a Möbius strip and try to negotiate your way so you can give non-Aquarians the better part of yourself. That way, the rest of us can explore with you with real pleasure.

AQUARIUS
exploring

AQUARIUS & ARIES: It could be love at first sight for this combination. But you should know that Aries happens to have quite a volatile personality. An Aries could connect with you in the first second or, just as easily, take an instant dislike to you. If the latter happens, you are in trouble. Heraclitus, the ancient Greek philosopher, is quoted as saying that "a man's character is his fate." Both of you should study this.

AQUARIUS & TAURUS: Don't get stuck in little arguments with a Taurus, because both of you could blow up at the same time or in different corners. If you're nice, Aquarius, you'll give in first and make a tiny new idea play like music to Taurus's ear. Harmony is what Taurus is usually seeking, so try to find out what that is and give it to him or her.

AQUARIUS & GEMINI: The great thinker and writer, Virginia Woolf (an Aquarius), found a tune in the zigzagging flying pattern of a moth. You and Gemini can do the same by exploring unorthodox ideas or perhaps inquiring about something unimportant or trivial that is related to your negotiation. The point is to find a reason when others say there is none, and you're on your way.

AQUARIUS & CANCER: One of you might have a chip on your shoulder—and it probably will turn out to be Cancer. So it is up to you, Aquarius, to work things out by softening your stance, even if only slightly. Appearances can be important to Cancer, so dress for the occasion. Both of your signs do well when you are in a sociable mood, so get out there and mingle.

AQUARIUS & LEO: Because you are Leo's opposite, only you can curtail the strong needs of Leo's ego. You, Aquarius, could even help Leo organize these needs, but you are going to have to do a lot of smiling and maybe even play dumb. Try coming to terms by cutting and pasting your ideas, as on a computer. Be flexible and creative. You might come up with something better than Windows '95.

AQUARIUS & VIRGO: Virgo can easily bring to your attention a precise observation and Virgo will probably be right. But you can be a pathfinder for Virgo if you arrange affairs ecologically, which means finding the right place and time for every need. This also means Aquarius could get Virgo to enjoy some frenzy. Wow!

AQUARIUS & LIBRA: If you can get Libras to translate whatever they are planning to do into actions, you will be doing them a big favor. Figure out a way to materialize negotiations instead of talking about them. Otherwise things could get uncomfortable. Once you really get rolling, however, you are assured of instant gratification.

AQUARIUS & SCORPIO: When negotiating with Scorpio, repeat the following question to yourself: "Do my proposals in this negotiation make sense?" It will be much better if Scorpio takes the first step. Now take a deep breath, dare to pry open Pandora's box (in mythology she was supposedly a Scorpio), and let Scorpio's ideas fly out. Catch what you can, and use it.

AQUARIUS & SAGITTARIUS: Aquarius, you should let Sagittarius guide and advise you, for Sagittarius knows instinctively what can work out, especially if the negotiation has something to do with signing, sealing, or delivering. The more material things are involved (like the material girl), the better for both of you. Your outlook should be, live and learn.

AQUARIUS & CAPRICORN: One of you (probably Capricorn) needs to explore the possibility of being a real citizen of the world, and you are the best sign to help Capricorn see how it feels to be on the other side of the fence. If this doesn't work, put yourself in Capricorn's shoes and don't give in to small-mindedness.

AQUARIUS & AQUARIUS: You both have a great feeling for newfangled ideas, so let them take the foreground and put anything that you consider old hat into your bottom drawer and lock it up for now. Forget about wise insight. Instead, both of you should concentrate on exploring the unknown. The more outlandish the idea, the better for Aquarius.

AQUARIUS & PISCES: Inner chaos is quite common for Pisces and for Aquarius. The big difference lies in the fact that chaos may be easier for Aquarius than for Pisces. So it is up to you to help Pisces open up. You might even get more out of this negotiation than you counted on, and Pisces certainly will.

PISCES
ideals
"They can because they think they can."

—*Virgil*

Sharing one's life with a Pisces can be a blessing. As a Pisces, you should, ideally, convince those around you of their good fortune. Not that life always works out as it should, or that convincing others is easy, but as a Pisces, you should negotiate proving this idea all through your life, whether you want to or not. It's like trying to find the definition of the word "ideal" itself. *The Oxford Companion to the Mind* says that "the concept of an ideal seems to come from extrapolating from that which is seen as inadequate to some relatively perfect state." This definition is almost impossible to understand in itself because who can agree on a personal ideal? This will never stop a Pisces from trying define his or her own ideal.

How can you not negotiate toward that ideal state, knowing that it could be there? You know what should be done, but can you make it happen outside your mind? Pisces, you are an allegory to yourself, and the other eleven signs must learn to let you be. You can be a link to everything else. Maybe that's why Pisces is the twelfth sign of the zodiac, encompassing everything that came before it. And maybe that's why whatever you construct can be so creative. You can negotiate with words in such a way that the other signs will end up believing that you are presenting the best part of any situation.

Pisces, you are a book of answers to yourself. Ideally, we would be lucky to have you negotiate for or with us. Whatever you think we need should be worked out. Negotiating can take a long, long time, Pisces, because you first have to talk things over with yourself. This internal discussion could be the perfect endeavor, even if it goes on forever—and it very well could! When you negotiate, it seems like you are starting a conversation with all the possible outcomes you can imagine. But do others understand? Ideally, others should take a promise for all it's worth when dealing with you. However, it doesn't always work out that way. Whatever the outcome is with you, Pisces, the negotiation will give us all deeper meanings and open up windows to our souls.

PISCES
ideals

PISCES & ARIES: Pisces, don't let Aries rush you, and remember to keep your focus on the matter at hand. These two signs can complement each other in the best possible ways during the best possible negotiations, which actually seldom exist. But a solid basis is good enough.

PISCES & TAURUS: Let Taurus do the talking, and make him or her get straight to the point. You can open up Taurus's eyes to new ideas, if you are strong enough (or pretend to be). Practice pretending and don't give up. Keep pushing, pulling, molding, and always remember that hug!

PISCES & GEMINI: Gemini can outshine you by talking faster and longer, so let the dice roll and don't be as truthful as you would in other circumstances. Use your intellect, because it could be the lubrication of your soul here, and even if you aren't too sure what you are talking about, try to ad-lib. P.S. Be punctual.

PISCES & CANCER: Be ready with two possible endings, because one of them could fall through. Take turns being the boss. And remember: if Cancer can give a little, so can you. Ideally, this combination could be sheer perfection. If it isn't, find yourself another Cancer!

PISCES & LEO: Don't worry if unpleasant surprises pop up; they're not as bad as they seem. Yet if the process of bonding with Leo doesn't seem at all difficult, don't trust your insight. You could suggest some physical teamwork here, like going together to a gym or running around the block. Strong energy is good; you just have to find the right outlet for it.

PISCES & VIRGO: For both of you, a good laugh is the best antidote to what is actually a silly argument. Pisces, you have to accept the fact that there is nothing certain under the sun, except that its light takes eight minutes to reach the earth. So give in, at least a bit!

PISCES & LIBRA: If it seems financially safe, go ahead and negotiate. If you have a vague feeling of some kind of artificiality, drop whatever you are about to negotiate and go out and have some fun on your own. Until there is a change of heart, you might be taken for a ride.

PISCES & SCORPIO: This combination could be pure magic, so you both need to give unconventionality a chance, because Pisces and Scorpio are tuned into rather ebullient vibes. You might find yourselves going to the same hypno-tist or New Age dietician. Give your Chi (cosmic energy) a chance to work.

PISCES & SAGITTARIUS: Both of you need to come down to earth here. Pisces, you must not indulge in Sagittarius's reveries unless you are absolutely certain you will not allow yourself to be led astray. Sagittarius might just think that you don't know what you are talking about, so take the time to prove him or her wrong.

PISCES & CAPRICORN: You should enjoy whatever it is you are negotiating together, and if this has not happened yet, find out what Capricorn really like, loves, or pursues for happiness by asking around. Then use it like bait. Pisces, you could win out by giving in.

PISCES & AQUARIUS: Meet, converge, expedite, agree, and then put ideas, things, money, or plans in one large shaker and mix them into something new and delicious, like the best of all possible martinis. This, of course is a metaphor, which means that you understand perfectly how to assem-ble ideas and improve them.

PISCES & PISCES: Even if you don't speak Latin, two Pisces need to work on having *"mens sana in corpore sano"* (a sound mind in a sound body) before you start anything. Once you achieve this, you can pool your conscious and unconscious resources and end up showing everybody else how great things can be! You both deserve great things and we deserve to watch you two enjoy them. Whatever you do turns out to be an interactive negotiation.

CHAPTER 5

BONDING

Bonding is perhaps the best part of it all.

Bonding connects us to the exact present and should make us pleased to be in it, to be here! We should be completely aware that if we are wishing, hoping, planning, looking at our watches, and waiting for the right time, then no matter what we are doing, we are bonding. Now! When you bond, you can build, confine, restrain, strengthen, link, secure, ensure, condition, provide, connect, hold together, solidify, or bridge. Bonding allows you to "hold infinity in the palm of your hand," as William Blake said, because time has no limit to its action.

But perhaps bonding, since it can be the most rewarding aspect of human relations, is also the toughest part, especially if it stops when we don't want it to or if we bond to the wrong thing. If you are not careful, you can find yourself bonded to a question mark, meaning that you will be forever asking yourself "What if I did?" or "What if I didn't?" We will always be rethinking possibilities if we let ourselves stay in this "what if" mode. Once we do bond, the course of our lives is altered, for better or for worse, no matter what happens.

The good news is that we can always work on our ability to build strong, rewarding bonds. Astrology can guide you on this path, helping you develop and face whatever challenge your personal growth pattern needs. While you are trying to connect and interact with others, it is important to understand how to do so in the best possible way. Through astrology, you can get a glimpse of the intimacy that bonding implies and use your knowledge as either a decorative device or a calculated, perceptive move. Astrologically, bonding has a rhythm and each one of us puts it to our own rhyme, poetry, or music. When you bond, there is an exchange, at best an even one: you give of yourself and you get something in return. But ultimately, regardless of the outcome, there is always some kind of a reward, because bonding will undoubtedly make you grow.

As you bond with the myriad people who cross your path, you are constructing your own personal and intimate address book—the one you carry within you. Bonding should help you feel and be more assertive as you decide how much glue you want to use in your bonds with others. On a grand scale, humanity bonds with any passing comet that illuminates the sky, whether it be now or one that traveled through the sky four thousand years ago; call it bonding with the *anima mundi* if you like. The act of bonding person-to-person, even within everyday interactions, has such emotive power that even by saying a simple word such as "Wow!" to another person, you can accomplish something important or create something lasting.

Bonding can make you feel as if you are part of the object of your desire, thought, or situation. It can be a physical or a mental experience, but it definitely taps into your essence, into the nature without which you could not be who you are. And since, by reading this book you are finding out about your nature, exploring and understanding your astrological makeup, combined with your discovery of the natures of the other signs, you are giving yourself a chance to evolve, reveal, and perhaps revel!

ARIES
to work
"The empires of the future are the empires of the mind."
—*Winston Churchill*

If you are an Aries and you have not yet come to terms with the fact that it is by enjoying your work that you work things out, take a good look at yourself, for something is wrong. You, Aries, will always have to work on the way you bond, because Aries is unique. You may think people do not understand that you are actually trying to bond with them. However, let yourself go and show how your creativity has something to do with what you are working on. For this is the link between yourself and your work, Aries. Creativity is your life's pursuit. In one way or another you need to have that special dynamic input in your life because showing your originality has to do with using your incredible strength, both mental and physical. Never forget that your inner cosmological core is made up of the stuff that drives leaders. You have to tap into the possibility of being a leader and subtly let others see it. No easy task!

You may at times appear childish. You sometimes act on impulse without even thinking about other's wants or desires. This tendency has far-fetched consequences. As a child playing in a park, you could push someone off a swing—with luck, into a sandbox—just as easily as you could catch a person who falls. Both of these reactions are examples of Aries' impulsiveness. Fueled by your strong drive, your work moves forward by itself, sometimes leaving you in the background, which is not your favorite place.

Work, however, should somehow liberate you. It actually helps you understand what bonding is all about so you can take the next step and bond to a place, a person, a group of people, or a situation. Whatever it is you are connecting to, in your own way you should be working toward something and envisioning a better situation, for it is through this process that you give yourself the time to curb your impulsive tendencies and come into your own. While you are working, you are unconsciously considering everyone around you, and therefore tapping into your best part. Strange as it may seem, you bond just by being in a given interaction.

There should be a universal law that prohibits Aries from being out of work, because you are capable of mischief when you are idle. Because of your creativity, you can improve the outcome of any task that you take upon yourself; in fact, you can always achieve more. You are a whiz at working yourself up to excellence. Lucky you! Not only that, but if you help others, your glow might rub off. Lucky them!

ARIES
to work

ARIES & ARIES: One of you might try to outrun the other, so you go first, unless you have already decided that the bonding is much too important for you to actually care about who will get to sit at the head of the table. If you are in a good mood, just take it at as first come, first served and promise yourself that your mood won't change if you are elbowed around.

ARIES & TAURUS: Think of your relationship, whether personal or professional, as a workshop. During this process, you and Taurus can maneuver your emotions into any mode you want or need once you actually work out all the possibilities. Just don't trust your gut feeling at first, because you will hurt Taurus without even understanding why.

ARIES & GEMINI: Aries, let yourself be led if Gemini tries to lead you because you can learn a lot by listening. You, on the other hand, could invent a new way of adding, subtracting, or multiplying if you wanted to. You just have to let go a bit because Gemini needs to feel that you are with, not against, him or her. Even if Gemini bores you, let him or her talk a blue streak.

ARIES & CANCER: In this combination, form must usually come before substance, or you, Aries, will lose out on a good thing. The form could be like rainy weather, and the substance could be a raincoat or an umbrella. Remember, if Cancer feels threatened (and if it is a full moon, he or she might), forget it—for now. But don't give up: Cancer sometimes does better the second time around.

ARIES & LEO: The outcome of you and Leo bonding could be as good as gold (even though the gold standard at Fort Knox is no longer what it used to be), because you both do well as long-term winners. Be sure that what you are working on is for a good cause, though, so egotism doesn't get in the way. Otherwise sparks could fly and actually kindle an unwanted flame.

ARIES & VIRGO: If you dare to be vague with a Virgo, he or she might wipe you off his or her screen. Make sure that you can back up your promises with real words. If not, you might find yourself back where you started—alone! You might not enjoy hearing criticism, but Virgo is good at giving it, so you should listen, even if the words seem harsh. Wait a bit and then let the dice roll.

ARIES & LIBRA: Since Libra is your opposite, you'd better be careful if you find that you are bonding with an "all work and no play" mode because both of you will end up feeling stifled. Try using a dual-screen approach, meaning "I see it your way and you see it my way." If you think you know best, you just might be mistaken, but then so might Libra, so don't make any grand assumptions.

ARIES & SCORPIO: Analyze the situation three times over and then let Scorpio be as selective about it as he or she wants. But don't lose the real meaning of things or of what is actually going on. Give in for once, and let Scorpio remind you of the deeper reasons that brought you together in the first place.

ARIES & SAGITTARIUS: This combination thrives when it is oiled with fun. You, Aries, must decide what kind of fun to have. Do you want to pretend you are having a good time? Do you want to learn how to have a better time? Or are you simply going to disguise your feelings? For Sagittarius, it is usually easy to work anything out. For you, Aries, that is not always the case. So why don't you just let Sagittarius get the better of you in a playful way?

ARIES & CAPRICORN: While Capricorn waits, you, Aries, can mature if you give yourself the chance. Waiting is almost a cosmic antimatter for you, Aries, but with a Capricorn, you can get on that great long-term wavelength.

Capricorn can teach you the fun there is in counting, whatever . . . even if only numbers.

ARIES & AQUARIUS: A master plan cannot go wrong if you both allow yourselves to see the ridiculous side of absolute certainty. There is even a Chinese proverb that states that it is ridiculous to be certain. I wouldn't push it that far, but while you're at work, do have a good laugh! The bond has been in the heavens forever, even without certainty.

ARIES & PISCES: Have you ever heard of Ouroboros? It is an emblematic serpent of ancient times that is represented with its tail in its mouth, believed to express the unity of all things. Aries, work on beginnings because Pisces understands all endings. Whatever Aries starts to work on, Pisces can add the finishing touches. Allow yourselves to lean on each other.

TAURUS
to believe
"Mysteries are not necessarily miracles."
—*Friedrich Wilhelm Nietzsche*

As a Taurus, you wish first; then you believe. However, if you then determine that what you now believe in is distracting you from what you consider your rightful power to command, or if you feel that what you believe in doesn't have long-term potential, the bond will lose its strength and you will lose interest. Not that Tauruses will not end up doing what they want to do anyway (just look how British Prime Minister Tony Blair, born on May 6, fared once he bonded with his constituents), but if you can't believe, your heart will not be in it. And Taurus's heart is something to be believed in!

You need to immerse yourself in the belief that the bond is a shared experience, regardless of the actual outcome, for as a Taurus, you enjoy the process of doing things more than the final result: the bonding more than being bonded! Emotions are of paramount importance to you, Taurus, at any point, at any time. And if the ancient astrological sages of past millennia were right when they claimed that we are all born under the sign we choose, then given the chance, you would choose to be a Taurus so you could put your feelings first.

Did you know that a human being breathes about 21,000 times a day? Taurus, you connect to the whole universe just by breathing. A life-giving natural process becomes a way of bonding for you. You interact with the world without really thinking about it, but with the deep inner knowledge that each breath you take involves the senses. It is not that complicated: all this means is that Taurus bonds with emotions in an unconscious way, just as you bond instinctively with the five senses and carry within you an intimate illusion that feeling is believing. You see the illusion, you hear the illusion, you probably even believe you can touch it with your bare hands, that you can smell it, and you believe it tastes just as it should. Bonding comes after Taurus has come to terms with this basic need before anything else. Luckily, time is usually on Taurus's side no matter how long it takes.

TAURUS
to believe

TAURUS & ARIES: Like an electrical current, the bond between you two can work wonders if you are on the same wavelength. Think about what happens to electrical appliances when they're plugged into the wrong voltage: They blow a fuse. Aries needs to learn not to be too pushy and you, Taurus, need to take the time to comply with what Aries suggests.

TAURUS & TAURUS: The important thing here is to define what you both are actually looking for. Why not try dancing? Once you figure out what dance steps to take, you then might find a latent, unexpressed force within yourselves. If you work this out, you can, could, or may just watch things happen with a bang—a big one!

TAURUS & GEMINI: Ask yourself if you really want to get involved in this bond. You could also tell Gemini that if you *are* around, it is because you do really want to bond. Once you decide either way and then inform Gemini of your decision, the relations between you should be smooth riding with quite lovely results, even if the word "lovely" is not to Gemini's liking.

TAURUS & CANCER: There is a lot going on between the lines for both of you. You, Taurus, must dare to mention things that Cancer hasn't dared talk about, or maybe even think about, for that matter. There is an unwritten coopera-tion between you that could light up each other's feelings. Maybe it is written in the stars, so put it to good use!

TAURUS & LEO: Leo might seem a bit too authoritarian for Taurus, but the Bible says, "Nothing is secret that shall not be made manifest," meaning that you can use whatever you know. With this in mind, you, Taurus, need to take a bit of Leo's pushing and bide your time until you believe you have bonded.

TAURUS & VIRGO: Cooperate. You do each other good, but there has to be a give-and-take. For instance, Virgo could pick the time and you could pick the place. If your data are clear and there are no misunderstandings, you can either create a strong bond between you or contribute to the bonding of things around you.

TAURUS & LIBRA: Once again, we can talk about Venus, the ruler of both your signs. Venus embellishes whatever it touches, so try to outdo each other. A little competition is good for both of your inner fires. Also, never forget, that with this combination there is always more than meets the eye.

TAURUS & SCORPIO: Since you are opposite signs, one of you will have to grin while the other bears it. You can bring out either the best or the worst in each other within the first couple of minutes, although every time you get together might be different. Don't let go, because at least it will never be boring.

TAURUS & SAGITTARIUS: As in an open relationship, the bond between Taurus and Sagittarius has to be an open bond, which acknowledges the fact that things change and that change might improve things. The key thing to remember here is that there is always room for improvement.

TAURUS & CAPRICORN: Once you get past the nitty-gritty details, the bond between you two could last as long as your favorite poem touches your imagination. It should rise to become an eloquent and meaningful bond, even if you somehow clip each other's wings. The final result should always contain some reasonable doubt enhanced by good feelings.

TAURUS & AQUARIUS: Taurus might believe that Aquarius's adventurous spirit is just too far-fetched, but, Taurus, if you are watchful, you can find out something that has to do with

caring: taking care of yourself or taking care of Aquarius—
you decide. The change that you might feel can be very
tempting to you: is Aquarius revealing something you didn't
know?

TAURUS & PISCES: Some exaggeration by either of you is
good for both of you. At times you are kindred spirits, the
wind beneath the wings of what could turn out to be a uni-
fied form. The bond here is never futile. Go for it!

GEMINI
duality
*"Everyone is as God has made him, and oftentimes a great
deal worse."*

—*Miguel de Cervantes*

Gemini, you usually have a double perspective. Not only
can you see the forest from within the trees, but also you
can see each individual tree within the forest. That's because
you are a double sign: the twins. One side of yourself bonds
with the other before you even dream of bonding with anyone else. To make things easier for yourself, use this dual
approach to coast down the two-lane highway of life. Since
bonding also has to do with more than one person, it gets
very complicated if you start trying to be all things to all
people. You can call it the melodious aspect of your potential or call it a part of your functional dichotomy. Yes, I
admit, I am using vague words, but I am doing this because

you listen and learn at the same time. You were born with this talent, which at times makes things happen so fast that when any of the other signs are bonding with you, you are already on another wavelength. You may call it elasticity; they might call it superficiality. Whichever it is, you have a flexibility that is admirable.

Most other signs would love to have the privilege of your double-edged bonding forces. Your twin persona is the perfect example of bonding without the need to feel safe and you can show others how to apply this in their own lives. Does this sound confusing? That is what I'm trying to tell you, and let me be blunt: you are the happy owner of the possibility to bond without the need to feel that this is the right thing to do. Why? Because you can talk almost anyone in or out of almost anything. With your quick-wittedness, you tap into whatever you need without having all the tools that most other signs count on. You are the champion of bonding even when you are doubtful, for you can turn any shortcoming into something valuable, or at least worthwhile!

GEMINI
duality

GEMINI & ARIES: Aries will have to understand that for a Gemini to bond, or to bond with a Gemini, one word will rarely be enough. The more words, the merrier, the better, and the easier for you, Gemini. Fewer words can get you to

be more precise. On the other hand, Aries can always teach
you to cut down, cut up, or sum up, so why not try out a
new way of bonding in any context and treat yourselves to
a double dose of generosity?

GEMINI & TAURUS: If such a thing as a spell exists, use one
to get Taurus to believe in whatever you say, whichever way
you do it or say it, and your shortcomings could turn into
enticing dualities. If you don't believe in spells, you will
have to add a triple spark to your dialogues, Gemini,
because believe it or not, Tauruses are not easy prey! Think
of doing, saying, or presenting something that will light up
things.

GEMINI & GEMINI: Since your sign is a twin (double), two
Geminis together mean you are blessed with four ways of
looking at everything. Just make sure you don't lose yourselves in a world of make-believe. Pick the most realistic
way and either Gemini will have it made big time. Never
give up on each other because Geminis are even better the
second, third, and fourth time around.

GEMINI & CANCER: Your asset of being doubly blessed
could be your biggest disadvantage as far as Cancer is concerned, because he or she will see right through you. There
is no way for you to manage your dualities without giving
up something in return, Gemini. Even if you get away with

it, Cancer might end up feeling better by bonding with someone else.

GEMINI & LEO: Either of you could actually save each other from bonding in the wrong way. You will just have to work out your very own personal way of using the word "save," as in saving to enable, saving to store, saving to look out for, or saving time. But whatever saving you choose to do, make certain you give Leo a chance to save face!

GEMINI & VIRGO: This bond could be an "oh"—an "Oh, no" or an "Oh, wow!" Or, if the stars really are on your side, one long "ooooh." The tone does not depend on astrology; it depends on what you do. The stars will take no blame, because the choice is yours. Just be prepared that if you do cause a bond to happen between you, the stars will provide the right punctuation.

GEMINI & LIBRA: Give yourself a break. Being seduced can be one of the most delicious experiences in life. Since both of you are skilled in the art of seduction, you should decide between you who is the seducer and who is the seduced—on any level. The duality comes into the picture if both of you decide to switch roles, which I would definitely not recommend.

GEMINI & SCORPIO: I could be sounding a false alarm, and feel free to disagree, but unless each of you has a real feeling about this, things between you two could get messy. Remember, because of the potential in bonding, you can find yourself either trying to hold together or trying to hold back. If you are lucky, you will prove me wrong.

GEMINI & SAGITTARIUS: If you are looking for answers, as Sagittarius usually is, watch out! You are opposites, and if you are not careful, one may nullify the other and much will be done about nothing. The worst scenario is that you will take a rough guess and come up with zero; the best could be a double dose of good fortune. Too many cooks improve the broth, in this case.

GEMINI & CAPRICORN: Do not count on Lady Luck traveling with you all the way through this possibly enticing but also slightly worrisome relationship. Your first impressions may be the best ones, especially for Capricorn. As for you, Gemini, you should take a long shot for a better chance to get something done.

GEMINI & AQUARIUS: Something really special could be in the making between you two. If people say that what you are working on cannot last, don't listen to them. Plunge into it anyway. You will certainly have a good time if nothing else, and if you really bond with Aquarius, you will use the better side of yourself. The bond is a good test for your wills.

GEMINI & PISCES: Always write things down, bring the contract with you when you go to bond with Pisces, and be sure that you enlist the help of a mediator, even if all you want is a good time. A reasonable facsimile might be just as good as the real thing if you can decipher what it is that you are really looking for. Don't be too hard on each other. You might just find some much needed support from each other.

CANCER

giving

"One must be poor to know the luxury of giving."

—*George Eliot*

There have been some extremely serious studies of astrology written all over the world. One of the best, *Petit Manuel d'Astrologie* by André Barbault (whom, together with Michel Gauquelin, we have to thank for creating the first computer astrology), claimed that the creation of the very first human cell was produced (symbolically) within the sign of Cancer as a result of the union (represented by Gemini) of the ovule (represented by Taurus) and the spermatozoid (represented by Aries).

Cancer, your sign is commissioned by the stars to represent the gift and initiation of life. The act of giving is inherent within your cosmological soul. You give in order to bond, as well as to do so many other Cancerian things. The big question for you, Cancer, is this: *What* do you give? Do you give over, give place to, give your hand, give forth, give ear, give and take, give up, give back, give the slip, give away, or just give way? The answer depends on the bond that the other person deserves. Those who have anything to do with Cancer must understand that they will get a part of what they give—and this is something I can vouch for, as a Cancer person. When you are compromising, you are bonding. When you bond, you relinquish and divulge yourself. Your giving is a reaction to that which is due (even though the other person might not yet have noticed), so the other signs should take this into account when trying to bond with you.

Before taking the first step toward bonding, you, Cancer, need to have a gleam in your eye. Otherwise you will find yourself simply exchanging or trading, instead of bonding, because you probably submitted *too* much of yourself. For Cancer, any bond is usually forever, even though with the approaching millennium, we probably will find out that forever is not as long as we think! So take heed: since you, Cancer, always give away a big piece of your own illuminated self when you bond, you have to consider that the other person might not be able to take it, even though you may wonder what more anyone could want. You need more because as a Cancer, you give more. If you are a lucky, you might even get it.

CANCER

giving

CANCER & ARIES: Try to understand, Cancer, that Aries sees things through a completely different eyepiece than you do. Even if you have a karmic link with Aries, you still will not see eye to eye. Thank goodness for the difference, because it can do both of you a tremendous amount of good. Remember the nursery rhyme about Jack Sprat and his wife? Well, you and Aries can bond by making up for what each of you thinks the other one lacks.

CANCER & TAURUS: Do not leave things to your own imagination. You might think that you have explained everything while Taurus has understood the exact opposite of what you actually mean. Be clear and don't judge Taurus. Try to find mutual pleasure in satisfying at least one of the five senses. And remember that Taurus is the best hugger in the world (there is "touch" right there!).

CANCER & GEMINI: Bonding between you two can get complicated because Gemini will usually interpret what you say and do in a completely different way. For instance, you might think you are giving a lot, whereas Gemini doesn't even see how much is there. Try rearranging priorities, as you do with furniture. You'll be doing Gemini a favor if you remind him or her what to avoid.

ASTR⊕L⊕GICAL INTELLIGENCE

CANCER & CANCER: If you act out of habit, you could detonate a very real reprehensible, yet rewarding feeling. Sound funny? Dissect the words, take them to heart, and give new energy to the situation, the feeling, or the relationship. Then, by bonding, you will both improve upon yourselves. (Don't we all need a bit of self-improvement?)

CANCER & LEO: In this case, Cancer, you should ask instead of give. Put your foot down and beg if you have to, but the relationship can only get better if Leo offers more than you do, which is something that Leo usually finds difficult to do. If this doesn't work, you may end up sighing, "It's bigger than both of us," so give up.

CANCER & VIRGO: You need an alarm clock or something with a ringing sound that reminds you that time does fly! Meaning, don't try to rush a Virgo, especially if you are a Cancer. Of course, if you and Virgo are having fun, the bond could be perfection. Keep in mind that even if one of you is driving the other one a little crazy (especially if there is an eclipse or a full moon), the bond is worth the trouble.

CANCER & LIBRA: Try to be objective if you are thinking about giving to a Libra. As you work on combining your signs, you might find yourselves waging a quiet war of wills. Coming to terms with some unacknowledged truth might sound difficult, but doing so would clear the air.

CANCER & SCORPIO: First step—Cancer, don't be upset by anything that Scorpio might say. Second step—remember that Scorpio needs you. Third step—take everything in stride. The fourth step—and all those that come after—is up to you. If you learn this by heart, you will come to understand that if you two just give each other a second thought, the bond is already there.

CANCER & SAGITTARIUS: Let yourself be taught by Sagittarius. Start off, Cancer, by using some health-promoting guidelines. Remember that Sagittarius is a good sign to teach you a thing or two about shaping up, especially physically. Count on a Sag to get you on the right fitness track; then you can bond through your experience.

CANCER & CAPRICORN: Capricorn will count on you, but it might take him or her a very long time to understand how much you give of yourself when you bond. Watch out: you might burden yourself with hidden undertones that are not easy to clear up. Maybe you could do yourself a favor by giving a little less to your exact opposite sign, until Capricorn almost begs for mercy.

CANCER & AQUARIUS: You'd better make sure that you are quite clear when you offer to give Aquarius something— anything but never everything—because Aquarius often takes things for granted. Yes, things could get complicated, but Aquarius usually likes to help others get into a better position, which for you, Cancer, is a bond in itself. What-ever the outcome, consider yourself lucky.

CANCER & PISCES: Ovid, the Roman poet, born on the last day of Pisces, said that "to give is a thing that requires genius." Keep this in mind when dealing with Pisces. You can indulge yourselves by getting involved in worthy causes as your bond gets deeper and deeper, or better and better.

LEO
having fun
"He who laughs, lasts."

—*Mary Pettibone Poole*

Nobody in any civilization at any time had more fun than the gods of ancient mythology. Retelling these legends bonds us to our history with fabulous allegories, colorful stories, fantastic situations, and amusement galore. We cel-ebrate with them by spending at least a couple of minutes every day searching for Eros on a bridge to our own Xanadu. The essence of Leo has been weaving in and out, up and down, around and inside these tales ever since humans first looked up into the sky and saw a lion shining, glowing, or winking down at them. Someone, at some time, devised a way to entertain people of all ages with endless possibilities of how to go about our search. We call it fun. And each one of us is creating our own personal lore as we grab, latch on to, or catch that unpredictable illuminated moment that gives us joy. Thank goodness that having fun comes in spurts because it is addictive. And no one is a better moderator than you, Leo.

Leo, you are at your enthusiastic best when you use your unique ability to connect to a certain inner harmony and show others how they can enjoy, divert, make merry, celebrate, romp, go on a spree, recreate, be as playful as a kitten or as roguish as an alley cat, take control of their world, amuse themselves, and have fun. But the degree to which you can truly let yourself go depends on taking hold of a moment of enthusiasm, packaging it, and—if Leo is around—supplying a good dose of this basic energetic force. Lucky us! If you are a Leo yourself, you know even more about it than I do.

Leo, once in a while try to point out to each of your friends the best way that you think that they can have more fun or perhaps brighten their day. You will be doing them a great favor because this is actually the best way to channel that little bit of bossiness that comes with your sign.

By now people should understand that when they are bored or want to plan something spectacular, they should call upon the nearest Leo. They should be so lucky as to have a Leo nearby. If not, they should lighten up and do it on their own! It's easy, if they use part of the Leo spirit that everyone carries within . . . but that is another story.

LEO

having fun

LEO & ARIES: This bond could be extremely creative and so much fun that it might actually seem to have been made in heaven. However, you must give each other a chance to use your survival skills, because you, Leo, might have several irons in the fire, which is good for you if you remember that Aries will almost never wait as long as you might think he or she should.

LEO & TAURUS: This bond could be like trick or treat on Halloween. What you actually do will depend on how clearly you focus—which, as far as Taurus is concerned, might not be clearly enough. So try to understand what Taurus's definition of "fun" is. Instead of trying to bond, try to work things out, have a duel, try low-key competition, and don't think too much about outcomes.

LEO & GEMINI: Leo must remember that Gemini's moods can change in the snap of a finger, for no apparent reason (at least the reason won't be apparent to you, Leo). For a Gemini, place might be more important than time, so let him or her choose the place and you choose the time. Then you can try to show Gemini that he or she can have fun within any situation. This just may be the easiest way to create a lasting bond.

LEO & CANCER: The energy between you two must be smooth, like a well-oiled race car. Otherwise, forget it. For you, Leo, the fun is taken out of anything if it isn't spontaneous, so if you are going to tune something up in advance, do it by yourself first and then invite Cancer into the passenger seat.

LEO & LEO: You should have a real field day bonding with a fellow Lion. Did you notice, Leo, that the letters in your sign also spell "Olé"? I think that this exhilarating expression is some kind of cosmic message that has to do with the exuberance of your sign. A bond between two Leos can be dynamite as long as one of you doesn't taunt the other.

LEO & VIRGO: The smallest feeling of distrust could cause Virgo to anguish over whether or not he or she is actually making the right choice by bonding with you. Luckily, you, Leo, can provide reassurance and give Virgo, the sign right next to yours, a pat on the back. Virgo will not only be grateful but will loosen up and really start to have fun.

LEO & LIBRA: When Libras are having a good time, they show the best side of themselves. When you show others how to have a good time, you, Leo, bring out the best in yourself. If you combine one with the other, this combination may reveal a new side of an old feeling. When you two are together, there is always room for more.

LEO & SCORPIO: Leo is an expanding sign, which helps others grow personally—emotionally, mentally, and spiritually. Scorpio, on the other hand, gets rid of anything extraneous. Imagine the down-to-earth fun you can have together, once you bond with the right energy-balancing factor. But take care not to let this energy get out of hand.

LEO & SAGITTARIUS: Oddly enough, each of you will feel that you can outshine the other—and you probably can. But instead of competing, you should pool your strengths to come up with the two different sides to each of your bonding stories. You will probably find that in your case, two is really better than one. Your bond could actually be very enlightening.

LEO & CAPRICORN: Try to fit in some kind of athletic bond or sport as you relate with Capricorn. Without looking, you probably will find some kind of healing process as you bond through physical exertion. The fun part is actually not that important, although it will probably pop up time and again. Maybe the first step could be asking a question.

LEO & AQUARIUS: Opposites can make a big splash in each other's sign, and Leos do best when the splash is a big one. If you feel off-balance, don't worry. Use your fast-beating heart to test out the plot and give in to the ploy. Your popularity might be an important factor in making things go smoothly.

LEO & PISCES: You could almost get addicted to each other's way of having fun, because you can bond with Pisces in a deliciously exaggerated way. Why not share some fine wine or expensive chocolate, if you, Leo, can't think of any-thing else? You probably can, though. Pisces can help you grow if he or she accepts the fact that you have something that Pisces wants. Once you clear this up, go public!

VIRGO

to answer

"Truth is generally kindness, but where the two diverge and collide, kindness should override truth."

—*Samuel Butler*

Virgo, you thrive when answering questions, asking for answers, or finding out exactly what any other signs would enjoy if they would explain what they actually prefer. And if others give you the right answer even once, Virgo, they will have bonded with you forever.

It sounds simple. It is not.

Because what you, Virgo, consider the right answer is far beyond anyone else's comprehension. You are exquis-itely programmed for perfection and like beauty, perfection is in the eye of the beholder. When the beholder is you, Virgo, others should be careful. For any other sign, an answer can be excellent or it can be an irreversible error, while you, Virgo, browse through existing conditions and take a dreaded chance, a purposeful hint, or a responsible point of view. You may remark, argue, or object. You also have the liberty to imply, counter, or plea. You may enjoy giving solutions, explaining perplexing cryptograms, or examining files, and you could wittily retort or remonstrate.

Virgo, deep down, you know the right answer, which for you is always a method of bonding. You also have the intuitive knowledge that may not be better than anyone else's, but it connects you to the intellectual side of discussions. You probably don't remember, but your sign was once called the representative of the Seven Virtues (faith, hope, charity or love, prudence, justice, fortitude, and temperance) in ancient astrological texts. You can dissect information as a Windows 3098 might one day, and wait for the right answer, no matter how long it may take. When you ask someone else something, you are bonding with him or her. If someone else asks you something, be sure to prepare that person to hear your two cents, for you are usually very opinionated. Virgos can go *Around the Day in Eighty Worlds*, as Julio Cortazar, an Argentinean writer and a Virgo, explained in his wonderful collection of short stories.

Words, bonding, and answering are part of a big crossword puzzle for you, Virgo. You can see right to the point, and yet sometimes you don't dare to give others the answer for fear they might be hurt by your insight. To answer is complementary to Virgo's nature because it opens more doors for Virgo than for any other sign, which is something that the other signs should remember. You, Virgo, should not let go of the distinctiveness that your answers can

bestow on all those who happen to cross your path. They
are the lucky ones, and you must carry the burden of knowing that your answers count.

VIRGO
to answer

VIRGO & ARIES: Virgo might seem a bit baroque to Aries.
You should pretend that you are writing down your answer
to an essay question, and then look back, reread, and take
care that your words carry no grudge. Try to simplify any of
your suggestions so that Aries can act quickly instead of
having to think about what you would wish to hear.

VIRGO & TAURUS: The two of you could actually use
each other to the hilt and come out all the better for it. To
find out how, try entertaining together—it should go
smoothly. Even if Taurus actually gives answers incor-
rectly or thinks that the answer is wrong, there is an
underlying current between you that should make you feel
like family.

VIRGO & GEMINI: Virgo, you'd better get your priorities in
order if you contest a Gemini's call; Gemini can really make
you stumble if you are not careful. You will have to work a
bit harder to bond than you thought in the first place. You
might feel that it is not worth a try, but go ahead anyway
and see what happens.

VIRGO & CANCER: The more you invest in this bond, the better the answer. Investing usually has to do with material things, so you should keep this in mind, even if no money is involved. If you can meet a deadline, one of you will probably get more out of the transaction than you were counting on. You nurture each other in the right way.

VIRGO & LEO: Leos don't like having their schedules changed, but when you are involved, they just might realize that the change is doing them some good and that it might bring them some relief. You also might be able to emphasize the fact that complaining will do neither of you any good. A bond between you could mean some good times together.

VIRGO & VIRGO: Try as much experimentation as you dare, which is probably not much. You two could bring out the best in each other. One possible goal could be optimal function, which is a daring way to say "perfection." Just take care not to overreact if one of you procrastinates, as Virgos have a tendency to do. If you do get stuck, ask a third party to help you out.

VIRGO & LIBRA: The outcome of this bond could be success if you let Libra do the talking. Dissect all the possibilities that come with success, and once you have done this together, allow Libra to take the first step. Be sure to make yourself available to each other so that you can share the burden of any difficulties—the sweet smell of success will be so much greater for both of you.

VIRGO & SCORPIO: Working together could help you survive any question, any answer, and any bond. If you let Scorpio make the opening statement, he or she can convince anyone that you, Virgo, have the strength of a rising star! Keep your eyes open so that you can envision any kind of possible perspective.

VIRGO & SAGITTARIUS: Let Sagittarius sound off, and make your terms as simple as possible. Remember to start with the promise of what could come next. Language and its form are extremely important to Sagittarius, and if you can fascinate him or her, you can wake Sagittarius up to the vast possibilities of your bond. For once, don't give Sag an answer.

VIRGO & CAPRICORN: Trying to build castles in the air might do wonders for both of you, but you probably will be called down to earth by a third party before you get the chance to finish. A real brouhaha could ensue because this third party will want to latch on to a good thing: your answers. Take my word for it: answer only to each other and you might find yourselves proving that Virgo and Capricorn are a good combination.

VIRGO & AQUARIUS: Give yourself a break if you need it and let yourself change sides, because there are two to every story. You might be caught in some kind of uproar, but Aquarius does well in unstable situations, so don't get angry or worried; just stay cool. Subdue your feelings and let Aquarius take the initiative.

VIRGO & PISCES: Decide which one of you is responsible and then take things in stride. Pisces is your opposite, and so one of you actually could end up being the other's role model. Don't rush things. You and Pisces can always find a way to fix, to answer, or to imply much more than you think. If things aren't working out, try something that Pisces thinks is new.

LIBRA
compromise

". . . the one thing that everybody wants to be is free, to talk to eat to drink to walk to think, to please, to wish, and to do it now."

—*Gertrude Stein*

A brief smile is a compromise; so is a glance, because by giving or receiving either, you are making a promise or agreeing to something. Catching a glimpse of your own reflection as you walk about is a testimony about yourself. As a Libra, you are the best at compromising the infinite ways of working out how to get a comfortable feeling from that reflection or that smile. Even if it shocks you, you will find a way to manage, because this is what you are good at.

When you are threatened, criticized, or shaken, you survive through your innate ability to compromise. Compromise is a component of Libra, just as a nose is a component of a face!

Libra, you know how to get the best out of yourself—be it in business, pleasure, relationships, or physical output—because you adjust to the course before you. I could be fancy and call this ability rapprochement, or I could be accommodating and call it conciliatory. But one way to understand what you are capable of, Libra, is to read what Saint Augustine said: "Thou hast touched me, and I have been translated into thy peace." Libra, you can do just that, and others have to admit to themselves that if they find out how to tune in to that part of themselves, it will work for them, too. No "help" button is needed. Help is there, within them.

When others are fuming, feuding, looking for a friend, or giving something a last chance, you, Libra, can show them how to adjust. They will discover that the thing that was inhibiting them was actually their own unwillingness to compromise. When others finally get to the stage of making concessions—when they finally find the middle ground, they should thank the stars that helped them illuminate the Libra part of themselves.

Libra, you are putting everything into place when bonding, even if the bond is spontaneous. You can easily show others how to come to terms, because you know how to make matters better and how to make things work—or at least understandable. Now, I know there is no panacea for everything and we are all aware that there is no big book of answers to all questions. But we should also know that "us" is Libra's perfect word, and each and every human being, whatever your sign, needs to find some sort of equilibrium when the "us" word comes into play. The world is filled with an unlimited number of possibilities to make compromising bonds, sometimes in the strangest ways. Give yourself the chance: try a smile, a glance, or the challenge of filling your sail with a gust of fresh air, to make things a little better. A compromise just might be the right thing.

LIBRA

compromise

LIBRA & ARIES: A bond between you could be fire and ice because you are, after all, opposites. But it can be a wonder of wonders if it works, and to make it work all you really have to do is try—both of you. Once you start rolling, the bond may not last forever, but you could romp and make merry until Libra gets tired or Aries gets bored. Or not.

LIBRA & TAURUS: Try not to get on the wrong side of Taurus by pushing. Both of you might convince the same person of two different things, and because you are the two greatest charmers in the zodiac, it all just might work out regardless. Taurus could be a bit too funky for you, and you,

Libra, can be a bit of a riddle to Taurus! Try to be nicer than you normally would.

LIBRA & GEMINI: Each of you should try to guess what the other dreams about. You will find some interesting interpretations there. After the first guess, look up at the night sky and find out about yourself by figuring out how the sky feels resting on your shoulders. If it is comfortable, Lady Luck is probably around the corner. If she isn't, start over tomorrow night.

LIBRA & CANCER: Don't worry too much about truth or its consequences. In this case it is okay for one of you to fib. Self-confidence can help you recover your poise, even if you find that little white lies are bigger than you think. Everyone deserves a second chance, so work on that idea and reach a compromise to put it into action.

LIBRA & LEO: Don't try to surprise Leo. You could unintentionally break some rules in your attempt to bond with Leo, but you will have to take a chance to begin something, so try to look your best. If you are the one who gets floored, show Leo that you have been taken completely by surprise.

LIBRA & VIRGO: If you keep things between your two signs rather low-key, good things can happen in a compromising bond. Remember that Libras often are a riddle to themselves and Virgos are rather good at figuring riddles out. Don't hesitate to find the simplest and easiest way to get what you are vying for.

LIBRA & LIBRA: I would love to be in the middle of whatever it is you are working at, and any other sign, even a third Libra, could get a thrill out of this as well. On the other hand, if you give in to being too opinionated, we all could find ourselves in a never-ending argument that wastes everybody's time. Watch it!

LIBRA & SCORPIO: Is there an undertone of sexual innuendo between you, which actually might do both of you some good? I'm not saying you have to do anything risky, but I am saying that you shouldn't miss out on the possibility of using your feminine or masculine wiles, almost to the hilt, because the resulting bond could be such a good one.

LIBRA & SAGITTARIUS: The process you use doesn't even matter. You can actually achieve more than you counted on if you make yourself available to Sagittarius and keep your promise. Some of your favorite things are also the favorites of Sagittarius, which means you have more in common to bond over than you think. Never give up, but do give in when it doesn't hurt too much to do so!

LIBRA & CAPRICORN: Holding back is inadvisable, Libra, especially when you are dealing with a Capricorn. You should learn to say "for your sake" to Capricorn. If that doesn't seem to work, try a little pushing from a peer—someone whom you respect, if possible. If you don't give in to something with a Capricorn, you probably won't get very far.

LIBRA & AQUARIUS: Perhaps the word "Wow" can bond. Try it out. If it doesn't work, go for something else that has three or four letters at the most, and that needs an exclamation point to get the message across. Exaggeration will get Aquarius's attention even if the bond only has to do with memories. Your experience is not what counts; the firmness of your conviction is!

LIBRA & PISCES: Don't waste time by doing things on your own. Do things together, and if possible, do things that have to do with other people's joy. There's no room here for egotism; it can only make you overanxious. Would it sound better if I just said that group therapy could work wonders?

SCORPIO
searching
"What a wonderful life I've had! I only wish I'd realized it sooner."

—Colette

The word "searching" is so much better than "looking for." Searching brings things into view while it endeavors to find something. When you search, you travel through things, people, situations, and experiences, and that is the way that you, Scorpio, bond. Not to be taken lightly, the act of searching is part of your inner need to relate to yourself and to other people and things. It also encompasses knowledge about yourself. Such a thorough effort!

Scorpio, you can agglutinate experiences and put them all into two big piles: the good ones and the bad ones. Then you can take your pick for later use, especially for intense situations. In fact, others usually don't realize how intense you are, Scorpio, especially when you are searching for that which bonds you to any situation. Your intensity, Scorpio, comes from bonding one way or another with almost every action, deed, and feeling. You make your emotional living by discovering what makes things tick! It is usually well worth other's time to travel with you on any journey, from eating an ice-cream cone or drinking coffee together to sharing a lifelong bond, because they usually will find out something new about themselves, thanks to Scorpio's inherent, tireless search engine.

Your only trouble is that you are usually not very user-friendly. You like to take time after the search to thoroughly examine an individual or a situation. You can't be bothered to explain things that other people don't see because, for you, Scorpio, the whole searching process happens in the blink of an eye. Just as Big Blue can decide which chess piece to move because it has the ability to choose from more than 100,000 moves in one second, so do you, Scorpio, have the instinct to choose your strategy in split seconds. Done.

The search is on, and the rest of us must get on with our lives and, perhaps by searching with you, learn how to make the most of our own search mechanisms. You sometimes see right through what others take ages to understand, but don't write off all those people because they have so much to learn from searching with you.

SCORPIO
searching

SCORPIO & ARIES: If you can fit some passion into the search, you've got it made with Aries. Aries has the match to kindle Scorpio's inner fire. The only thing you have to worry about when doing things together is the possibility of getting scorched. Since second impressions don't even count with Aries, you should make sure the fire is kindled the first time around.

SCORPIO & TAURUS: Taurus will probably have to shape up a bit, but you are not the best person to tell him or her as much. Your forceful inner vibes can go so far as to turn you on, and that is good, considering you two are astrological opposites. Sex doesn't always have anything to do with it, although it very well could. It would be in your best interests to bond with one of the arts in mind and allow yourselves to make mistakes—even silly ones, like choosing the wrong color.

SCORPIO & GEMINI: Scorpio, you have a lot to teach Gemini about going past the surface and not keeping the bond at a superficial level. Find a way to show Gemini that digging deep can be worthwhile. But don't write him or her off, because Gemini can really liven up your life. Once you combine forces, you can achieve memorable things.

SCORPIO & CANCER: A real quest is the best thing for both of you, but beware of sudden changes in the atmosphere. Either Scorpio or Cancer can be bothered by little things that the other considers unimportant. Both of you could benefit from rummaging in your own conscience to make space for little upsets that usually are worth considering.

SCORPIO & LEO: By letting Leo get away with what you would never let anybody else get away with, you will be doing yourself a favor. Perhaps your plans will not work out as you thought, but it doesn't matter. If you do learn something new, it will have been well worth it. You are both much more creative than you think.

SCORPIO & VIRGO: Just be certain that you won't be caught in a lie, a fib, a falsification, or even an exaggeration, because it could be misinterpreted. Virgo will never forgive you, which means that the search will be over before you even begin. On the other hand, you might find that the insight that one of you reveals to the other could be earth-shattering, great, or perfection!

SCORPIO & LIBRA: When you have a Libra around, you should act as if you always needed him or her as your personal defense attorney. Recheck and reconsider what you were looking for in the first place. Give each other all the chances you can and ask each other a simple "why?" before making any final decisions. The decisions should work out. The bond is a maybe.

SCORPIO & SCORPIO: Practice sneaking around each other like two investigative reporters on a scoop. You have the world's greatest stage at your feet—life itself. If this seems too big, there is no use trying to stop the world, because you can't get off. Any answer is better than none.

SCORPIO & SAGITTARIUS: If you hear each other say something like "What the heck?" it might mean that the other one doesn't quite get it or that he or she is actually interested. But if you open up a bit, you, as a Scorpio, could get more from Sagittarius than from practically any other sign, and the bond would be conclusive.

SCORPIO & CAPRICORN: Experiment, try out, compare, investigate, and take a real risk, because the final result should work out for both of you. Even if you find yourselves pitted against each other, give the bond a try. What you can work out together is almost like a mathematical equation, and lucky for you, Capricorn is good with numbers.

SCORPIO & AQUARIUS: If you can't join Aquarius in the search, certainly don't trust him or her. Even though things would be unbelievably boring without some palpable difficulties, exchange views and wait for the skies to clear, as they usually do. The more metaphorical you get with each other, the better.

SCORPIO & PISCES: Take the "soft answer" approach. To bond with Pisces, you will have to wait a while, test, and maybe even be asked to prove something that you consider rather strange. This bond is a bit like what Shakespeare says: "compare dead happiness with living woe," meaning nothing is perfect.

SAGITTARIUS
relating
"What is now proved was once only imagined."
—*William Blake*

We should think about the sign of Sagittarius as relationship to inspiration—a way of relating to what we aspire—from outside in if you are not a Sagittarian and from inside out if you are one. Sagittarius, the ninth sign of the zodiac, is almost certainly a distant cousin of the nine Greek muses—

poetry, history, love poetry, music, tragedy, hymns, choral song and dance, comedy, and astronomy, which at that time included astrology. These muses presided over learning and the creative arts, which are Sagittarius's bond to any illuminated choice.

When you bond, Sagittarius, you do so with this heavy-duty relationship to the muses in your psyche or subconscious. The need to relate to your creative spirit is always paramount for you, Sagittarius, even in the most banal situations. Could it be that when you bond, you are in effect re-creating some historical event on a smaller scale, creating a link between the past and the present? It is by trying to understand this that you do yourself as big a favor as you do for those with whom you are relating because you open doors to everyone's creative spirit. When somebody says, "Nobody does it better," it means that the muses are bonding with you, Sagittarius.

Relating to the logical connections that should exist between cause and effect is another thing you are great at doing. You have been chosen to find the direct link between one's "self" and the person you choose to be your significant other (and why). Some people would say, "It's called wisdom, stupid," but I find it much easier to relate all the above to your inspiration from the past—the mythological past inhabited by the muses.

You are part of a wonderful whole that is probably foretelling what so many of us should be. When one is inspired by Sagittarian traits, it is like dipping into a melting pot of nontraditional sources in which one finds his or her own uniqueness. Most signs connect. Sagittarius relates. Relating means that you are right in the middle of something that could be important, is usually remediable, and should one day help you improve.

SAGITTARIUS
relating

SAGITTARIUS & ARIES: Try not to compare people or objects because the bottom line is that your bond with Aries should be restorative and rejuvenating. Take turns at giving each other a break. Take everything into account, and for heaven's sake don't throw anything away, not even a bad idea.

SAGITTARIUS & TAURUS: Physical looks have much more to do with the outcome than either of you would like to admit. There is an underlying transference of unclassifiable yet invigorating feelings between you. You, Sag, might be able to fix something that could actually improve Taurus, although Taurus will hate to admit that anything about him or her needs improving in the first place. If things get bogged down, take a walk in the park.

SAGITTARIUS & GEMINI: Incredible excitement could be the result of this bond—after all, you are opposites. But you could have so many good laughs together that it would really be a pity if you don't have some quirky plans for a future rendezvous decided within the first half hour of your relating!

SAGITTARIUS & CANCER: *Relax.* You could make each other a bit nervous, so let Cancer settle down and feel good in his or her place, so that you will have the time to show how invigorating you can be. You should be able to find a consanguineous relevance while trying to work out something together. Remember those six degrees of separation . . . and try narrow it down to three.

SAGITTARIUS & LEO: I promised not to use words that can be translated only by astrologers, but both of you have such vibrant rulers that I can't resist! In this case, your rulers are the sun (for Leo) and Jupiter (for Sag), both of which shine and illuminate whatever you choose to relate to—unless you are downright neglectful, which would be a crying shame. Be ready to take advantage of anything that comes your way.

SAGITTARIUS & VIRGO: Don't go overboard with your enthusiasm because Virgo just might discard your exaggerated expectations and deem them incoherent. Instead, approach Virgo with calm, measure the temperature, gauge the wind speed, and proceed with caution as if this were a litigation instead of a desired relationship.

SAGITTARIUS & LIBRA: F. M. Amiel, a rather forgotten, wonderful writer from the past century, said that "In every union there is a mystery—a certain invisible bond which must not be disturbed." He was not an astrologer, but he perfectly described the bond that these two signs could forge. So if you don't find a common denominator, don't worry. Relax and enjoy the mystery.

SAGITTARIUS & SCORPIO: Put on your most diplomatic smile, and be as laid back as you can. Sagittarius can do this easily. Scorpio actually can never do it because it is not in Scorpio's karma. But you, Sagittarius, can help people get past any difficulty with ease, which makes room for the relating part to settle in. Try talking about things over a bottle of wine.

SAGITTARIUS & SAGITTARIUS: This combination might add up to eighteen muses instead of the nine basic ones, which means the two of you have an increased opportunity to invent, create, and use all of your versatility to bond. Alas, the bond might not last as long as you would like it to. Your one disadvantage, Sagittarius, can at times be a lack of continuity. Never mind; the memory of relating can be just as powerful as you would like the bond itself to be.

SAGITTARIUS & CAPRICORN: Speak up and speak out. Do not let Capricorn get the upper hand, for he or she can rule you right out of the picture. Actually, this might not be so bad, because you will most likely find out that what you thought you were or think you are relating to is not that hot! But if you don't connect, there will always be other possibilities for you, Sagittarius.

SAGITTARIUS & AQUARIUS: The symbols of both your astrological signs include an artifice—Sagittarius has a bow and arrow, and Aquarius has a water jug. You should take this to mean that getting together will work best if you rely on the pertinent tools. In order to start bonding with Aquarius, make sure you have a we-can-do-better self-improvement attitude. Don't take anything for granted. This combination could be great for both of you!

SAGITTARIUS & PISCES: You need to learn how to appreciate each other. This is something you can work on over a lengthy period of time. The more time you give yourselves, the easier it will be to settle into an easy rhythm of relating, which will then help you bond with Pisces. Once you take the first step, the relationship could have boundless meanings.

CAPRICORN
adding
"As a general rule, nobody has money who ought to have it."
—*Benjamin Disraeli*

Capricorn, if a certain bond adds to your stamina, your life, or your possessions, then it is a must for you. This bond is

especially good if it is a planned effort to increase the possibilities of a voice: your own. Besides enlarging things, the
process of adding needs to form substance and gives you,
Capricorn, the possibility to control whatever it is that you
are summing up. Then you bond. It might seem like a
roundabout explanation, but time is, was, and always will be
your ally, Capricorn.

The sign of Capricorn was once represented by an
anchor that was connected to life. Although you might
spend time trying to convince others that your feelings do
not interfere with your thoughts, you do best when summing up your feelings. You Capricorns are so good at keeping things to yourselves that others need to really reach
your inner structure to be able to connect with you. And
since the spirit of Capricorn can last forever—many of our
most-respected elders were Capricorns—once you add
something to others' lives or others add to yours, those
people will be able to increase something within themselves, if you allow them. You, Capricorn, insert and almost
never delete, for if you do, the deletion is forever. Others
should never forget that for Capricorns, "forever" is written
in the stars, unconquerable and immeasurable, unless someone creates a computer that only adds and adds and adds,
reaching at least past the year 5000.

Adding should reinforce and never detract from your
ability to bond. It's as easy as that for you, Capricorn. For
anyone else, to add in order to bond foments feelings. Not
so for this wintry sign that can keep whomever he or she so

chooses warm in the cold weather. Be fair and remind those close to you that if they don't add up in one way or another, you can freeze them out better than any other sign. So for you to add anything new to your life, you must get back to basics in order to show others, or add to yourself, what really counts. Before you go on to the next step, you constantly reevaluate the cost-effectiveness of a feeling, a person, or even a doubt. If it doesn't add up, out it goes. If it does add up, after all these calculations, you might, perhaps, make it a permanent addition to your life story. Then you can begin to bond.

CAPRICORN
adding

CAPRICORN & ARIES: Don't make any assumptions or take anything for granted. First you need to argue for or against whatever. Then and only then you can propose an addition. Don't worry about minor issues. Aries usually does you some good, so give him or her some slack by letting Aries skip some steps. Remember, you are a good teacher, so make yourself available.

CAPRICORN & TAURUS: There is a theory called Gödel's theorem that associates any number with any formula of a logical system. It is used in mathematics as a way of proving that you do not need to prove things, and this is what both of you need to add to a relationship if you want to bond.

The next step could be sheer happiness. In fact, Taurus can show you, Capricorn, that perfection can be an emotional thing.

CAPRICORN & GEMINI: Capricorn, you can show Gemini how to reach higher, and if Gemini is straightforward enough, you just might make it through the night. The evening hours are a better time for you two to try to bond. If worse comes to worst, try out some evening music—it's better than elevator music!

CAPRICORN & CANCER: This combination should always keep an account of the percentage of effort that each of you puts in and takes out. Because you are opposites, the bond will get the best results only after you have figured out what the percentage actually is—and I mean on paper. And puh-leese, Cancer, don't get overemotional about anything. More is less here.

CAPRICORN & LEO: In this astrological combination, as in a computer, there is hardware and software. Even if you happen to be computer-illiterate, you can understand that these are two separate things. This metaphor is relevant because you need to make up your minds who takes the "hard" position and who takes the "soft" one. Capricorn, if you happen to read this first, take your pick; the advantage is yours.

CAPRICORN & VIRGO: Your two opinions about what happiness actually is might be extremely different, but even though you are not opposite signs, you can fuel each other's desires to such an extent that the number of occasions of pleasure will always add up to more and more and more! Just remember that to count from one to one million actually takes three weeks, but you can always get there if you persevere.

CAPRICORN & LIBRA: Things could get a bit complex between you two, because you, Capricorn, find it hard to loosen up, and you can be a bit of a stoic. Maybe I can help you out. Did you know that the word "stoic" actually comes from the painted portico in ancient Athens where doctrines were taught? Why don't you try being a mentor for Libra? Your bond will be stronger if Libra can lean on you.

CAPRICORN & SCORPIO: Whatever you state, Capricorn, will be judged by Scorpio. So leave out all the possible "howevers" and be clear about what you mean. Then you and Scorpio can add your forces and practically conquer the world, even if nobody else notices. Actually, you could even rush into something here and never be taken for a fool for doing so!

CAPRICORN & SAGITTARIUS: Wait for your turn because a Sagittarius does not like to be pushed. You may need to fill in some gaps with a bit of sensationalism by being loud and perhaps lewd. There should be an easy point of entry; you just have to fish around a bit to find it. This may sound fishy to you, and fishy is not your thing, but in this situation, do give it a try.

CAPRICORN & CAPRICORN: One of you will have to outwit the other. One of you might even exhaust the other. But so what? Just countermand the order. Don't let yourself feel isolated, and don't isolate yourself. Anything that has to do with material things might make you worry. One worried Capricorn plus another worried Capricorn can only can only add up to something advantageous.

CAPRICORN & AQUARIUS: Don't estimate anything; instead, count it. The "it" can be esoteric, metaphysical, obscure, occult, transcendental, cabalistic, or symbolic. Even if you are feeling evil vibes, count them. Whatever "it" is will turn out to be much more unconventional than you are used to, but that could actually be great.

CAPRICORN & PISCES: Each of you is an asset to the other, but at the same time you could hinder your process of adding up, just because you might lose your keen sense of direction as you go along. So try piling up practical details that can help you continue. Lots of little bonds can be just as satisfying as one big one.

AQUARIUS

anticipation

"A fact in science is not a mere fact, but an instance."

—*Bertrand Russell*

You, Aquarius, should be well aware of and extremely well acquainted with expectation and intuition. At worst, you thrive on it; at best, most synonyms of these words are at your disposal. The first computer with human feelings will definitely be an Aquarius! (Don't balk! I look forward to it.) Then you will be able to explain perfectly how anticipation relates to you and everybody else, and I will not have to strain to pull the words out of this great big illuminated cosmological grab bag, which helps us construct the association of ideas in a personal and helpful pattern.

Aquarius, you can sense things before they actually happen. You might even find yourself saying, "Time doesn't matter"—possibly because you are always one step ahead of it. For you, time is irrelevant; it usually depends on wishes! You carry the weight of other people's—and possibly the world's—problems on your shoulders and you mold yourself accordingly, at times to people's dismay. Do you find yourself recalling a part of your former self that you put on hold because you knew it might be needed later? Does this sound far-fetched? You *are* far-fetched. Others should listen to some of what you have to say about what is to come, because they can use this foreknowledge to their advantage.

All the other eleven signs carry some part of Aquarius within them, in the same way that we use only one-eighth of our brains while the rest is still being studied by neuro-scientists. We should all welcome your presence, Aquarius, in anticipation of bonding with you.

I hope that, while others wait for the right time and place to bond with what might make them a bit more venerable, you will summon them to your side and help them along. You are neither better nor easier nor abler than others, Aquarius, but you have the faith that others need in order to experience that certain, precise moment that informs a kind of inner sensibility, overriding all others. You know how to identify the perfect "now." You are one tiny step ahead in anticipation. Aquarius more often than not holds the key to what is coming. Perhaps mythology was born under your sign, but nobody dares to acknowledge it. You make hype possible. Others should jump on your bandwagon and go for it, because doing so can enhance their bonds in every way!

AQUARIUS
anticipation

AQUARIUS & ARIES: If you try, you can knock anybody, including Aries, off his or her feet with your fabulous flair. So what are you waiting for? Pool your energies and don't worry if things don't seem that clear at first. You will probably get more answers than you ever anticipated. Don't let Aries ground you, because that would spoil the fun.

AQUARIUS & TAURUS: This is not an illuminated choice; this is an illuminated meteorite. The issue will probably not be your choice but the bull's. Don't take too much to heart, and remember that Taurus usually gives the very best of all hugs, so give it a whirl if you can and if it seems right. Otherwise, anticipate small treasures and some losses.

AQUARIUS & GEMINI: Future studies by the next generation of sages might prove that you and Gemini are actually made for each other, even if you don't speak the same language, read the same books, or like the same things. Just don't do anything that Gemini could consider to be premature, because it could turn into an enormous anticlimax.

AQUARIUS & CANCER: If you both give yourselves the time to work on your health, you could find the perfect diet, the proper exercise, or anything that has to do with a healthy outlook on life. This is actually the most important thing for this combination to do, because by anticipating how to maintain your physical and mental fitness, you could lengthen your bond on life. As an aside, dress for the occasion.

AQUARIUS & LEO: Opposite signs can boil over from scalding cauldrons, but those very pots can hold alchemy, so with this combination, princesses may turn into heaps of straw, frogs may become princes, and pigs may learn to sing. It all depends on what you are waiting for and whom you might have left behind. Show Leo that your imagination can always impress.

AQUARIUS & VIRGO: The best way for the two of you to bond is to join together in some meddling. Find out some hidden information about someone, disclose a secret, or initiate some juicy gossip. Then you can use your mutual interest to get one step ahead, which is something you are both very good at. (Have you ever tried being ostentatious?)

AQUARIUS & LIBRA: Perhaps you'll dislike each other, but it would be completely wrong to write yourselves out of each other's light, life, or business. You and Libra were made to work together—in some form. Give the potential of your bond with Libra as many chances as you can and use the words of all the other signs in this chapter to bond if you need to—work, belief, duality, giving, having fun, answering, compromise, search, relate, add—and maybe you will be lucky enough to end up creating.

AQUARIUS & SCORPIO: Take it easy whenever you try to bond with a Scorpio. There may be some kind of rotten apple around trying to choose discord instead of an encore. Use a different figure of speech in case you are not understood, which well may be the case. And before you even think of beginning, be sure you are not doing so under a false pretense. Or could Scorpio be guilty of doing so?

AQUARIUS & SAGITTARIUS: Prepare more than a day ahead of time so you won't be caught off guard. You and Sagittarius could show others how to anticipate the future by using ancient practices in modern ways—like calculating an astrological chart with a computer program. I would call in both of your signs to fix the possible crash of all computers in anticipation of the year 2000.

AQUARIUS & CAPRICORN: There are gamma rays and gamma ray bursters; the latter emit energy for a couple of hours and then disappear. This happens 25,000 light-years away but can be measured on earth. All of this has to do with inconceivable energy: You, Aquarius, can be the inconceivable part and Capricorn can be the energy. Take it from there.

AQUARIUS & AQUARIUS: One of you could be the actual or virtual aphrodisiac of the other. It's up to you to decide in which way and how. Once that is done, the bond is within. If this sounds kinky or quirky, it should. If it doesn't, you're out of sync, so try again some other time.

AQUARIUS & PISCES: Break down the barriers between you. Even though only one of you is a water sign (not you, Aquarius), both Aquarius and Pisces have water in your astrological symbols. This means that you can find the right shape to help you become whatever form is needed for the time being. The time being could last much longer than you think—or much less time. But at least you will have become something that you didn't even know existed! You may bond with feeling and create new forms.

PISCES

to create

"The creation was an act of mercy."

—*William Blake*

Pisces might just be the most enigmatic and sophisticated sign. Pisces, you are also very good at dissimulating these wondrous characteristics—sometimes because you want to, but you often do it without knowing. So many things have been related to this last sign of the zodiac that Pisces sometimes seems to be an allegory of itself! Stories have it that Pisces is the signifier of all primal chaos and then the first ever sound, which probably came from the Big Bang. Pisces is great at making something out of nothing, which is how you, Pisces, come close to creating. You have so much to give. Pisces, you are a great example of how things can be seen from different angles and how images can be turned into visual messages that mean different things to different people. For instance, we create a bond with ourselves when we look at our own image in a mirror. Images are processed by the optic chiasma (the part of the brain where the optic nerves meet), so we can see not only what is there, but also what we want to see, or what others would like us to see. Thank goodness that subliminal messages are created under the sign of Pisces; otherwise we all would have become Big Brother to ourselves.

Everybody is creative and capable of creating. We create by performing an act of grace. We create by changing our moods. We create just by thinking. Creating can be an artistic endeavor or it can have something to do with "investing with a new form, office or rank." When you approach an unknown relationship, you are creating something new. Actually, even when you are reading a book, you are creating your own personal document. Pisces can tune others in to the space around the creative process and give all of us the necessary breathing space to bond in. Perhaps not everything has a cause, but everything does have an effect, and you, Pisces, are great at taking things up from there and showing all others how to create what that effect may turn into. I don't mean to imply that only Pisces can manipulate the act of creation; I am just pointing out that Pisces is extremely adept at doing so. Let us all create our very own conclusions and produce, construct, generate, deliver, unfold, blossom, evolve, grow or outgrow, compose, structure, or generate our bonds and create something better while asking Pisces to stick around and help us see through, or just see things under a different light or perspective. All of us, when we believe in ourselves, are creating something better, and that is what this book is supposed to be all about!

PISCES

to create

PISCES & ARIES: Pisces, you can help Aries be a little more flexible and let go more easily. Pisces (the last sign of the zodiac) and Aries (the first) together could set an example of how things should be if you give each other a chance to create freely. There is usually much more between you than meets the eye. Somebody once said that these two signs provide a perfect psychoanalyst-psychoanalyzed combination. It's up to you to figure out who is who.

PISCES & TAURUS: Pisces, you can show Taurus how to improvise, and it will do Taurus good to listen to you. Remember, Pisces, that Taurus is master of the five senses, so take some time and create the right atmosphere. Once Taurus learns to enjoy listening, the sound of your voice will become a pleasure. The next step is pure heaven.

PISCES & GEMINI: You two could create an everlasting argument that would go on and on for a whole lifetime. It makes no difference if you don't agree, however, because the more you have to say to each other, the more you will learn. Investigate, find out, and use your knowledge to separate myth from reality; otherwise Gemini will corner you!

PISCES & CANCER: Whatever you plan to do together could be close and comfortable and should have an easy familiarity about it, but you must not dawdle. If you do, both of you could just sit in your own little corner and let time pass by. I'm sorry to say that with this combination, thinking is not doing.

PISCES & LEO: If you can get a Leo to believe that dreaming is creating, you have done the impossible. Getting Leo to believe in something that he or she has not created is harder than you think. Turn things around by creating an opportunity for Leo to push somebody else around. Otherwise, do yourself a favor and forget it.

PISCES & VIRGO: Don't let Virgo get away with being a conformist. In fact, as far as creating is concerned, do not let Virgo get away with anything, just because he or she is your astrological opposite. You could take Virgo to an art gallery or a fine restaurant and then propose something wacky. It would do Virgo good to meet you halfway!

PISCES & LIBRA: Play a bit with Libra's mind, even if you start off with a game like Scrabble. If you get Libra's attention, you'll have it made. If you bore Libra, you'd better shape up or ship out! Let your mind wander, imagine, daydream, and speak to the stars without asking for answers.

PISCES & SCORPIO: Measure for measure, tactics, a real timetable, and nothing fancy, just something simple yet tangible can get you two going. You could end up showing the world that anything can be creative—even setting a table. If you let Scorpio exercise a little more power, you might be doing yourselves a favor.

PISCES & SAGITTARIUS: Use *The Old Farmer's Almanac* or ask your grandmother for some folk wisdom to help solve life's little everyday problems in a low-tech, old-fashioned way. Try not to see those unexpected things that happen, like getting your finger caught in a door or stubbing your toe, as bad omens. To be able to bond, you might have to take more knocks than usual, Pisces, but remembering to listen to and learn from Sagittarius could be a good start.

PISCES & CAPRICORN: You can confide in each other and help each other create whatever the other signs expect of you. Letting yourself go and leaning on others is the best thing you can do for yourself, Pisces. I dare you to do so. Capricorn usually needs a bit of molding to be able to let go of inner frustrations. You, Pisces, are perfect for the part of molder. Go for it!

PISCES & AQUARIUS: When you try to create a bond together, the order of the process you undertake to do so has nothing to do with the final outcome. This is actually the best of all possible combinations for inventing new things because both of you can see clearly into the future (especially if it isn't your own). Don't forget to keep track of who actually begins what because your bond could get so big, that millions will want a piece of your action.

PISCES & PISCES: As long as you don't forget what you promised to deliver to each other or to others, you're on the right track. However, your right track may be obliterated by the noise around you. So don't let yourselves get carried away by what you think you may be doing. If you are more concrete, then everything might be at your disposal. Stand and deliver.

CHAPTER 6

BUILDING

By now we've gone through a lot together, so much in fact, that not only is this the last chapter but we could see it as the jumping off point to the great beyond! As you have been illuminated by working with and through this book, you hopefully will also have started to feel better about your choices because they are more on target.

You are now ready to keep moving forward using a dynamic free-association approach. Your decision-making process should have more of a flow than it did before you started using this book. You have made it through the chance of approaching, the idea of questioning, the possibility of strategy, the excitement of negotiating, and the permeability of bonding and you now approach the hopefulness of building as well as withstanding while you cope with everyday decision-making. You are mobilized and on your way to taking personalized cosmic measures. If you have hesitated for a while, worked out how to ask yourself certain questions, or figured out why you want to ask them, you have extended your horizons or your level of chance. You are now building up your strength to cope with the results better than you thought you could. I hope you now understand a bit more about your limits, for this understanding will definitely take you farther along the continuum. This next but not final step will be a wonderful accomplishment, if only because you have made it this far! You have reached up into the friendly skies, where I hope you have found some astrological tips that you can use to approach others, because you now know that the energy that the stars and planets emit is part of our basic selves. You have taken the first lessons and have learned a new language. With this newly acquired knowledge, you can construct sentences, form questions, and maybe even become fluent with your own inner prose. The twelve astrological signs form patterns in all our psyches—no matter what sun sign we are—that help us through each day of our lives. Aries, Taurus, Gemini, Cancer, Leo, Virgo, Libra, Scorpio, Sagittarius, Capricorn, Aquarius, and Pisces all help to open windows to other opportunities and illuminated choices.

Remember that when you make an illuminated choice, you are subtly backed by an astrological craft that includes Akkadian, Babylonian, and Assyrian sages, Zarathustra, Democritus, Aristotle (who, don't forget tutored Alexander the Great), Ptolemy, the encyclopedic writer al-Kindi, Thales, Spujodhvaja, Kepler, Pope Clement VI, Petrus Alfonsi, Copernicus, and even many of the great modern minds, all of whom contributed to this natural and philosophical art. The next step is yours. By choosing anything with an astrological sign in mind, you enhance your own mythological powers.

Your faculty for connecting with ideas, places, and people is your personal link "to build." One last time, let me remind you that astrology does not pretend to show you exactly what you should do, but it does illuminate the quality of what you can do, while directing your attention to the quantities you can supply for yourself. You are creating your destiny, in small or large doses. "Building (Coping)" is in some way the wrap-up chapter, but just as when you get a gift, you unwrap it and proceed to use whatever is inside, your choice is the outcome of the use you make of a word or an action that gets you going. Adding your spontaneity to cosmic harmony should help you move forward.

Perhaps you are building up or building toward something. Are you assuring yourself how to build something new, or are you taking a chance that you can cope with what you have already built? Are you building up your rage or coping with a pent-up feeling? Did you just happen to relate because you stumbled into something, or are you starting to think of tearing it down? Does it seem possible to reconstruct what someone else has already destroyed? Whichever and whatever you find yourself building toward or against, your consideration should help you relate to the world around you. Quality built upon qualities can be transformed into coping in the best of all possible ways!

ARIES

to obtain

"Days are scrolls: write on them what you want to be remembered."

—Baya

If absolute justice existed, your sign would have received it as a gift for one of your early birthdays. Despite the speed of the earth, you, Aries, should arrive at places before anyone else, only because you are at your best when obtaining the right to be first. It would be just. As an Aries, you might spend a large amount of time dealing with the fact that even though you deserve to be first, you will perhaps have to wait longer than you would like to or are counting on. If, as cosmologists say, there once was a time, some 40 billion years ago, when everything in the universe was so crowded together that there was no room for galaxies, atoms, or stars (there were only particles of matter and antimatter), you, Aries, were there waiting around to leap into existence! Perhaps a millionth of a second before that Big Bang, Aries was already there, anticipating the proof that the wait was unnecessary. Yours is the all-encompassing significator for this, the first sign of the zodiac!

You were not randomly chosen to be the first at the Big Bang, since your sign practically invented the verb "to obtain." Just remember that that doesn't mean you are completely in charge of this word. You will just have to deal with this fact as you plan ahead and build, or decide whether one thing or another is worth your time to have or to hold, before you arrive at the coping part of the process. And believe me, you're the best at finding out quickly whether something is worthwhile. You are the human accelerator that brings forth the immediate desire to obtain the strength to succeed or to continue. You cope better than most because you carry within yourself an everlasting flame, which was lighted the moment you were born and which kindles all kinds of coping, especially the kind that helps you obtain success.

Build to your heart's content, Aries, for no matter what happens, you will obtain something worthwhile. You can be certain of that.

ARIES
to obtain

ARIES & ARIES: The mind has to convince the brain that something can be done. An Aries mind can convince any other Aries' brain that this immediate goal is obtainable. Then it doesn't really matter if your other bases are covered, for the end will always be the beginning of a new means. This, by the way, is a proven fact.

ARIES & TAURUS: If a future endeavor broadens your horizons, you should be able to make a promise of fulfillment that might be faithful to what you first believe in. (If, on the other hand, you feel hindered, leave the endeavor where it is.) This might be a rather roundabout way to read about coping, but it is the best one if you want the outcome to last. By the way, Aries, it is always worthwhile for you to show your clout—believe it or not, it brings out the best in you.

ARIES & GEMINI: You may think that there is an absolute urgency to resolve feelings, meetings, or plans in this combination. There is none. When you give each other the time you don't think you have, these plans, meetings, and feelings will come to fruition. Trying too hard to cope, Aries, might be a waste of time. Sometimes, Gemini might seem sort of ditsy, but that is only because he or she has a different way of settling into things.

ARIES & CANCER: If you pick the wrong words at the beginning—or in the middle or the end—you will probably have to start building from scratch, which might be too much for you to cope with. So, Aries, get a thesaurus, lean on Cancer's emotional interpretation, and then try to work things out. The more observant the two of you are, the better.

ARIES & LEO: Faithfulness means two different things to you two very different people, but once you acknowledge this discrepancy (if you manage obtain Leo's interest), you probably are in there for the long haul anyway. Has it been fun? If so, you really should hang in there and plan some fun for the times ahead.

ARIES & VIRGO: One of you should be a lawyer—if it is Virgo, you are probably safer—and then all will work out just fine, even though you will need to obtain copies of everything so that when you, Aries, cannot find things, Virgo will have copies to put under your nose. Both of you must strive to be as coherent as possible.

ARIES & LIBRA: You, Aries, need to be hardy enough to stand the sometimes intolerable niceness of one particular Libra or another. Libra could sweep you off your feet without you even knowing that he or she has done so. You are opposites, which you must know by now, and sometimes by doctoring each other, you can achieve your long-term goals.

ARIES & SCORPIO: There is no real nutshell advice when Scorpios are involved because twists and turns can change things from one minute to the next. But that also is the fun of it! So the best thing to tell you is to have other irons in the fire, even with other Scorpios.

ARIES & SAGITTARIUS: If something isn't working out, rethink your course of action, because this combination should be as good as a free membership to your favorite club or volunteer group. Recombine, reinvest, redo, but don't leave it at that, even if once in a while your two strong egos get in the way.

ARIES & CAPRICORN: Ask yourselves if you are able to get down to favorable facts and figures. And you, Aries, need to keep cool. If you are able to combine those two things, you are onto a good thing. But—and this "but" might be a big one—if one of you gets upset while you are trying, remember to observe and learn, and one of you will probably have to get out of the way.

ARIES & AQUARIUS: Aquarius should think of a way to copy the best characteristics of Aries. Then, since Aries is next alphabetically, you are next in line to do the same (sorry, Aries, with Aquarius you will always have to wait a bit, so get used to it now). If one of you can find a way to improve the health or the figure of the other, you will be on the way to attaining perfection.

ARIES & PISCES: Both of you are treading on thin ice here. In order to build something that will give you great and lasting results, take turns at doing whatever you are up to, even if it happens to be heated arguments. They could turn out to be gratifying in the long run.

TAURUS

to have

*"A man's worst difficulties begin when he is able to do as he
likes."*

—*Thomas Henry Huxley*

If you review the terms that have fallen under the umbrella
words for Taurus—caution, strength, possessing, endurance,
and to believe—you probably will come to the same conclusion I have: that you, Taurus, have it in you to have whatever
you need to hang in there! Taurus, you know best of all what
to do with what you have. Others should watch and learn
how acquisition traditionally forms part of your better self.
Your plans, hopes, desires, and dreams should gratify your
five senses so you can relate your own personal experiences
to your inner joy. Taurus, you have a bounty of strength and
enough sensitivity to spread around when it is needed by
others. One of the best examples of how much Taurus can
have in store for others is William Shakespeare, a Taurus who
had a way with words, to say the very least. The buildup of
his having so much to say while so many others cope with
his legacy means that we still find ourselves building on his
saying, "That that is is."

Taurus, you can set things in motion that others never
thought would work again, and from ashes you can rebuild
relationships, ideas, cities, countries—you name it! Taurus,
you have such a capacity to be heroic that if the opportunity
to be so does not arise, you simply turn little everyday situ-

ations into things that are inarguably worthwhile. Others had better not break an agreement with you, Taurus, for they may be lucky enough for you to forgive them, but they will have to show a tremendous amount of creative power to regain your confidence. You have a huge amount of tension within so you need your resoluteness in order to cope with yourself. Others have to have a Taurus nearby to help them add to their own tree of life. Taurus, you know better than anyone what it means to have such a tree. Because you are around, Taurus, because you teach others how to believe in themselves, they have to continue, and so do you.

TAURUS
to have

TAURUS & ARIES: Taurus, you would do well to learn the lesson of detachment here. By putting yourself in the "to have not" position you will clear the way for luminous understanding of the saying "less is more." If you don't, you might almost seem unintelligible to Aries and you'd be losing out on a whole new series of opportunities.

TAURUS & TAURUS: Claim what is yours, and let your counterpart have the right to claim his or hers as well. Ownership might be an issue. You both could respond to the same needs, but not to the same wants, because where you are at this moment in your lives will sway Tauruses in a definite way. So build on having to give.

TAURUS & GEMINI: It all depends on whether Gemini has a clear conscience or not, and you have to have the guile to find out. Your safety depends on it. Don't worry, because the kind of safety guide you need is the one this relationship is built on. Taurus, you can help conjure up the best feeling to give it a lusty try!

TAURUS & CANCER: Intuition can work wonders in this combination, especially if you give each other a chance to work things out while you are having a tête-à-tête or rendezvous. Taurus, when you deal with a Cancer, you should rely on your intuition to provide you with the insight you need to count on having some darn good old luck! Luck does pop up now and then when you two are together.

TAURUS & LEO: Remember the children's game, "rich man, poor man, beggar man, thief"? You have the opportunity to juggle all four of these around, but only one of the four will work to your advantage. The other three will work against you. So take your pick of the winner and cope with that. The sooner you choose, the better.

TAURUS & VIRGO: Taurus, avoid sentimentality. Ultimately, Virgo will thank you for it and will greatly appreciate your approach. Rest assured, there very well could be a positive undercurrent in a grander design as you come closer. To have something to build on or to cope with can only do both of you a lot of good.

TAURUS & LIBRA: A little bit of beauty is worth building something on, and if you have to spend to get some for yourselves, just grin and bear it. You are both ruled by ageless Venus, so do take what is more pleasurable to one of the senses into account and then have a little safe fun. Either of you could be a great catch for the other.

TAURUS & SCORPIO: If you are working together, you should stamp "handle with care" all over whatever it is you are working on or with. Scorpio needs to know this before he or she even starts. So don't try to take Scorpio by surprise. You two are not as easygoing as you think, although you, Taurus, can find easier ways in and out of situations. If you show this capability to Scorpio, you will really have something to deal with!

TAURUS & SAGITTARIUS: You don't have to stamp your foot, Taurus, but you should show a bit of hard-heartedness here. Then things will probably work out much better than if you just gush, because Sagittarius very well might see you as gawky! You need to build things up in a precise way; otherwise Sagittarius could bow out.

TAURUS & CAPRICORN: This combination can at times be too good to be true. So look for a willing significant other or a contented, friendly companion who will help you plan how to accumulate sound judgment with measured time. You, Taurus, have a spark within you that most Capricorns would love to copy, use, and even own, so turn on your charm and count your blessings.

TAURUS & AQUARIUS: This combination is a navigational challenge. If you are able to maneuver through the difficult currents that can rock your boat, one of you might show the other his or her true mettle. Do take into consideration, Taurus, that you will have to let Aquarius do a disappearing act once in a while—and I'm not too sure you can cope with that, Taurus.

TAURUS & PISCES: Have a party, have a ball, have a family, have a support group, have it in one second, have the strength, have the knowledge, have it done with, have the willingness, have the courage, have boundlessness if you can, have a heart . . . but don't have a doubt. Not here, please.

GEMINI

to translate

"No one means all he says and yet very few say all they mean."

—*Henry Adams*

Translation is possible even if it is not perfect. There is an Italian saying, "traduttori, traditori," which means, "transla-tors are traitors," that is just about as true as the sky is up and the earth is down. Recently some scientists agreed that there is an up and down to the universe and that we earthlings are the right way up, which makes the Italian saying even more relevant. However, translating is a necessary function that starts out when a newborn baby cries before learning how to speak (and his or her mother translates the need to be looked after. . . . see Dr. Spock). In order to understand one another, we can always count on a Gemini, who is usually at his or her very best when it comes to making words fit into the right place, as well as accessible.

Gemini, you translate ideas, language, and entities that are difficult to understand, and you convert them into reference notes. Walt Whitman gave us an example of this ability when he wrote, "How shall I know what the life is, except as I see it in the flesh?" That poetic question can be translated a thousand ways by anyone, especially someone who has a Gemini at his or her side. Gemini, you know how to get in or out of any and every circumstance with one single word. You are the perfect word catcher, who can easily translate word of mouth into a word to the wise. "To transfer," which can sometimes be a synonym of "to translate," also goes well with Gemini's sense of building.

Gemini, you have the uncanny ability to trespass on other people's feelings and somehow make them believe they should feel good about it. You know exactly how to focus on bits and pieces, so that your description of the same comes rushing out of your mouth translated into something valuable. While others are coping, you are composing the next step. Gemini, you might even overstep yourself and yet find the perfect way to convince others that you have not been checkmated after all, that you are simply building a new language out of forgotten words and that to lose the king in this new game is actually a victory.

GEMINI
to translate

GEMINI & ARIES: Building together could be like finding a buried treasure—a stash of novelties, goodies, and riches, within which you will find new knowledge that you never before thought you could use. It's like starting over. Aries usually prefers to start anew, but once again, Gemini, you can overcome.

GEMINI & TAURUS: Be as transparent as you can, Gemini. Otherwise, one of your novelties might backfire. Haven't you tried this before? Be careful with your accountability because somebody might remember something you would rather have everyone forget. I don't want you to end up with a slightly bitter taste in your mouth, Gemini, so remember, you may be king or queen for the day, but Taurus is the proud owner of a lot of common sense.

GEMINI & GEMINI: If you could find the right word in your own personal dictionary to use as an analogy for the other Gemini to play around with, you just might find yourself on the right track. Then you could convince each other that unanswerable questions are your best bet in any language.

GEMINI & CANCER: Most of the time, Cancer will be subconsciously influenced by his or her emotional habits—and if you don't know what I mean, you're in a bad way. So, you, Gemini, need to find something that Cancer can translate into an almost visible appreciation: an appreciation of what Cancer is doing, not what you are pushing for. Then you will have the pleasure of doing something worthwhile, such as building a relationship.

GEMINI & LEO: To get you back on track, the best thing that could happen to both of you is to learn a lesson in impermanence, which will show you how to cope with new perspectives. This lesson could help both of you work things out, even if you just happen to be so different from each other that your "large" translates into Leo's "medium."

GEMINI & VIRGO: The two of you are probably on wavelengths as different as AM and FM. Only with real appreciation will you be able to get in sync. But it can be done, especially by you, Gemini, for you usually owe your organization to Virgo anyway. Once you are in sync, you will have found a new way in or out of a controlled situation. Translate "give-and-take" into "giving in."

GEMINI & LIBRA: You, Gemini, may take anything out of context, use it as you wish, transform it into something else, and build up a real transformation scene that will actually work. You and Libra can render a valuable service to each other, just by being together, so keep working on it. Libra should get some of his or her friends involved.

GEMINI & SCORPIO: Let Scorpio explain, and give him or her all the time in the world to do so. Even if at first Scorpio does not seem interested, you, Gemini, can count on charming him or her into at least one date. Work on building up Scorpio's interest, and then take the plunge. Reinforce something very down-to-earth or basic, and don't forget to listen.

GEMINI & SAGITTARIUS: You should not count on getting away with murder or being careful when Sagittarius, your astrological opposite, is around. Even if you think you can, in the long run, it won't be the case. Sagittarians can see right through you, so watch it. You might get away with something by finding the right words. If you do, you might get a big smile from Sagittarius, but you won't get a future recommendation.

GEMINI & CAPRICORN: Gemini, if you convey the clear-cut possibility that a place or condition will change from one thing to another, then you just might be establishing a long-lasting relationship. If Capricorn believes you have something remotely close to farsightedness, he or she will move forward, which is a good first step toward building something up.

GEMINI & AQUARIUS: You could use something like hyper-text markup language, the html mode on a computer screen, and you will be doing yourself, as well as Aquarius, a big, big favor. When you two work together, you are tuned in on a frequency that makes anything over wires exciting and makes anything related to computers work out brilliantly.

GEMINI & PISCES: You two are probably not speaking the same language. Gemini, you have to understand that your concept of freedom is completely different from that of Pisces, although who's to say that you can't have a good time? Find a sheltered place and sit together quietly. See what comes out of that silence. Perhaps it will be something worthwhile that you can both understand, cope with, and build on.

CANCER
finishing
"No man is weak from choice."

—*Vauvenargues*

If it were possible, Cancers should start at the end. That would make the process of finishing things so much easier for you, especially since you can be so emotionally plugged in when it comes to saying good-bye. Just look at the huge, heavy suitcase you carry around instead of a simple overnight bag. Your suitcase is usually filled to the brim for no other reason than your being the proud carrier of this grandiloquent sign. If, for some strange reason this is just not true for you in particular at this point in your life, just you wait! To come into your own, you need this baggage— you just have to know how to fit everything in. Having this baggage builds your character, because to finish arranging things is proof that you are coping well with yourself.

Cancer, you are related to finishing as a search engine is related to a Web site. One finds the other. And for you, Cancer, the finishing mode should always leave changeable options at your beck and call. In fact, you are at your best just before you finish something, when your expectations are running high, because it is the time just before you have to say good-bye that always leaves you with memories to deal with. Perhaps it is because as a Cancer person, you have this great nurturing vein within your psyche, which tunes you in, more than anyone else, to what the Jesuit astronomer William Stoeger of the Vatican Research Group said at a gathering of cosmologists in 1997: "Scientists now know the atoms of human bodies were forged in the stars, [and] modern cosmology shows how humans are woven into the entire cosmic network." He was definitely not thinking about astrology when he said this, but he did all Cancers a favor by putting a finishing touch on our cosmological language.

Others should consider how difficult it is to end anything with you, Cancer. Once people are caught up in the delicacy of entrapment within your tenacious grip, they are in it forever! No finishing touch allowed, unless you, Cancer, make the decision to let them go. Cancer, you are a whiz at reassessing, realigning, reaccommodating, redoing, and showing what happens when others don't finish as they should. Just look up any of the fables of Jean de la Fontaine, who was a Cancer, and find out for yourself. Every story has a moral at the end.

CANCER
finishing

CANCER & ARIES: If you, Cancer, give in to your emotionalism, you might end up getting Aries to feel that all he or she wants to do is run in the opposite direction. Try to find a way for situations to slide smoothly into place, and suggest that Aries take the reins: "Do you remember that good idea you had a while back? Why don't we go for it?"

CANCER & TAURUS: Listen to what Taurus has to say and try to accept the fact that Taurus knows something that you don't and might help you out if you give him or her a chance. What you are working at could last forever, because you two can complement each other. However, Cancer, you will have to give in a bit even if it is against your better judgment.

CANCER & GEMINI: Here is another case of troubleshooting, but instead of turning to a certain page in the instruction booklet, you need to start all over again. If Gemini convinces you that returning to the beginning is good for both of you, just grin and bear it. In most situations, a stumbling block could actually reinforce your efforts. You can work very well together!

CANCER & CANCER: Jean de la Fontaine wrote eighteen books of fables, each of which had a clear moral at the end. The fables are fun and funny, and la Fontaine uses words in a fresh way. The important thing for you to know about these stories, Cancer, is that la Fontaine always leaves room for his readers to make their own interpretation, and because he was a Cancer, you two Cancers should always have his book close at hand. You will find advice, inspiration, and solace in his words, no matter which fable you choose to read.

CANCER & LEO: Try, Cancer, to be as brief as possible with Leo. When you start seeing how things might evolve, give Leo a chance to spill out his or her personal resolutions, which will probably not have anything to do with what you are working toward at the time. Let Leo ride on the crest of the wave because you can definitely turn out to be the winner in the long run. And don't forget that Leos are the best ones to call up on a rainy day.

CANCER & VIRGO: The best way for you and Virgo to deal with each other is to complete a task and not make it into an issue! Once you do this, don't allow yourselves to be swayed into other temptations—in other words, don't let yourselves (note the plural here) fall under the spell of somebody else who could mess things up. Your relationship should be fool-proof and hardy.

CANCER & LIBRA: End any fraudulent possibility or matter with a smile on your face, even if you hold a grudge in your heart. It might be a tiny, tricky matter, Cancer, but don't let it hinder what could end up as a good conversation piece. What about finishing with a laugh or a chuckle?

CANCER & SCORPIO: Lucky you! Both of you are water signs. As such, you have the right to muse, delay, and fall into particularly poetic states under this guise. So don't worry if things take longer than you would actually like them to. "Trust" is a meaningful word to remember here.

CANCER & SAGITTARIUS: Just throw the dice and may the luckiest one win. Take it from there and build up a tendency to modify or give in when things don't seem to be working. Even risky business can be good for both of you. Be sure that you can physically take what Sagittarius is offering.

CANCER & CAPRICORN: If you want things to last with Capricorn, you have to clear them up first. To do that, try having long-drawn-out conversations over the phone or taking walks in quiet places if you can get Capricorn to pay you the attention that you feel is due to you. Once you are in sync, the combination of you as opposites can work wonders. The longer it takes, the better. You will have to understand, however, that your frustration is just a reality check, not a reason to call it quits.

CANCER & AQUARIUS: Both of you have to be careful not to end up swimming in opposite directions, unless you are actually on a stage or in some kind of artistic endeavor and have been directed by someone creative to do so. The two of you can work wonders with unusual or New Wave ideas. Make long-term commitments so you always keep in touch, for both of you do have that magic something.

CANCER & PISCES: It is a known fact that everything gives off energy. The kinds of energy fields vary, as in magnetic fields and gravitational fields. Together the fields of Cancer and Pisces give off an energy that can turn into a perfect interaction. The important thing here is not to let go of each other, because the one thing you might disagree on is your timing. The more you work with each other, the better for both of you.

LEO
self-expression
"No one can make you feel inferior without your consent."
—*Eleanor Roosevelt*

Is self-expression an oxymoron? Not when dealing with Leo it isn't. Leo, you are your own best agent, and as such, your self is usually behind everything else you talk about. Since squandering is so good for you, this could be an upper as much as a downer: an upper if you are bettering your personal experience; a downer if you have overvalued yourself and are caught in the act of doing so. You usually think that you can do anything better than anyone else. Perhaps you can. Believing in yourself must come naturally, and the only thing that you should never let get in your way is self-reproach. You are at your best when your self-esteem allows you to feel elated, assured, proud, self-loving, motivated, and strongly enhanced by your own character. Medically speaking, however, only two moods are recognized: one is elation and the other one is depression. And when you are depressed, the feeling interferes in a drastic way with your self-expression. Not to worry, Leo. You can remedy this quite easily if you set your mind to it, especially when you are building. To really cope, lean on the phenomenal sign you were born with by finding solace in the inherent understanding of what self-expression can do for you, while you create your own technique for doing this, which is like adapting your own legend to what you believe in.

People need you, Leo, which is why you are a role model for others as they search for the best way to express themselves. Others should have the phone number of their favorite Leo. You have to exhibit the style of how to build things and be good enough at it so that others can hook up and follow your pace in their own celebratory way. In order for others to learn from you, you need to tick off what can and cannot be done. For instance, you always find the right thing to say, do, or wear at the right time, and others can follow your example. Then they will continue to build something—a dream, a quest, even if not always with whom they wish—as long as you are around to remind one and all how well you cope. So I thank you, Leo, for everyone. Napoleon, by the way, was a Leo. He is always quoted as having said, "If you want a thing done well, do it yourself." Perchance this is the best way to cope if a Leo can offer some last-minute advice!

LEO
self-expression

LEO & ARIES: You can, could, and should get ready to light up the sky for each other. You can easily show Aries how to pour on the charm, which is something that Aries usually plays down. Remind Aries that Hercules and Gilgamesh were supposedly Leos. Strength and superiority are two traits that are always related to your sign.

LEO & TAURUS: Anything can happen when you two titans clash or just get together. Let us hope for the best, because you do so well when you do get down to building together, yet you could get lost in vagueness if things aren't working out as well as either of you think they should. Try writing things down as you pick up and keep on going.

LEO & GEMINI: Here is a combination that can surely make all other combinations wish they were one of you. Gemini needs the booster shot here, so give Gemini a fighting chance to show what he or she can render. Express your belief in Gemini so that he or she can feel the flow with you, Leo. Work out together, work it out together, or just work on it.

LEO & CANCER: Try to understand that if Cancer uses slightly more romantic symbolism than you would like, it can work—even if you feel overwhelmed or do not agree. People do like to be loved, cuddled, warmed, and coddled, and Cancer has the insight to sense just when you, Leo, need one or some of this kind of TLC. Don't say no or never to Cancer's tender and kind offer, because you will probably enjoy the attention more than you think.

LEO & LEO: Take care to tap in to your own shrewdness and use some of the wit that should have its own chapter in your book of self-expression. If outshining others is a great sport for Leo, one of you two will just have to do better than the other. I don't want to be around when one of you falls behind, even though I know that in the long run you can cope.

LEO & VIRGO: You will have to take Virgo for granted, even if he or she complains that you are doing so. You, Leo, are the right person to give Virgo a nudge in the direction that seems evident to all, except Virgo. Virgo needs to hear what you have to say to help him understand what he has been musing about. Don't give up on Virgo!

LEO & LIBRA: The two of you can interact well and should do so often. The more the merrier here, and more is much the better for expressing joy, which is just up your exuberant alley, Leo. ("More" can be quantity or quality.) If ever someone should be picked out of an astrological lineup to get a party going, it would definitely be you, Leo, and Libra should be the one to pick you. Never criticize Libra's outfit, though, because what he or she wears is a form of self-expression.

LEO & SCORPIO: Neither of you will ever agree on how to show what you require when you are in dire straits. You, Leo, might be overwhelmed by the strength of this possible opponent, so take turns expressing your doubts, which is just another way to say "Let it be." Both of you carry a mighty sword and are perhaps too eager to use it, especially when you shouldn't. There should be a better way to work things out than that, and if worse comes to worst, you can count on the survival of the fittest.

LEO & SAGITTARIUS: Distill as much as you can from your first idea, then try for a much more ingenious, expressive manner in your second idea. Then you can try to diversify and create many more outlets than you had thought of at the beginning. Diversification is a great way to build a new role for yourself, or even for Sagittarius.

LEO & CAPRICORN: If you hear rumbling in the background, it could be plain old mismanaged judgment that makes any Capricorn so angry. And in addition, if Capricorn thinks that you are scrutinizing him or her, the rumbling could turn into thunder! Try working in the background, for this is the one combination in which you'll do yourself a favor if you let yourself be led. Then you can go ahead and build by leaps and bounds.

LEO & AQUARIUS: Yours are two lines that should never cross, like high-power electrical cables. You two should make certain that you never clash—ever. Opposites seem to attract, but if you and Aquarius actually do, just remember the above advice. Why don't you try to figure out how to deal with the little things and leave the big ones to better times?

LEO & PISCES: If ever a miracle could happen, it should between you two. With a little bit of pushing, welding, and improving from one of you (Pisces can always help Leo find his or her form), you could find the right expression for any sentiment or creation. Both of you should take a third sign into the fold to keep up the good work.

VIRGO
understanding
"It is a luxury to be understood."

—*Ralph Waldo Emerson*

It seems that the question, "Don't you understand?" is asked often in families all over the world. If it isn't number one, it very well might be second or third. According to Sigmund Freud, a large part of the mind is unconscious. Even though the unconscious mind is quite similar to the conscious mind, the unconscious does have wishes, fears, and anger. So we should assure ourselves that the unconscious mind understands as much as the conscious mind, which should give us some solace and relief. Whew!

Unless you are Virgo. You, Virgo, want the unconscious to understand the conscious as much as there has to be an up to go down or you wish your optimism was around to counteract your pessimism. Virgo, you perceive minutely misinterpreted adversity and understand within seconds how to put things into their rightful place. You don't even need to ask, because you will know in a flash where the question stems from, and you'll find hidden qualities that you can turn into comprehensible interpretations. Virgo, you can seem to make a mess of things and then get everyone to understand that you are actually coping while you build or turn piles of waste into something extremely useful. You can show anyone how to make something good out of something bad, and you understand why it is worth doing

so. Others need to have you around, Virgo, even if sometimes they can't stand you or it hurts to have you there.
When you misbehave, they must understand that you are
actually contributing. And you will not forgive them for not
understanding.

Perhaps the neurons in the brain are all tiny Virgos that
push and pull things into place so that the mind can finally
understand what the whole big shebang is all about. This
word, "understand," does not belong to you alone, Virgo,
but you have your own unique interpretation of it. You can
style, drop, change, or object to whatever there is to understand. When once "somebody" said, "Let there be light,"
Virgo was the one to turn it on.

VIRGO
understanding

VIRGO & ARIES: Don't cop out if Aries is distasteful. Be sure
to give each other a second chance, because a misunderstanding between you could have a much deeper effect than
an understanding, since you both are truth-seekers. Try
harder to give each other personal space, please. In fact, try
harder at everything you do together. The most important
thing is to set your priorities on the right track.

VIRGO & TAURUS: One of you can fuel the other's thoughts.
The "other" is whoever is the first to appear. There is something very visual as well as physical between your two signs,

and you'd better get used to the idea, because otherwise coping might turn out to be a bad idea. You can find out much
more about the world with a Taurus at your side.

VIRGO & GEMINI: Between you two, all work and no play
will actually be all right! If it's too much play and a little
work, it will be so-so. If it seems as easy as pumpkin pie
(why people say this I don't know), then it is sure to bring
some kind of trouble that only you, Virgo, will understand,
and this will give you the upper hand when building something with a Gemini. I'll let you in on a secret, Virgo: you
deserve to have the upper hand.

VIRGO & CANCER: Combine, mix, intermingle, jumble up,
and even mock if you must, but do not let Cancer go on without understanding that you need him or her by your side.
Your modus operandi and Cancer's insight can move mountains, change the weather, and lead you to the big payoff!

VIRGO & LEO: If you let Leo begin a monologue, you can
just sit back, relax, and watch the ball roll. Virgo, take Leo's
advice or consent, which should be part of any mutual
agreement. It will be great for you to be seen with Leo by
your side. Get him or her to understand this. Mutual respect
is imperative for this combination.

VIRGO & VIRGO: If you work out your plan to build
together to the right degree and whatever you want to

build seems affordable, financially or otherwise, support whatever your significant equal has to say. Don't get over-wrought if you hear or see any warning sign. You should be benevolent by understanding how your coping can soothe hurt feelings.

VIRGO & LIBRA: Be unashamed about asking for things, for Libra can surprise you in many ways. If he or she has the slightest feeling that you are not interested or that you understand things in a different way, Libra will speak too softly for you to hear. This could leave you out in the cold, where you'll be losing out on a good thing or a pleasurable one, which you need more of.

VIRGO & SCORPIO: You might find yourselves in a wild-at-heart mode, which is good for both of you. Letting go is an understandable way of dealing with everyday problems. Scorpio can be good at letting go, while you, Virgo, need to work on it. Prepare yourself for answers that pop up in your brain while you are busy doing other things.

VIRGO & SAGITTARIUS: Try not to bring Sagittarius into your home while you two are working toward an under-standing. If you do so (just because the word "never" doesn't apply to either of you), provide whatever Sagittarius thinks is necessary to feel at ease, something that you rarely care about, Virgo. Sagittarius is a great person to help wipe away gloomy thoughts, so let him or her try.

VIRGO & CAPRICORN: You have some stored information that can get Capricorn right on track, open him or her up, and work things out with a far-reaching plan that can do both of you a lot of good. A faint feeling of sensuality may give both of you a surprise, hopefully a pleasant one.

VIRGO & AQUARIUS: I dare you to imagine what Aquarius looks like without any clothes on! Then tell him or her what you envision, and maybe you two will actually have a good time. If you don't want Aquarius to know why you have a twinkle in your eye, never mind. Aquarius just might have been turned off by your ideas.

VIRGO & PISCES: You two should ask your spouses, best friends, or significant others to help you wade through troubled waters. That would make four of you, instead of just the two of you, which as far as understanding and mis-understanding are concerned, changes the hue of things or brings out an illuminated shade of gray.

LIBRA
solve

*"The greatest mistake you can make in life is to be
continually fearing you will make one."*

—*Elbert Hubbard*

The ability to solve, resolve, find a solution, or to carry out a balancing act is not only Libra's premier talent; it also makes you, Libra, more desirable. Many drop-dead gorgeous women and a few tremendously attractive men are born under this sign. They are not really any better looking than anyone else, actually, but a Libra will always know how to solve and resolve the meaning of his or her presence and play it up to the hilt. There is no getting around the fact that this illuminated action belongs to Libra's domain. Libra, you should never have to resolve to choose; instead, you should be chosen. When you are called upon to solve or to decide something, you can easily prove to all others that you are right; actually this is possible only because you are a Libra. The reason that your sign is always represented by a man who can balance weights is because you could even carry the weight of antimatter on your shoulders, which is a lot or nothing at all (because scientists do not yet know how much antimatter actually weighs).

I must admit that you, Libra, can drive people a bit crazy if they love you, because you find magic solutions that turn out to be riddles for everyone except for you. Puzzles seem to work out to your advantage, Libra, the same way that you know how to resolve any unbalanced account in your favor. Libra, you can also be so pliable that others think you are too tender to be true or so composed that they are afraid you don't really care. Sometimes you solve situations instead of feelings, and yet at the same time you can make others feel better about themselves. I can assure you, Libra, that you will never lose out in the long or short run, because you usually make good use of compromise.

With a snap of what is usually a handsome and well-groomed finger, you turn good ideas into perfect theories and bring consensus to your side. Usually people feel that their lives are better because you have included in them in your solution. Others need to be included by a Libra as you solve your own well-being, which can only broaden their horizons.

LIBRA
solve

LIBRA & ARIES: Opposites trying to solve a problem, especially when Aries and Libra are the opposites in question, have to scrutinize the situation right down to the last detail to make sure they can be innovative enough to see things through. Do not jump to conclusions. As long as the solution doesn't seem to recede further and further away, working on building something with Aries can be well worth your time and energy.

LIBRA & TAURUS: Think beauty. Think peace and quiet. Think about both of you having the same lovely ruler, Venus, and be assured, Libra, that by getting things to act nicer, look prettier, or by turning on a bit more charm, you are already more than halfway through solving the problem with Taurus. Good for you, good for Taurus, and good for whoever else happens to be around.

LIBRA & GEMINI: Be objective and tell the truth. Doing so will solve any problem because these two things come from you, Libra. Both of you should clear the air of any nonsense, which is something that Gemini is good at doing. (He or she also can make nonsense seem logical.) If you pool your resources, you can overwhelm any other sign so completely that you will not need to solve any problems, because things will fall into place all on their own!

LIBRA & CANCER: Before anything is resolved, before you agree to commit, before you think of coping to build or building to cope, get behind the scenes and stick to the basics as much as you can. Cancer can dupe you, so try not to get lost in absurd thought patterns. Erase any memory connections that tie you to the past. Get with it, get to it, take the most direct course, and rely on solid information.

LIBRA & LEO: You both thrive on recognition. Do what you can to attain it—the more you receive, the better. If only one of you can take center stage, give Leo that chance. You can stand just behind him or her while Leo takes a bow and thanks you publicly. Then go out and celebrate, have some fun, take a break.

LIBRA & VIRGO: The trouble you have making up your mind or deciding on something might come to the fore when you deal with Virgo. Picky Virgo might ask again and again, "But suppose we look at it this way. . . ." Deal with this by drawing on your great capacity to put yourself in another's place and perhaps even by giving up for now. That should solve the problem!

LIBRA & LIBRA: For the encounter between two Libras' souls, read and dwell on the Doris Lessing saying, "Some sort of divorce there has been along the long path of this race of man between the 'I' and the 'We,' some sort of terrible falling away." Yes, Doris Lessing is a Libra. Yes, do read that sentence again.

LIBRA & SCORPIO: Work together to circulate some good ideas from some older scholars among yourselves. Go back as far as Cervantes—*Don Quixote*, for instance—and pick among any other intellectual giants for inspiration, which gives all of us, and you two in particular, a way in and out of solving any question. To build with a Scorpio is always an advantage.

LIBRA & SAGITTARIUS: Ask yourselves if the issue would be the same if the season were different. There is a big probability that there would be a huge difference, only because Sagittarius is so tuned in to nature. First-class clues are all around: in the weather, in the sky, in the leaves that are on or off the trees. Look for them, as if this were a riddle in itself.

LIBRA & CAPRICORN: You might be able to keep Capricorn enthralled just because you are charming enough. But if this doesn't work, you'd better resolve the problem of how to seem as serious as this clear-minded person will usually expect. Perfection is sometimes not enough for Capricorn, and you just might not be up to delivering that yet.

LIBRA & AQUARIUS: Try piecing things together, even if you are not too certain of correctness—as in political correctness. Timing means little to Aquarians, because they are in their own time zone. Consequently, things sometimes seem to be out of control when they actually are not. They are just waiting to happen, to solve themselves when the vibes between you two are right.

LIBRA & PISCES: It doesn't matter if you do not have a strategy when you are solving problems with Pisces. It does matter that you have the stamina to survive the long run, and you also need a closer understanding of the short run. Both of these things will convince Pisces that somehow you are serving mankind, even if only in the most roundabout way.

SCORPIO
to know
"To know oneself, one should assert oneself."
—*Albert Camus*

Scorpio is the astrological sign that is supposed to be the transition between the individual and the collective being. This is a heavy load to carry, but somebody has to carry it, and Scorpio can bear more than the other signs. Scorpio, you help others test their personal alarm systems, which give them the knowledge that something is wrong. You also help them get to know themselves. It seems sometimes that Scorpio is the sign that gathers information about everyone else and then spreads out the knowledge so that conclusions can be drawn. Scorpio, you provide access to the personal records of others, which are then made public. This information, which is a part of our everyday lives, includes the details of where and when all of us were born and what information we carry in our DNA. Since you carry such a heavy load, before you even start dealing with yourself, Scorpio, you should first spend time with yourself to identify the unique recognizable individual that is inside you so you can connect with all that goes on outside. Once you acquire this knowledge, it will be a godsend, for it will make you respect other's self-knowledge in such a way that you are the proud carrier of the verb "to know" in this illuminated-choices tool bag. This knowledge is your luxury; it is worth more than its weight in gold.

Knowledge is often acquired through problem-solving, and this includes trivia or useless knowledge, which is so subjective that I wouldn't dare go into it. Facts and figures have nothing to do with the kind of knowledge that others can acquire by being at your side, Scorpio. "Is that the case?" or "Is this the case?" are the only questions that you, Scorpio, have to be wise about when weighing your knowledge about yourself or others. People need you to be around so they can ask you, "What is this knowledge that is gnawing at my soul?" and you, Scorpio, can ease them into the best of all possible strategic moves when you answer. I would trust whatever you, Scorpio, have to say on the subject. I know that you know what kind of condition to add or subtract to make things work.

Let's say that you, Scorpio, are the best bridge the zodiac has to offer for other signs to figure out "finding out." Your other key umbrella words (passion, mystery, falling, imagination, and searching) can be casually counted on to get the knowledge everyone needs as we all relate. Perhaps no more than that is needed.

SCORPIO
to know

SCORPIO & ARIES: If you don't believe in alterations, you might find yourself believing in something firmly yet falsely that will get you nowhere, such as the wrong fax number or Web site address. Take sheer chance as a tool before you use something else to fix the order in your personal survival kit. This means anything goes, except evading issues.

SCORPIO & TAURUS: Have you given yourself the chance to trust a reliable belief by accepting it as true "just because"? You might give in to the whims of Taurus, your exciting opposite, but even if they are your own whims, Scorpio, count on yourself to exemplify the knowledge that comes when you let things be.

SCORPIO & GEMINI: When you are dealing with a Gemini, Scorpio, you will have to relate to his or her senses, which should actually be common sense! Then cross your fingers and hope that when Gemini says, "Trust me," you actually can do so. Whether you can or not will depend on whether you can or not rely on the wisdom of prediction, which sometimes makes no sense!

SCORPIO & CANCER: This can be a very advantageous combination if you give Cancer time to settle down and you accept issues that come with illogical connotations. One of many of Cancer's complaints might be a misunderstanding. You, Scorpio, don't have to be convinced, although you should be prepared to accept how extremely delightful Cancer can be as you settle in with him or her, especially for you, Scorpio.

SCORPIO & LEO: If you feel misguided by Leo, you are probably right. Just don't let things go so far as to cause permanent structural damage, for Leo will blame you for not expediting knowledge in the correct form and thus causing loss, lack, or slack. Try making amends before things break apart. Remember that all work and no play is not a good thing.

SCORPIO & VIRGO: Some people call the simple comma an inky comet. Knowledge like this is well worth the time for either Scorpio or Virgo to ponder. This should open up a path of thought that you can use as quirky knowledge to settle any differences that might pop up as you consider tackling the future together.

SCORPIO & LIBRA: You might just find yourselves analyzing to such an extent that you end up knowing you know nothing, which has been said by so many people that it is not even worth dwelling on. Instead, Scorpio, try to be a bit more casual and enjoy your surroundings while you're with Libra.

SCORPIO & SCORPIO: Information gets stored and hopefully turned into knowledge in various ways. *The Oxford Companion to the Mind* refers to these ways as "accounts," which have three main access routes: the proper channel's account, the causal account, and the reliability (law-like) account. If you can sort this out with another Scorpio, you might get yourselves included in a future edition of that book, if you're lucky!

SCORPIO & SAGITTARIUS: Do you know that the k in "know," besides being the eleventh letter in the alphabet, is also a "unit vector parallel to the z-axis" and it can be a cryptographic subscript or a symbol of kalium (potassium). It can even be an ionization constant. So now you know.

Either play around with this knowledge or have some other kind of fun with Sagittarius.

SCORPIO & CAPRICORN: You should always take the time to prepare, Scorpio, especially when you are trying to get to know a Capricorn. If you want to build something and if you have to cope with a Capricorn, you will need to do this to find out not only why but also how. Probably, Scorpio, you will spend most of your time trying to acquire this knowledge, which is something that Capricorn does not enjoy divulging.

SCORPIO & AQUARIUS: There is much more going on here than you know. Have you taken into account that you see only a part of what goes on around you? For instance, you cannot see a broken bone without an X-ray; you cannot see in the darkness, as some animals can, and in fact, even the visible spectrum differs between man and animal. Aquarius instinctively has knowledge about what is going on around him or her that you, Scorpio, would be wise to latch on to.

SCORPIO & PISCES: You both could easily start your conversation by asking each other if you believe whether or not man is the measure of all things and how much knowledge you think you have to acquire to make a plausible reply. Then you can decide if you want to include anyone else in your reply. All of this could take more than a lifetime to build up, but it would be well worth the effort. If you come too quickly to the point, start another conversation.

SAGITTARIUS
ambition

"Ah, but a man's reach should exceed his grasp, Or what's a heaven for?"

—*Robert Browning*

Lucky you if you are a Sagittarius. When non-Sagittarians start turning their adventures into feature films, they are surely drawing on their Sagittarian feelings, no matter what sign they are. Sagittarius, you help others grow as they approach idealism, you bring pleasure into any situation just by being there, you can show the people around you how to continue in a good strategic mode, you simplify negotiations by using your clear mind, you bond because you know how to relate at the right time, and you inspire others to find an outlet for their own ambition. Sagittarius, you can point out how all other signs can use ambition in the right way.

Sagittarius, your sign is half mythological centaur and half man. This symbol epitomizes adventure, and there *is* no adventure without ambition. Ambition gives everyone a chance to aspire. Who doesn't want to do better, get a bit more, make a wiser decision, have a better time, get healthier, take another journey or prove that they can be more worthy? Everyone does, but you, Sagittarius, have always had that arrow, drawn in your symbol, showing the other cosmological signs how easy it is to reach for the stars because that is your intention and aspiration. Anyone can be ambitious, but it takes savvy to have the right ambition entwined with your quests. To be and to have are as different as to wish and to hold. Sagittarius, because you are so good at fashioning the right tool to help you reach for more, you are also good at showing others how to have ambition without letting envy intervene.

Sagittarius, you are the grand and eloquent optimist of the zodiac (usually), and ambition comes as a natural part of the whole package. Maybe this is because the sign of Sagittarius is supposed to have been built of two-thirds divine source and one-third common man, but is perhaps forever aspiring to make that human third into a perfect godlike being. This all means that you will forever carry a healthy share of that ambition to be superhuman in your mythological soul. While you are in action (which is one of your favorite states of being), you manifest ambition. However, when you are not in action (which, for you, is like an affliction), you feel useless and lost. You shouldn't let that happen, Sagittarius, because everyone needs your stamina and your spirit. All other signs can use the way you put sophisticated words into their mouths, and they should also watch how you choreograph an idea that can at times break molds. If others want something to happen very badly, they should get close to a Sagittarian, try to get him or her in a good mood, and ask him or her to point the way. Ambition will come naturally and work wonders if others listen, watch, and try it on their own, the way you, Sagittarius, do so elegantly. With Sagittarius at their side, they can cross any bridge or find out that maybe there is something better to aspire for. Sagittarius, you make things worthwhile.

SAGITTARIUS
ambition

SAGITTARIUS & ARIES: Your ego, Sagittarius, can find its equal with an Aries. The enjoyment you find together should spread out over countries and continents and provide you with bits and pieces of nice things, swell things, great things, and wondrous things. Aspire to no less, and when you are building together, never accept no as an answer from each other.

SAGITTARIUS & TAURUS: Some people say that illusions are discrepancies from the truth. But you two have found your match in each other. You might go off on some illusory wild-goose chase that Taurus can enhance and that might turn out to be just what everyone else aspired to have or to do but never dared to. You shouldn't care at all about either illusions or discrepancies, unless you can use them.

SAGITTARIUS & GEMINI: You could find yourself disappointed, Sagittarius, or maybe you'll wish you had the same things or possibilities as Gemini has, but Gemini feels the same way. You're opposites, remember? The ambition of one of you to try beat the other one to it may surpass your better instincts. Perhaps, being the opposites that you are, you should take time to find things that have been either lost or previously not dealt with and put them back in their rightful place.

SAGITTARIUS & CANCER: You should give Cancer a little advice, Sagittarius, so that he or she can actually give a better performance than Cancer thought possible. Cancer should have no need to try for anything better than a radiant look and a great attitude and should ask Sagittarius how to go about achieving that. What could be more ambitious for either of you than to look greater than you feel?

SAGITTARIUS & LEO: Dodge anything that looks or seems less than perfect. Both of you can make perfection a reality, Leo for Sagittarius and Sagittarius for Leo. Strive for Ambition with a capital and well-heeled A, so that you both feel not only right about getting what you want, but also reassured that what you get will last.

SAGITTARIUS & VIRGO: Think things over together, and only then try to reach as far as the moon. Don't rush into an ambitious plan without making sure you will be able to keep tabs on each other. Virgo will always give you a perfect, if curt, opinion. Ask for outside help if you have the slightest doubt about reality.

SAGITTARIUS & LIBRA: Have you ever wanted to see your face on the cover of a national magazine? Well, all things considered, if you really try for it, you could attain that or something similar with a Libra around because you actually light each other up if you give each other the chance to do so. This combination is great for a public relations gig!

SAGITTARIUS & SCORPIO: Decisions, decisions, decisions— so many choices are available to you, and Scorpio can help you see them for the first time. Soften your stand or get Scorpio to soften his or hers. It might be wise to consider pledging to each other what you will do once you actually get wherever it is that you have the ambition to go after.

SAGITTARIUS & SAGITTARIUS: The two of you have all the options in the world at your beck and call to make things work. You do need prudence, because if you try too hard to meet a self-imposed deadline, you will make mistakes. You run the risk of physically and mentally exhausting yourselves. Remember that ambition is not the mother of all virtues.

SAGITTARIUS & CAPRICORN: Your reputation, Sagittarius, is worth more than anything you could aspire to achieve, so you'd better let Capricorn know how much it matters to you. Capricorn might feel the urge to take you for granted or to use what you represent. Make your demands clear to Capricorn. Possibly high visibility will come for you in due time.

SAGITTARIUS & AQUARIUS: One of the few things you really need to aspire to is the hope that the weather will be right so you can enjoy the glorious outdoors. Give yourselves a break by taking time off to think about some nonsense and a bit of disorder. In the long run, this time-out and its consequences will fuel your fire. A third party's ambition will settle down peacefully in the process. You, Sagittarius, and that third party have a lot to thank Aquarius for.

SAGITTARIUS & PISCES: Compare. Distinguish. Connect. Distribute. Listen. Note. Attend. Then take one wild guess and plunge right in. Either of you will appear to have captured the attention of some ambitious so-and-so, so try working things out together but in your own separate ways. You will do best when you go on by yourselves, if you give each other a chance to wonder but not to wander.

CAPRICORN
staying
"I shall stay the way I am because I don't give a damn."
—Dorothy Parker

Staying means coming to terms with being compatible with something. We stay because we are free to do so. External forces and natural selection should have nothing to do with it. "I asked not to stay," said the poet Muhlenberg, which shows us that the idea of staying can be as illusory as time itself. Hopefully we stay in the minds of those we love or admire, and since this has to do with duration, Capricorn is called forth to be the everlasting bearer. Capricorn, you are at your best when you are not going back and forth, because you strengthen yourself just by being there, being around, or supporting anyone's role—by staying right where you are, sometimes, unfortunately for others. And yet, Capricorn, you always know how to help other signs stay in place, in their place, or how to show them the place in which they should stay.

Time is your playground, where others find themselves fenced in! Capricorn, you have no problem staying within the limits of eternity, meaning that you know how to sojourn surrounded by the tiniest or the largest of all possible outcomes, because despite all possibilities that exist in all the signs, Capricorn remains the best judge of time.

Capricorn, you know better than anyone how to put to use the critical side of your soul and thus orchestrate your own up-front and personal staying power as if it were your designated prize. Capricorn, you can, if you put your mind to it, mold intimacy out of the waiting game and have people brimming with expectation while you do so. You usually help others while you get them to stay, whether it be staying in shape, staying calm, or just staying around, even if only for a while. You will do yourself a favor, Capricorn, by using this intrinsic power to stay involved and not back out of situations, especially if the situation has something to do with building relationships. In all fairness to you, Capricorn, let's hope all the other signs stay by your side forever!

CAPRICORN
staying

CAPRICORN & ARIES: Having different styles is no excuse for you, Capricorn, to be inattentive to the changeability that Aries might be displaying. He or she could ask you to stay quick on the trigger and help each other through what might be a rocky start. Some meditation at the beginning of each day that you will be working together is advised.

CAPRICORN & TAURUS: The prize is yours, Capricorn, if you can get Taurus to stay at your side. Even if you can arrange only temporary, brief meetings, persevere until you can say "Gotcha!" You are both in good company when you're together and can work things out extremely well, especially if Taurus can get you to loosen up and drop your restraints.

CAPRICORN & GEMINI: There has to be a good motive for you to strive to stay together, one that lets you, Capricorn, take the supportive role. In the worst case, employing a bit of superficiality would not hurt you, Capricorn. Don't let Gemini get too hyped up about his or her own sudden reactions to your powerful rigidity. And don't let anything become too much of a bother to you. The best case is a long shot here.

CAPRICORN & CANCER: You two could work so well together if you, Capricorn, try to emulate Cancer's gentle nobility. It might seem like an extra effort to you, but what it really should come down to is being intelligently nice to each other. Cancer is quite malleable when given a pat on the back. So now that you know this about your opposite, Capricorn, put your knowledge to some good work.

CAPRICORN & LEO: You may find Leo to be capricious, but it actually is good for Leo to be capricious, so if you help him or her to be more comfortable in that role, you will be doing yourselves a favor. Perhaps, Capricorn, "whimsical" is a word that you should stay around once in a while.

CAPRICORN & VIRGO: The keynote here is "Stay within the framework of moderation." It seems that the latest news is that intelligence cannot be defined, but avoiding stupidity can. This information is better than any famous quotation when you are coping or building something together. So do just that (to repeat the advice would be foolish).

CAPRICORN & LIBRA: If you are able to find a peephole to look through, you will also find that at the moment, smaller is wiser. Get back to basics and don't make a mountain out of a molehill. You should be able to add up situations without having to prove that you have actually been there, done that. Just take it a bit easy because Libra sometimes can be hard on you.

CAPRICORN & SCORPIO: You definitely do not need a common denominator to be supportive of each other. You can pick things up from anywhere and guide each other through any storm. If you have decided to work things out together, things should fall into place. That might happen slowly, it might happen surely, but it will definitely be in a way that you both want to stay in.

CAPRICORN & SAGITTARIUS: Assess which steps you need to take to work things out so that other things will either stay as they are or get better (though hopefully not worse). The important thing to remember here is that the assessment is much more important than the actual outcome. Why? Because when you two put your minds to a task, you can work wonders together.

CAPRICORN & CAPRICORN: If you are able to discover what gives you the most satisfaction without misleading yourself about it, your doubts and your fears will subside and even disappear. Nobody can do this better for Capricorn than another Capricorn. Don't pretend, because without realizing it, you will become an easy target as an example for poor excuses.

CAPRICORN & AQUARIUS: Do not think that because you have the feeling that there is nonsense in the air, there actually is. Just because you do or do not like one kind of music doesn't mean that someone else can't, so use some of Aquarius's nonchalance to loosen up and stay out of silly discussions. Take some time out either to teach or to learn something for or from your Aquarian companion of the week.

CAPRICORN & PISCES: You, Capricorn, can actually be quite a conformist. Pisces can at times be the opposite, even though you are not opposite signs. If you are able to stay in line with each other, you will find an outlet for anything you want while working together on something that can turn out to be quite creative. You are the best sign to stop Pisces from hiding in his or her elusive mode.

AQUARIUS
vitality
"The biggest sin is sitting on your ass."
—*Florynce Kennedy*

If you don't have enough vitality, you'd better find out how to get some more. If you are an Aquarius, you were born with know-how, and even if you think you lack vitality or if you've ever been accused of being lethargic, it's only because you haven't found the right venue in which to show how much strength you actually have. Aquarius, once you are doing something or are in a situation that you have promised to work on or that you find interesting enough to deal with, nobody can stop you. Your vitality turns you into the cream of the crop. When you are asked, "Where are your limits?" you usually can't give a satisfactory answer because you really don't know if you have any. There is a doctrine called vitalism, which is something that you should look into (superficially to save time) because it might suit you. It is "the view that life, and all consequent biological phenomena, are due to a vital force." You, Aquarius, are the object and the subject of just that.

Alexander Pope, the eighteenth-century poet, uses the phrase "vital spark of heavenly flame" to describe life. He was not an Aquarian, but he says more in those few words than any other lengthy description I can think of to point out how strongly that word "vitality" throbs in your being.

However, you would do well, Aquarius, to tame a bit of your vitality so that you can strengthen that of all those around you. This special gift is inherent in your sign, and it would be a damned waste for you to not make good use of it. It's as simple as that, especially if happiness has anything to do with building other people's lives. The potency of your energy can at times run amok, but it matters very little in the overall scheme of things. Your vibes are perhaps a bit more difficult for you to control than those of other signs, which may be the shadow-traffic side of being lucky enough to have been born an Aquarius. When you figure out how to direct the independent channel within your vital spirit, you can turn into a wonderful cosmological vitamin for all the other needy astrological souls. Inwardness is one of the most difficult things to explain, but something in your inwardness can somehow help to arbitrate others' fortunes, luckily for those around you. It is perhaps like being blessed, which we all are just by being here. So here you are, Aquarius, and now you have the opportunity to make the most of your such-ness, your vitality, and your propensity to help. Never miss out on such a benevolent opportunity. It would be a shame if you did, because that might leave the rest of us in the dark!

AQUARIUS
vitality

AQUARIUS & ARIES: "Beware lest you lose the substance by grasping at the shadow," wrote Aesop, perhaps 2000 years ago. Celebrate the coming millennium by grasping the core of this meaning, as you two can do so very well together! Let your spirits rise above all adversity and use anything and everything that comes your way to better somebody else's situation. You and Aries will both feel good about your-selves while you are at it.

AQUARIUS & TAURUS: Do not give in to anything that is not substantial. You, Aquarius, can be as blunt as you want and as pushy as you need to be in order to get Taurus to come down to earth. If you are working within a tight schedule, Taurus could very well cop out because he or she will feel too constrained. Be careful, Aquarius, and get him or her to see how important a realignment of his or her per-sonal vitality is!

AQUARIUS & GEMINI: This combination can be so energizing that you may find yourselves showing everybody else how to cope with the right spirit, in the right place, while having the most fun! If things don't seem to be working out, you probably have your signs mixed up, or you, Aquarius, are being taken for a ride by Gemini.

AQUARIUS & CANCER: With one single outlandish idea, you could give Cancer enough sustenance to keep a worthwhile train of thought going, all the way up to winning a big jackpot! Combining your vital forces just might be well worth a try! And while you are doing things together, don't forget to partake of some of those healthy fads that could benefit your health.

AQUARIUS & LEO: Oops, watch it! Don't raise any objections if Leo asks you to be a bit more submissive than you actually care to. This doesn't mean you have to give in to Leo; just pretend to. You two opposites may feel as if sorcery is involved here—and it very well could be.

AQUARIUS & VIRGO: The best way to approach any vital statistic is with a Virgo at your side, no matter what your sign. So conform for once, Aquarius, and be careful not to act up in a way that doesn't become you. Try getting together with Virgo when there is a religious celebration happening. Or try to turn back time and create your own happenings.

AQUARIUS & LIBRA: When you are thinking about building, coping, resolving, or using something with a Libra, being faithful is the most vital of all the virtues. Certain archaic rules are well worth using as you come around to submitting to the little difficulties in life. Libra might not give you exactly what you are expecting, but you will be wise to try to work on all of the above with him or her.

AQUARIUS & SCORPIO: Take five or a breather before you commit to doing anything vital with Scorpio. Not that you can't or shouldn't, but you certainly should do so with a bit more skill than your sometimes overindulgent, carefree spirit would allow you, Aquarius. Scorpio can sometimes shut down and close off all access to himself or herself, but you should just keep trying to get in. Both of you should shape up, and you can do so if you take a deep breath.

AQUARIUS & SAGITTARIUS: The two of you almost don't need any nutshell advice, because building things together should come almost too easily or in such a normally vital way that neither of you should have second thoughts about moving forward. Good. Heaven knows, if you keep trying, you probably could even churn out a new Big Bang theory!

AQUARIUS & CAPRICORN: If you feel hindered in any way, Aquarius, stop now and wait for another opportunity. Both of you are so finely tuned to weird things like ionized particles, unorthodox vibrations, and electromagnetic waves that if they are charged the wrong way because of some silly temporary sunspot, the two of you will be thrown off track. If and when things finally do start to go smoothly, try smiling at each other.

AQUARIUS & AQUARIUS: You might find yourselves involved in some kind of rendering of unintelligible signs, but then again, you might be together when life from outer space chooses to tune in to our world and prove its existence. One way or the other, I would bet on you, Aquarius, being there—which one of you, I don't know!

AQUARIUS & PISCES: Keeping things going, even if the two of you don't agree, should be an accessory to making things better or filling up wasted time. You can find out more about a person's inner core when you talk things over and give each other enough time, especially since Pisces needs to recharge his or her vitality every once in a while. You usually do fine while you are awake.

PISCES
pathways
"Teachers open the door, but you must enter by yourself."
—*Chinese proverb*

There is a method to all madness, even if the wrong way might seem reasonable at the time. (Thanks to Shakespeare and G. Moore for showing me the pathway to this first sentence.) But Emerson's exact wording is perfection: "There's no road that has not a star above it." This is the poetic essence of Pisces' role in building up, helping to cope with, and showing others which road they should choose so they don't miss the path that leads to the good things in life.

Pisces, you could probably take this book, open it up to any page, and point out how any particular illuminated choice can fit into any circumstance. You have the wisdom that builds a private driveway in and out of situations, which can be a pathway to and from the present. You can help all other signs feel better *now*, because now is the most important time. You don't require much to willingly provide others with this treasure; you just have to be asked. Pisces, you actually know how others feel, even when they cannot express it. By relating to others' joys or woes, you understand why they are where they are and how they got there. A vital part of your package is incredible insight, intuition, and at times even clairvoyance wrapped in the ability to handle feelings for others. You do better when helping others than when striving for yourself.

Pisces, you make it seem that on life's pathway, it would be better or wiser to use this precise moment to go on forever, because, for you, the present is so great that perhaps it will be a Pisces who will finally find the specific number that represents endless duration. (This is the pathway that I would like to choose!) Maybe all the other signs should build a Web site dedicated only to you, Pisces, so when you access it, you enjoy because you deserve to. Sometimes you forget to work out your own pathway, because you are working too hard helping others. Perhaps the other signs should never forget all that you do for them as they gamble through their days and notice what time it is: now. Just maybe, with your help, Pisces, they will choose the right pathway, whatever their burden. For wherever there is a Pisces around, there is help.

PISCES
pathways

PISCES & ARIES: You, Pisces, might find this moment in the world a bit strange. Aries might find it a bit hostile. But together you can find a way in or out of most situations that can carry you through anything you put your minds to! The more intellectual your approach, the better for both of you.

PISCES & TAURUS: You might not notice the time that passes when you are with Taurus, because you might forget to look at your watch. But don't worry—you probably will not be held accountable. Time will always be on your side, for perhaps your choice and your timing are written in the stars! Whatever comes up should be worth it. Whatever seems not to work out, you should leave on the side of the road. Good luck, forever, maybe.

PISCES & GEMINI: You will just have to be more picky, Pisces. Don't take any path at any time, just because you are charmed into it by Gemini. Let your mind imagine all possibilities so you can plan how to get out of situations just in case. In fact, you should have a couple of scenarios up your sleeve to handle "just in case." Don't hesitate to use them when necessary.

PISCES & CANCER: If you find yourselves pressed for time, make a point of taking it easy. There is usually much more to be said or done when you two pair up for a cause, and by tomorrow your priorities will probably have changed. A lack of definition or a laissez-faire attitude should give you more insight than you think. The more you let go, the better the long-term outcome.

PISCES & LEO: Stick to your basic skills, Pisces. The truth of the matter will reveal itself without too much ado, even though you might find yourself having worked a lot for nothing! The more specialized you get, the better chance you will have of not getting caught up in byways or dark corners that can lead you astray—not specifically by Leo, but with him or her. Do remember that you, Pisces, can do well when astray.

PISCES & VIRGO: As long as you don't forget the basic task at hand, the experience with Virgo could, if you're lucky, be

as simple as pressing the appropriate key. Now, don't jump
to conclusions. Remember, you are opposites and it's okay if
this turns out to be a flighty or a passing attraction because
you will be the wiser just by having spent time together.

PISCES & LIBRA: Begin by talking about your real dreams—
the ones you are counting on to come true. Then, little by
little, branch out, and if you strike unreality, keep going
anyway. Just don't force anything and keep jumping back
and forth until some suppositions, a couple of possibilities,
and one or two assumptions seem feasible. Libra can be a
big help to you, Pisces.

PISCES & SCORPIO: If you two could get together and create something artistic, it would be sheer perfection. Try to
come to some kind of agreement that brings you closer to a
creative vein, even if it's investing in a valuable work of art,
because this would be excellent for building up your sensitivity. You both have a lot of it, and associating yourselves
with something creative is like fueling a helpful fire.

PISCES & SAGITTARIUS: Can you find a way to make things
official between you? If you can sign something, commit to
something in public, or rely on actual rules and regulations,
you will be doing yourselves a favor, because you will avoid
incongruencies that can only befuddle your two signs. If
you feel that it's bigger than both of you, don't give up—just
be cautious.

PISCES & CAPRICORN: You should dare to experiment, Pisces, to get Capricorn to try something new, newfangled, or susceptible to trial and error. You would be doing Capricorn a huge favor, even though it make take you absolute ages to convince him or her of that. The alternative is boredom.

PISCES & AQUARIUS: You first need to be sure that your senses are coordinated and then take a plunge into something that needs a tremendous dose of adaptation. You two have the perfect combination to go off and spend a couple of years at the south pole, studying the language of penguins or something as outlandish as that!

PISCES & PISCES: Spiritualism. I could almost leave this word only and say nothing else, but I want to make sure that you take the pathway that encourages you to at least give it a try. You don't have to believe in it; just give it a chance. So once again: spiritualism.

NOW THAT YOU ARE A CONNOISSEUR, TAKE THE NEXT STEP

Generations and generations of stargazers, wishful thinkers, and men and women of daring and wisdom have looked to astrology for answers. As you move through this book and refer to it either on a regular basis or on the spur of the moment (which can be just as much fun when you are on your own or with friends), you should start to feel as if using astrology in this way is like having your own personal coach on-line, there at the turn of a page (instead of the click of a button) whenever you need a boost, some advice, or just another opinion. Using this book even once to make a more informed, star-influenced decision should spark your confidence in your own self and empower you to interact with some of the energy that the sun, the moon, and the heavens have bestowed on all of us, no matter what sign, sex, nationality, income bracket, or hair color we are. Consulting this guide should make you better prepared for what you can expect from those with whom you deal and help you focus your energies on making better, and perhaps more appropriate, decisions for yourself.

I hope that by now you have gotten your feet wet or at least dipped one toe into the wonderful and exciting range of possibilities that fill this book. If you have made one choice—even tentatively—based on the guidance of *Astrological Intelligence*, why not try again (and again)? Perhaps you feel yourself becoming a bit of an expert—an expert about yourself, that is—because you have used the sheltering, inspiring, and confidence-boosting combination of your umbrella words with the energy of your astrological sign to make several illuminated decisions. Good for you! Whatever the case, I hope you have seen how these tools have given you the power to light your way through the labyrinth of opportunities that appear and disappear along the path of your life.

You can use the advice in this book to start changing things in your life, or less ambitiously but equally importantly, to change your day. Sometimes a good choice can even make your day! As you—a Pisces, let's say—sit across the dinner table from your Sagittarius spouse, the two of you can find the best way to *approach* each other with baby steps, and eventually to *build* a mutually satisfying future together after the series of baby steps becomes one great stride. Or maybe you are a Libra who has to deal with a Gemini at work. So you choose Chapter 3, "Strategies," and find that you, Libra, relate to strategies through the word "pretend." Don't balk yet, for you go on to discover in the corresponding interaction between the two of you that your signs can get along better than you think if you give Gemini the space to grow. Instead of pouting, pretend to grin so you can bear it in order to make things work.

The point for everyone is that by finding the right balance, you will learn to cope better in your daily encounters.

Remember that by giving yourself a break, you always benefit. The time that you take to relate to your astrological sign, find the umbrella word that pinpoints a precise moment, and map out the perfect plan is time well spent. It is just as easy as tuning in your radio when all you have is static by moving the antenna an inch any direction. The more you use this book, the more of a connoisseur of yourself you will become. The process will soon be second nature to you, and eventually you will find yourself using this tool to your advantage. Give it a shot!

Your life has not been written in the stars in any preordained way. As Johannes Kepler, the famous astronomer, wrote: "Stars do not compel, they do not do away with free will, they do not decide the particular fate of an individual; but they impress on the soul a particular character." By making your own choices under the auspices of your sign, you are writing out your own story through blood, sweat, and tears, as well as with energy, vigor, and effervescence, using the knowledge that our ancestors bequeathed to us all. You are using a part of the landscape of the heavens to blaze a trail. If you take a chance and illuminate your choices in this way, you will attach to your side the power of a big chunk of history. I can think of no better bridge over which to cross into the future!

You should also be encouraged by the fact that there are no limits to what the mind can devise, imagine, or create. You are the architect of your own life, the author of your own story, and the creator of your own personal universe— every day or whichever day you choose to do so. That is a big part of the fun, excitement, and freedom of life.

INDEX